THE FISH LADDER

THE FISH LADDER

A Journey Upstream

KATHARINE NORBURY

B L O O M S B U R Y

LONDON · NEW DELHI · NEW YORK · SYDNEY

First published in Great Britain 2015

Copyright © 2015 by Katharine Norbury

The moral right of the author has been asserted

Artwork © Katharine Norbury & Eva Rae Thomson

This book is a work of non-fiction based on the life, experiences and recollections
of Katharine Norbury. In some cases names of people, places, dates, or the detail of
events have been changed to protect the privacy of others. The author has stated
to the publishers that, except in such minor respects not affecting the substantial
accuracy of the work, the contents of this book are true

Every reasonable effort has been made to trace copyright holders of material
reproduced in this book, but if any have been inadvertently overlooked the
publishers would be glad to hear from them. For legal purposes the list on
pages 289–294 constitutes an extension of the copyright page

No part of this book may be used or reproduced in any manner whatsoever
without written permission from the publisher except in the case of brief
quotations embedded in critical articles or reviews

Bloomsbury Circus is an imprint of Bloomsbury Publishing Plc
50 Bedford Square
London
WC1B 3DP

www.bloomsbury.com

Bloomsbury is a trademark of Bloomsbury Publishing Plc
Bloomsbury Publishing, London, New Delhi, New York and Sydney

A CIP catalogue record for this book is available from the British Library

Hardback ISBN 978 1 4088 5923 0
Trade paperback ISBN 978 1 4088 5924 7

10 9 8 7 6 5 4 3

Typeset by Hewer Text UK Ltd, Edinburgh
Printed and bound in Great Britain by CPI Group (UK) Ltd, Croydon CR0 4YY

MIX
Paper from
responsible sources
FSC
www.fsc.org   FSC® C020471

To Jean Norbury and in memory of Fred Norbury
with boundless love

Fish ladder (noun):

A structure that allows the natural migration of fish around an obstacle, such as a dam. Most fish ladders consist of a series of pools, arranged in low steps (hence the term *ladder*) that the fish swim and leap up to reach the open waters on the other side. The velocity of water falling over the steps has to be great enough to attract fish to the ladder, but it cannot be so great that it washes them back downstream, or exhausts them to the point of inability to continue their journey upriver.

PART I

It is no small pity, and should cause us no little shame, that, through our own fault, we do not understand ourselves, or know who we are. Would it not be a sign of great ignorance, my daughters, if a person were asked who he was, and could not say, and had no idea who his father or his mother was, or from what country he came?

Teresa of Avila

Font del Mont

'The theme for the summer is following watercourses from the sea to the source.'

It was the first day of the holiday and my nine-year-old daughter Evie reached for her journal. She transcribed my statement, and then underlined it, and in doing so turned it into a title. Beyond her a dozen crows, visible as sooty flecks, spiralled above Garn Fadryn's summit cone.

'What's a watercourse?' she asked.

'A watercourse is the path that water follows. It can be anything from a trickling stream to a mighty river.'

'What about the source?'

'The source is where it comes from.'

'Like a spring?'

'Maybe,' I said. 'It might be a pool, or a spring, or a crack in a rock. I've never really thought about it.' Evie looked at me, then put down her pencil.

'How shall we begin?'

★

This is the story of how I set out, often in the company of Evie, on a series of walks, or journeys. Our pastime began as a coping mechanism, a device that would get us through an otherwise blighted summer. Coping, because I had been pregnant the previous winter, but had lost my baby in the spring.

There had been tension in our household from the day a pink line appeared on the plastic wand of the tester kit. I was delighted, excited, and felt blessed. My husband, Rupert, was anxious. We had been living in Barcelona because the euro was weak against the pound, although that was already changing. Evie was thrilled, and wrote a poem called 'My New Brother', that was put up on the wall at school, but Rupert and I argued most days. I was nauseous, often sick, which I welcomed as a happy sign. Statistically, because of my age, I had a fifty per cent likelihood of miscarrying. But I was sure it would be all right.

When I felt the fizz of life slow down I stayed in bed, put my feet up, convinced myself the child was growing, although everything felt different from how it had with Evie. It was as though I carried a somnambulist, a sleeper, even now, when sleep was the natural state. Yet this rest was deeper, profound, dreamless. And then, one day, the baby's heart just stopped. My doctor tried to persuade me to have the miscarriage induced. But I loved him – I was sure the baby was a little boy – and I didn't want him to leave me. So I decided to let him rest as long as he would.

Most days I walked on Tibidabo, the rumpled mountain at the back of the city. One morning, after dropping our children at school, my friend Olga and I picked our way up one of the many narrow paths to join the track along the ridge – the Carretera de les Aigües – Olga swearing under her breath, and vowing to give up smoking, tucking her long hair behind her ear. Tibidabo was covered in pines, figs and prickly pears, populated with wild boar and herds of lost sheep and, occasionally, FC Barcelona footballers, training on the unpaved road above Camp Nou, as well as scores of joggers and morning walkers, some with dogs or baby strollers, and Lycra-clad cyclists wearing bug-eyed goggles. Swallows whispered in pulsing clouds. Cicadas creaked and buzzed. Despite the forest, the hill was bright, because the Mediterranean Sea, which was tacked like a veil to the hem of the city, acted as a vast reflector, and bounced light into all but the darkest gullies, driving out the shadows. At this time of year the mountain was dense with desert flowers, century cactus, scrubby pink roses, flat yellow poppies, the blue fluff of rosemary. Olga pointed out the places where, later in the year, mushrooms might be found, and wild asparagus in its season, bitter and thin as samphire.

At Tibidabo's southernmost ridge there was a freshwater spring, the Font del Mont, or spring of the mountain. It could be accessed by a road up the back of the hill, and every day a line of elderly Catalan men wearing wide braces and orthopaedic shoes, and leaning on gnarled sticks – for digging mushrooms – formed a line at the spring with their plastic water carriers. A stone cairn had been built over the spring and the water directed through a steel pipe where it spilled into a polythene ice-cream carton before running, profligate, onto the ground. Dogs that had run ahead of their owners formed a shifting community about the carton, tails wagging dust. The men waved us to the front of the queue to come and refill our water bottles, eyes darting to the smooth bump of my belly. We asked them if there was anything special about the water, if it contained healing properties. The old men looked at us as though we were mad, and laughed. 'It's water,' they said, 'and it's free!'

When we got back to Olga's house her mother was waiting

with a casserole of veal, eggs and peas. She spoke to me in Catalan, which Olga translated: 'Darling, you must keep up your protein. And replace your fluids.' At home, I stocked the fridge with isotonic drinks, enough to run a marathon.

The baby left my body in his own good time, almost a month after his heart stopped beating. We were at home when it happened, Evie asleep, Olga's number propped by the telephone. Rupert was in London for the premiere of a film, an adaptation of one of his books. There had been no way of knowing when it was going to happen; life couldn't and shouldn't stand still.

When summer came, and brought with it the realisation that our baby should have been with us, have been in my arms, warm and cuddly and smelling of sunshine, I found that I was struggling. It wasn't the first time that, grieving, I had found things hard; not the first time that the world had closed around me in a tight, hard sphere. I had been so afraid when it happened the first time that I declared, on my recovery, that I was more afraid of madness than of death. Although it turned out, in the end, that this was a luxurious boast, a terrible falsehood, and I would have the opportunity to revise my view entirely. So, because I had a daughter, and I had to be strong for Evie, I searched for something that would keep the air breathable, the sound of the wind audible, the smell of a bonfire or the smart tang of sea salt sharp on my lips and tongue. That might shut out the possibility of — depression is such a vague word — stasis. That would shut out the possibility of everything standing still, as it had stood still once before, when I was sad, and I never wanted to go back there, ever again.

So I came up with the idea of following a river from the sea to its source. The idea came to me in a roundabout way, which I will share with you, and for a long time I failed to achieve it. Indeed, the plan unravelled so fast that it very soon came to include anything with a watery theme. But I found, as the summer progressed, that I had accidentally embarked on a journey to the source of life itself. Not an abstract journey, or a metaphorical one, about who we are and what we're doing here. A literal one: a journey to the source of this, particular, life. Because, although my childhood had been a happy one, and my adult life fulfilling, if not particularly exceptional, or notable from the point of view of achievement, there had been a slight unorthodoxy about my beginning.

I had been adopted as a baby, brought into our family because my parents wanted to have a second child, and my mother had been unable to carry one after giving birth to my brother. I hadn't stopped to think about this in many, many years, although, at one level, I had always been aware of it. But for some reason, perhaps connected with, or triggered by, this new lost baby, I started to dwell upon this mystery. Of who I was, and where I'd actually come from. Of whom we speak when we talk about *our family*. And it turned out, as the weeks rolled by, and became months, and then years, that I discovered that there were places, empty spaces, *places in the heart*, that I simply hadn't imagined could exist.

Swimming Pool

On a huge hill,
Cragged and steep, Truth stands, and he that will
Reach her, about must and about must go

John Donne

The idea, of following a river from the sea to its source, had its origin between the pages of a novel – *The Well at the World's End* – by the Scottish writer, Neil M. Gunn. Unfortunately I no longer had this book, because I had given it to my friend Sofia, in Barcelona, just a few days before we returned to Wales for the long summer holiday.

At Evie's international primary school Sofia was, without doubt, the richest mother, being married to one of the wealthiest men in the world. We met when she overheard me complaining to Evie's teacher about an apparently armed man who had followed the children's bus to the swimming pool. Miss Linda had looked thoughtful. Bodyguards were the new black. One of the Russian families had one. Also one of the Bulgarian families, though theirs was more like a footman and doubled up as a chauffeur. A gentle-looking woman in a tracksuit then stepped forward and said that it was she who employed the guard, and she apologised for the fuss. A diamond the size of a penny glittered on her finger. The woman insisted that she thought it was better for all the children that there was a bodyguard outside the school, and I had been unable to think of a response.

In spring the knots of security already looped around Sofia pulled tighter. Her father-in-law stepped down from control of their family business, which was a bank, and Sofia's husband, with a minimum of fuss, slipped into his father's shoes. The daily walk to the school gates was accompanied by a huddle of walkie-talkied ex-marines and black-clad secret policemen. While the arrangement was clearly unsatisfactory, it was also short-lived, for during the course of the summer Sofia and her family would leave Barcelona for their own country, where the net of security could better enfold them, and the children would go to school in a four-wheel drive.

Shortly before she left, Sofia invited some of the mothers from the school gates over for supper. I was one of them. I pressed the buzzer by an electric foot-gate and her head of security asked me to state my identity and articulate the purpose of my visit. Overhead, a three-quarter moon competed with the intruder lights of the house. When the gate opened I stood outside the front door while the guard phoned Sofia, who confirmed the information I had given him. He admitted me to the hallway and opened a second door. I passed beyond him into a stylish, austere room where a glass table was set with damask napkins and ornate heavy silver. A centrepiece of unfamiliar flowers with beaded stamens, delicate as sugar, dropped ochre dust onto the table; it was like the powder on the wings of moths.

Beyond the table the women from the school gates sat talking on two low sofas. Sofia waved a greeting, the phone still in her hand. Behind her French windows opened onto a wooden deck. There was a swimming pool, filled with anthracite shadow. The reflection of the houselights crackled over its surface, illuminating bits of twigs and insects. The water looked cold despite the heat. It shivered with the vibration of the filters. Sofia had once invited me to come over and swim with her, and I had bought a black Calvin Klein bikini, the most expensive swimsuit I had ever owned, but the swim had never materialised, and now, I supposed, it never would. There was a tennis court, its bubble-gum surface speckled with pine resin and littered with fallen needles. There were swings and a climbing frame for the children. A high, bougainvillea-draped wall promised both shade and privacy. A slip of tyres and the hiss of brakes indicated the proximity of traffic lights on the other side of the wall. A magpie clattered in a tall pine and a blue-black feather curlicued to the ground. The place was reminiscent of a cloister, although a curiously secular one.

Inside the room the women sipped champagne from crystal glasses. A Lebanese butler attended to our needs. My eyes kept snagging, returning to his features, because he reminded me of a famous English actor. Eventually I asked him if they were related.

'Who is Steven Berkoff, Señora?' he replied.

The girls had fallen over themselves to give Sofia something to remember them by: a Hermès scarf. Gucci anything. Fleur de The Rose Bulgare, a perfume said to have been created by the House of Creed for the actress Ava Gardner, who fell in love with Frank Sinatra, Old Blue Eyes, in Tossa de Mar, an hour's drive from where we were sitting. I had had no idea what to give.

The most special thing that I had discovered that year had been the book I have already mentioned, *The Well at the World's End* by Neil M. Gunn. It told of a well 'whose water is so clear that it is invisible: when the two lovers first find it, they think it is empty ...' I had told Sofia about the novel, and she made me promise to write down what it was, and who had written it, and instead I gave her my copy. I gave Sofia my book because there was no time to buy another, and I was glad, because I had passed on something good.

And yet.

The Well at the World's End tells the story of a journey. The protagonist goes alone into the wild places of Scotland and tells anyone who asks that he is searching for the well at the world's end. His name is Peter Munroe, which may or may not be a play on *Peter the rock on which I will build my Church* and *munro*, as in a Scottish peak over three thousand feet. He is a successful academic, although now at the end of his youth. His wife's beauty is beginning to fade. Their only child – like that of Gunn himself – was stillborn. He is motivated by an indeterminate, and bittersweet, longing; the anticipation – were he to fail to act on this impulse – of something like *chagrin*, in the sense of both sadness and disappointment.

He is unable to articulate this feeling with any adequacy beyond the idea of the well. So he sets off into the wildest parts of the country, and finds adventure both in the land and in those he meets, discovering all kinds of different things about himself. Truth hovers at the corner of his vision, sometimes flickering in the landscape just ahead of him, sometimes appearing to one side of his path, only to disappear when he looks at it head-on.

In my heart I knew that Sofia would never make such a journey, even should she want to. It would mean bodyguards and chefs, servants and tents, tables and chairs and a four-wheel drive, cameras and digital surveillance. It would be like being on location with a heavily armed film crew. Sofia could never do it. But I could. My relative lack of wealth and absolute anonymity gave me a different kind of freedom. And the more I thought about it, the more I became determined to undertake Peter Munroe's journey, although I couldn't have explained why. I, too, had reached the end of my youth. I, too, had lost an unborn child. These were, possibly, the only points of connection between me and the fictional hero; but maybe that was enough. I certainly shared a sense that there was something beyond my grasp, something out of reach, and perhaps the idea of a secret well was as good a way of expressing it as any.

After Sofia left I tried to buy a new copy of the book, but discovered that it was out of print. In the three months since I had found it, *The Well at the World's End* had, quite literally, disappeared. I found a society associated with the writer, who was himself long dead. I communicated with people in his home town. I wanted to know if the journey described in the novel was real and, if so, where was it from and where did it lead? Did the places mentioned in the book exist? Was there a well that had inspired the writer? The general view was that the journey was real, that there had been a well, and that Neil Gunn had filled his kettle at it, but that no one, for the life of them, could remember where it was. Mr Gunn's nephew, Dairmid Gunn, was the one most likely to know, but he was away just now and no one knew how to contact him. I set the idea of the well to one side.

Gunn had written another book called *Highland River* and I was able to track down a 1975 paperback. It arrived a few days before

Evie and I flew to Britain for the holidays. I didn't have time to read it before we left, but I opened a page at random:

> *'And what will you do with yourself?'*
> *'Oh, I'll knock about and fish and that . . . Though actually I do have one small idea — I intend to walk a certain river to its source. It's a thing I have wanted to do for a long time. That's all really.'*
> *'Not a pilgrimage?'*
> *'Hardly!'*
> *'You mean that it is — slightly?'*

I stared at the words *one small idea*, and felt their weight as they passed beyond my retina, a stone disappearing into a pool, aware already that something had happened, was happening, alive to the new disturbance. *I intend to walk a certain river to its source . . . It's a thing I have wanted to do for a long time.*

So had I, though I had forgotten all about it. I remembered a geography lesson, my hair tied in plaits, my front teeth crossed. *The water table*, ladybirds beetling over the scarred varnish of my desk: they had got into everything that summer. Flicking their ruby bodies to the safety of the inkwell so I could liberate them at break-time, hiding them from the naughty boy who tugged out their lacy wings, so he could race them and they wouldn't fly away. Understanding that I had drifted, the words *porous* and *igneous* before me in looping chalk, but it was too late to ask what it all meant. I had missed hearing the part about where the water started, and the diagram in the textbook offered nothing. If I got a detention the ladybirds might die.

★

I closed the book, ran my hand across the cover, its aged paper smooth as chamois. I read the description on the back:

The Highland river with its dark brown pools and sudden rushing shallows is a magical playground for little Kenn and his fellows. Here he battles for salmon with home-made hooks ... With no conscious aim beyond satisfying the hunting instinct, Kenn's journey up the river becomes a thrilling exploration into its source and the source of himself.

I turned it over and studied the picture on the front: a photograph of a brown river, descending purposefully over flat slabs of rock, a few farm buildings in the foreground, some bluish hills beyond. The river was a real river. It was called the Dunbeath Water.

I slipped the book inside a suitcase.

When Evie and I arrived in the UK, we went first to our family home in Cheshire. Rupert had stayed in Barcelona to work on his book, and he would come out in a few weeks to visit us. I looked up the Dunbeath Water on a road map. It was very far away. And it really didn't look like much. About fifteen miles long, hunched in the top right-hand corner of Scotland, it was just a little way short of John O'Groats. There was no spring or loch marked on the map, no source or well – it simply vanished, a thin blue squiggle into a dazzling white page. It was in the middle of what appeared to be the emptiest part of the British Isles. I tried to find a better map, an Ordnance Survey map. But this seemed always to be missing whenever I was in a bookshop. And then I realised that to follow this river from the sea to the source I would have to make a return trip of around fifteen hundred miles, for a journey on foot of perhaps thirty. I decided that we would start closer to home.

Humber

f you look at it on the map Spurn Point appears as a bent hair-
pin, slightly to the right of Hull, curving out into the North Sea
and then back on itself. What it is, is a spit of land, of sand, of
shingle, that separates the wide mouth of the Humber from the
formidable North Sea. Towards the tip there is a lighthouse, which
has fallen into disuse because the spit, every quarter of a millen-
nium, breaches, and the whole thing starts again. Beyond that is a
lifeboat station; it too awaits abandonment. Spurn is felt to be
nearing the end of this particular incarnation. There is a road along
it, made of flat square tiles, and the spit, sinuous as a cat, shifts
constantly under it, so the road has to be remade, rearranged, in a
new place, wherever the spine of the land finds rest.

I had just kissed Evie goodnight.

'Where are you going?' she asked.

'I'm going to Spurn Point.'

'Where is it?'

'It's on the other side of the country. Pretty much in a straight
line from here. I'll be back tomorrow afternoon,' I said.

Evie arranged Jerome, a stuffed dog, next to her pillow.

'I thought we were going to the cottage tomorrow.'

'I know. We can go the next day,' I said. 'Will you and Grannie be all right on your own?'

'Yes!' she said. 'We're going to do baking.' She glanced at me sideways along her cheekbones. 'Sing long-and-winding?' I held her hand and began to sing 'The Long and Winding Road' by the Beatles. By the time I reached the end, Evie was asleep. I tucked a curl of hair behind her ear, then bent to kiss her forehead, rested my face next to hers. I listened to her breathing for a while.

I had always wanted to walk to the lighthouse, and Mum had encouraged me to go. I hadn't been alone all year, other than for the handful of hours when Evie was in school. Mum and Evie only saw one another in the holidays. Spurn Point formed the top lip of a river mouth, so it even fitted in with our holiday theme. Although the Humber wasn't a river one could follow from sea to source. Strictly speaking, the name referred to the estuary. There had once been a freshwater river, a long time ago, when the ice had first begun to melt. But the River Humber had been displaced by the rising North Sea, and today the name describes the conflu-ence of the rivers Ouse and Trent, joined later by the Ancholme and the Hull.

By midnight I had still not made up my mind to go. I sat on the end of Mum's bed, the two of us drinking tea.

'If you set off now,' she said, 'you'll be there for sunrise.' Her pale eyes were as blue as forget-me-nots. The bones of her hands in mine felt frail, yet pliant as feathers. She was eighty-one. A lovely lady, and an impassioned wanderer; Mum wouldn't have hesitated for a moment. So I kissed her soft cheek, and laughed, and went out into the summer night, made black by the glow of the street lamp. There was no need for a map. I started the car and headed east, past Manchester, towards morning.

Crossing the central ridge of the Pennines felt exciting – the M62 was the highest motorway in England – the journey surprisingly swift. But then the road passed along the northern bank of the Humber. In Hull the docks spilled on, mile after mile. I began to wish I'd brought a map. Although I knew where I was going: to the place that separated the sea from the river. If I followed the river, I'd get there. And yet . . . I hadn't thought the place would be so far beyond the city.

A flat landscape opened to the east, definite against the imperfect darkness. I passed through a hamlet: picturesque, sleepy. A triple-stretch white limousine parked jauntily on the village green. A farmyard crammed with Romany caravans where a wooden windmill powered the nodding head of a life-sized puppet clown. A nuclear power station. Wind farms. The detritus of extremities. I thought of Dungeness, where the filmmaker Derek Jarman spent his final years in a black pitch shiplap cottage, and dragged a garden from the blue-grey shingle as his once keen eyes foundered, then failed. There is a photograph of him as a smiling Canute, wrapped in a cloak with a necklace made of fishing floats, pitching himself between the land and the sea, ordering back the waves. Or perhaps it was King Lear. A fighter, against the dying light, the creeping sea. Despite the echo Dungeness seemed far away. Smaller, and harder. There was a softness about this new landscape, a vastness, which I had not anticipated.

I reached the village of Easington, and the signs for Spurn Point itself. There was a car park, although to use it seemed extravagant, given that there was no traffic, but I did so anyway. Next to the car park was a mobile-home park. I locked the car, went back, checked it. Was irritated with myself for doing so. It was, after all, not yet two in the morning. Who would come here now? I walked through farmland, past a number of houses, and was surprised by how many lights were on. I hadn't thought the place would be so populated, and had imagined that those who did live here would be sleeping.

I tried to suppress a panic, a rising fizz of anxiety. I felt sure it was to do with the unexpected proximity of so many other people, and the consequent vulnerability of walking alone out to the point. It was like walking the plank. I had acknowledged the possibility of meeting the odd birdwatcher, though at that time of year, and in a place so remote, I had believed it to be unlikely. And yet, behind the pulled curtains, I felt eyes fixed on television sets, sweating cans of chilled lager warming in the summer night. Young mothers with sleepless children, shift workers, the very old. I sensed their wakefulness.

Headlights approached: a police Range Rover. It stopped and the occupants – dough-faced, currant-eyed – peered at me; I raised a cautious hand. What were they looking for? Smugglers? Suicides? Vice? They seemed satisfied that I was none of these although did not reciprocate my wave. They drove on, out towards the point.

Where the arm of sand first lifted out from the body of the land – so that both the river and the sea became visible – there was a collection of prefabricated huts, of corrugated iron and precast concrete. A number of cars were strewn, rather than parked, outside them. There was an old BMW, its chrome lines glinting, its windows misted from within. One of the buildings, a Nissen hut, seemed to have been a café serving visitors to the point, but the signs looked old and abandoned. Yet the cars implied that someone still lived there, that there were other inhabitants of the fringe. My plan had been simply to walk out across the spit, to the tip, where the river met the sea, and then lie down, somewhere beyond the lighthouse, and sleep. I had thought that I could spend the following day there, exploring, absorbing, before going back to Mum's. But I hadn't comprehended how little darkness there would be. None, in fact. There had been a shadowing, a filling in, soon after midnight, but since then the sky had gradually lightened. At first dark blue, it was now streaked with lighter bands. It was easy to see the pale curves of sand ahead, the colours slowly emerging, like those in a developing Polaroid. The police passed by again. In just a few minutes they had completed the journey that I had driven through the night to undertake.

I walked over to the river mouth. Its shore was flat and fecund, green marsh, brown mud. There was a popping sound, as though a hundred mouths sucked bull's-eyes. Marsh gas, I supposed. And the Humber. As wide and real as death. A few miles upstream a single-span suspension bridge joined Lincolnshire with the East Riding of Yorkshire; it was a popular place for suicides. I wondered if any of them floated out this far, had washed up on this shore. I was afraid to look at the water, afraid of what I might see. A bloated dog, pale limbs like chair legs pointing at a sightless sky. Or worse.

My unease was accentuated by a sound, and one so distinctive that I would have known the place if I were brought back blindfold. It was a deep vibration, a plainsong, a confluence of many voices. At first I thought it was an accident formed by the architecture of the air, by the river-wind running against the sea-wind. And that may have been so, but in the paleness of the night I could see the instrument in which the notes were caught: the electricity poles that ran out to the lighthouse, and the cables strung between them. Any electrical current that passed through the wires was silent, or at any rate its gentle hum suppressed below the song, which was ceaseless, low, continuous as madness.

I turned away, and walked over to the other side of the spit, to the beach.

The more space I put between myself and the wakeful inhab-itants of the mainland, the better I felt. The sea shone pearl-grey, opaque, and the sky lightened above it with a bloom as soft as a plum. Sunrise seemed imminent but I knew it wasn't for another hour. A rusted raffia-and-metal chair retrieved from the sea and set up on the sand attested to the presence of fisher-men, or birdwatchers, but not now. I liked being alone. I settled into my gait, happy that mine were the first footprints in sand as new as snow.

Over the years there had been attempts to stop the spit from breaking, to protect it from the combination of long-shore drift and the river's passage that formed it, destroyed it, and will form it again. These various schemes now presented themselves as so many abandoned works. Ballast, in concrete blocks. The ribs of groins, each one made from a single tree, the bars of a giant cage along the shore. The horizontal planks had long since washed away, or been removed, as the futility of what they were attempting became apparent. The remaining upright posts had the gravitas of gods, each one as thick as a man, and twice as tall. I thought of Easter

Island, the unseeing heads that guarded the land. Or the skeleton of a Viking ship, its king and cargo turned to ash. I was delighted by the place, forgot about my fear, and was still running about between the forest of posts when the sun lifted out of the sea, orange into an indigo sky. I was surprised by the warmth as it lit my face. As though a stranger had reached out and touched me, in greeting, or reprimand. And shadows! Long, spidery shadows. Suddenly, to the right of me, I saw my own. Tall, and spectre-thin, my long hair blown sideways, my arms incidental above endless scissor legs. And suddenly my face was wet, tears from nowhere, my shadow. My shadow! I stood between it and the sun, it flooded from my feet along the earth and, for a little while, I knew I was alive. This moment, these moments, of recognition, they come so rarely; without hindsight, without forethought. Time passing even as we enter it.

I became accustomed to the day, relished the light wind, the turning tide, the water easing back. And now, outlined by the shadows, I could see each beach-combed fragment, each piece of rope, of driftwood, old toy, bit of net, and pram. Absolutely nothing unexpected. And then a ruin! A cottage, a bothy; without roof, or doors, or windows, half sunk into the sand. It must have been built on the spit, when the spit was somewhere else, and as the snakelike course shifted, the house, long abandoned, had ended up on the beach, disappearing under the water with each spring tide. I explored the bothy, its rooms cobwebbed in sand, but I wanted to get on and it was tiring, walking on the beach, my feet sinking with every step. I headed into the low dunes and was thrilled by snapdragons and sea holly, convolvulus and sea pinks. Saxifrage, pink – everything pink. *Rosa rugosa* flourished, arching sideways like a bramble, self-seeded from someone's garden; and then a yellow star-shaped flower, hypericum. I was enchanted with the softness of the landscape.

I saw the lighthouse. Something from a children's tale. And then I saw him. The man. At first I thought he was fishing. He stood, or rather acted, halfway between me and the lighthouse. I couldn't be sure of his age. I didn't want to get close enough to look. He could have been anything between twenty-five and fifty. I realised he hadn't seen me so I dropped into the long grass, aware suddenly how tired I was. He looked like Frank Auerbach, the painter, thick-set, wavy hair, energetic, strong. And yet he ran at the sea like a dancer, stopped – almost on tiptoe as his arms flew forward – and then hugged himself, ran back, but backwards, never once taking his eyes from the sea. He picked up a rock, ran again at the water's edge, hugged the rock to his chest, and then hurled it. It was this movement, I now saw, that I had mistaken for casting, for fishing. He was throwing. His arms fell, free of their burden, and he paused to see where the stone had landed. It was in the water. But he was still only for a moment. He seemed to rail at the sea, lift his arms in despair, or supplication, then run again, repeating his strange dance. And then again, another rock, hugged to the water, thrown, watched, the same backward, erratic movement. Every so often he reached the sea empty-handed, seemingly because he hadn't found an appropriate stone in the time he allowed for each circuit, and that's when the arms flew outwards, followed by the hug.

I was curious, yet afraid of him. I tried not to think about Virginia Woolf's novel *To the Lighthouse*, that told the story of a family and their holiday intention to visit a lighthouse; but they didn't actually get there until the First World War had happened,

23

and some of them were dead, and the children grown up, and it was all too late. I had no desire to pass this man to reach my destination. And I was so very tired. The dunes were full of indentations, clearings among the sea holly and marram grass, protected from the wind. Keeping one eye on the man, I moved behind him in an arc. A dusty green car was parked by the road, at my side of the lighthouse, and I thought it likely that it was his. The only footprints on the beach had been my own. There was a track leading from the road to the beach, between me and the car. There were no footprints in the dunes. So he'd either driven here, or walked, but either way he hadn't come over the ridge of dunes, or along the beach, which left the road, and the riverbank, as the spit was only a few yards wide at that point. And he was a creature of the most compulsive habit.

I retreated back into the dunes, keeping more or less equidistant from the track, the beach and the road, and scooped a hollow with my fingers in the warming sand, at the place furthest from where I felt he was likely to pass. I lay down in it, curled up, foetal. I could not see anything but grass and sky. I was below the lip of the dune. I could not see the man. Which meant, I supposed, that he couldn't see me.

The soft sand blew constantly. I closed my eyes. I remembered an event a few weeks earlier when I had met up with Rupert in London. We were staying in a hotel and I had woken early. I had walked over to the window and, while Rupert slept, had watched the hard summer light pick the shadows from the street below, first drawing detail, brickwork, cobbles; then bleaching it, until everything glowed and hazed with the promise of heat. I had watched a man come out of a mews house, as though to leave for work: he wore a suit, a flare of white indicating his shirt, too bright to see if he wore a tie. He had a cup in his hand, which surprised me. And then I realised: he was a smoker. I imagined a child in a high chair at a kitchen table, the mother or au pair in attendance. As he lit the cigarette, everything about him seemed to come together, his very atoms coalesced, formed a cloak about him, a swirl of testosterone. I watched him relax into himself, becoming a man, and for a while I had remained there, curious.

Later, I had walked past the house and seen that it wasn't a home but an engineering consultancy. This made more sense of his distraction, his abstraction, and also of his desire for the cigarette – when you want something, and you can't have it, there is tension inherent in the situation. I wondered what had happened to this man on the beach, what had brought him to this place, this erratic dance, this compulsion. But I was unable to hold the thread. Sleep worried at the fabric of my consciousness, loosened it, pulled at it before lifting it, so that it blew and dipped across the sand like a child's favourite blanket, carrying my thoughts away with it.

I woke up an hour or so later. The satiety only sleep can give. Sand covered me in shallow drifts; my hair was full of it. Warm in the hollow basin, heavy-lidded. I sat up. Cautious. I was incredibly hungry. I had brought food with me, but I was already ill at ease, and would remain so until I knew where the man was.

I walked to the tip of the dune, bending forward to reduce my height, the lighthouse to my right, the beach to my left and ahead of me. And there he was, still throwing rocks. I caught now the O of his voice, no words, the wind had shifted. It was as though nothing had happened (nothing had happened). Perhaps he was a little slower, but not much. I wondered, for the first time, how long he'd been there. Did we arrive more or less together? Or had he been there all the while that I drove, over the Pennines, along the estuary, under the deepening sky? But I didn't really want to know, not now, possibly not ever. I wanted to be free of him, away. I was very much afraid of him, afraid of his unquiet mind, and I felt this fear coiling in my intestines.

My heart pulsed at the base of my throat; my mouth was dry. I was still so tired. One hour's sleep was not so much and I was jittery with adrenalin. We were three miles into the North Sea, the murderous estuary to the west. At some point the man was likely to leave – I had hoped this would happen while I slept, leaving me to follow him, leisurely, off the peninsula. But no, it would be he who followed me. I didn't believe he had come along the beach, but the sand was too slow, and tiring at best, exhausting to walk along. The road would be in full view of him. In spite of this I decided to remain visible – he seemed settled for a while – and make distance. When I reached the road of tiles, I ran.

Because most of me suspected the man to be harmless, I could not find the necessary edge. My fight-or-flight-mechanism was folded, resting, just below the surface, and I could not access it. I was irritated that I was running away from a place that I had come so far to see. I simply could not believe the literary irony of not getting to the lighthouse, which was wonderful, full-bodied with black-and-white hoops, like an Everton mint, its decommissioned light held in a liquorice cage with diamond sugar panes. I knew that, if I was a man, and I was ten years younger, I probably wouldn't care. I was irritated that my long blonde hair and slight frame rendered me vulnerable, unexpected. I wished I'd brought a hat.

A hare appeared; huge, brown, with unmistakable black ears, the slightly devil eye. It seemed so large that it filled the road. I stopped.

Quite unperturbed, it loped off in the direction of the river. Had it come from the beach? What a thought. And I was happy – suddenly everything was all right. If I hadn't run away from the madman, I would never have met the hare. I followed it. The riverbank, so recently a place of terror, seemed, under the warm sun, quite lovely. The light on the water rendered it accessible, possibly this was also an effect of the receding tide. Even as I watched, a cargo ship entered the river mouth, brightly coloured and flat as cardboard, bound for Hull and full of purpose. On the far bank, impossibly far away, was a town, rows of towers and cubes, something made on a children's TV show, from matchboxes and toilet rolls. Not Hades, but Cleethorpes.

I walked along a narrow track through short bright grasses following the path of the hare. Every so often it reappeared before me, in exactly the same aspect, facing west, towards the river. Its hazel eye seemed to appraise me, before it turned once again and loped off, apparently as tame as a cat. Suddenly all around me were oystercatchers. I heard them before I saw them and laughed out loud when I did. They floated like an articulated carpet, like something from *Arabian Nights*, washing over the sand and onto the riverbank, pouring through grass, across the track, opening to circumvent a stone, or a bit of wood, and closing around it on the other side, their shifting pattern hovering above a movement smooth as castors. And their funny, chirruping, pulsing whistle – soft as mechanical birds'. I supposed they had gone to the river, because quite suddenly they disappeared, and it was as though they were never there.

I saw a fisherman ahead of me. Broad-shouldered, yet slender. My eye was drawn by the movement of his back. I could avoid him, he hadn't seen me, but I was not afraid. I continued to walk along the path. He was reeling in his line. He glanced at me and nodded. There was a smile implied in the gesture and humour in his expression, although that could just have been an effect of the sunlight, his eyes half closed against it. I returned the greeting, inclining my head fractionally, a Japanese quality to this silent exchange of nodding courtesies. I thought of the willow pattern, the blue-and-white plates, although they were from China and the figure on the plate carried a whip. The fisherman looked at the tip of his rod, and fiddled with it, the movement slightly exaggerated; I had probably surprised him. I knew that he was checking the whereabouts of the hook, and that this was for my benefit. So I looped behind him, allowing him room to cast. I walked on without looking round.

The hare had gone, the riverbank was not my demesne, so I made my way up to the road, then retraced my steps along the beach, towards the mainland.

I was curiously disappointed as I passed by the prefab buildings. It seemed silly, now, to have been afraid, to have abandoned my journey. I found the car. Noticed immediately that one tyre was low, and liquid seeped from underneath the engine. I reached down, touched the liquid; it was clear and had no smell. Water. That was something, then. I glanced at the wheel on the front driver's side, examined the tyre. It was soft, but not too bad and there was no obvious damage to it. I listened, but there was nothing, no hiss of air. The cap had been removed. So. Not a puncture. I opened the door and reached for a bottle of water; it was misted with condensation. I flicked the switch that released the bonnet. With one hand I held the bottle as I drank, long, slow, cool. With the other, I raised the bonnet. I flexed my foot against the bumper, watching for the movement of the water in the radiator reservoir.

It seemed OK. I checked the container that fed the windscreen wipers. Tipped the rest of my bottle into it.

A man appeared. I hadn't heard him approach and there was no sign of a car but, at this point, nothing surprised me. He was about sixty, heavy set, wearing baggy denim dungarees and a pair of Crocs. No socks, no shirt; indeed, he appeared to be naked beneath the dungarees, the sides unbuttoned to reveal pale flesh, but he wore a navy-blue-and-white bandana around his head, Hell's Angel fashion. Presumably to hide his encroaching baldness if the few wispy tufts that were visible were any indication of what was underneath. A large pair of binoculars hung around his neck, gold sovereign rings gilded the fingers that rested there. A twitcher.

'Someone's let your tyres down,' he offered, surprisingly well informed. 'And there's liquid coming out of your engine.' The pitch of his voice was light but nasal and this, in combination with his elongated Hull vowels, created an incongruously effeminate effect in such a big man. I noticed a large hooped earring.

'I think it's from the air conditioning,' I said. He was standing in the long grass at the side of the car park, and seemed unwilling to step onto the tarmac.

'That's good,' he said. 'Well. I can see that you're on your own, so I'll leave you in peace. Not disturb you.' And he set off in the direction of the beach. I smiled to myself, trying to work out what he'd have said if I'd had company, but was nonetheless touched by his gentle grace, and the implied understanding of what it is to be alone. I looked around me. How many pairs of eyes? What a curious place. I got into the driver's seat. I was about to turn the key in the ignition when I saw the hare again. Or rather, a hare. It was cropping grass on the bank ahead of me in more or less the place where the man had stood a few moments earlier. The word *psychopomp* formed in my mind. Meaning spirit guide.

I turned the key. The hare looked up at the sound, enquiring, deer-like, but unruffled. It went back to pulling at the grass. I put the car into reverse, and left.

Mersey

um unfolded a sheet of newspaper and spread it on the
table in front of us.

'I'd like to see this; I'm certain Evie would enjoy it.' It
was half of a page cut from the *Liverpool Daily Post* and showed a
photograph of a figure on a beach. There was a seagull standing on
its head. The headline read: *Fate Of Iron Men Decided Tonight*,
although the cutting was a few years old. It referred to Antony
Gormley's installation, *Another Place*. Evie peered briefly at the
picture, then went back to taking the order for breakfast on a
spiral-bound waitress's notepad. I said I'd like toast, as it was the
only thing she felt comfortable making, and she disappeared into
the kitchen.

'Are you sure they're still there?' I asked.

'I should think so,' said Mum. 'I don't think anyone will move
them now. We could have a picnic. And see anything else that you
think might be of interest.' I looked at Mum and then back at the
newspaper cutting.

'Anything?'

'Anything that you think we might like to see.'

I wondered how long Mum had been waiting for this moment. 'It's very close to the Convent,' I said. 'Did you know that?'

'Well, I remember you'd said it was somewhere near there. If you wanted us to have a look at it we could.' Mum had that slightly too wide-eyed expression that she always wore when she had an ulterior motive, or was planning some kind of surprise. Evie came back in with the toast.

'Would you like to go on a picnic?' I asked her.

'You said we were going to the cottage today.' Evie was frowning. This was true.

'What if we go to the cottage tomorrow? We can spend another day with Grannie.'

Evie agreed to the picnic, although warily, as though uncertain whether or not she had been cheated. She helped us to make sandwiches, pack apples, find the chocolate. We filled a flask, containing more chocolate, and then the three of us set off for Liverpool.

I parked the car close to the beach. Tall fences and razor-wire barriers marked one edge of the car park. On the other side were the docklands. Empty metal cranes clustered over cargo containers that were heaped like giant boiled sweets. Dunes the colour of sackcloth spilled beneath the fence, flowing north in rumpled bolts, until the coast bent them out of sight. Ahead of the dunes, in the river mouth, was a wind farm, but the blades were still. There was a boating lake, an oval lagoon, but it was empty. The only thing that seemed to move was the coarse, springing grass that grew all around us and pulled, tentatively, against the wind as though taking part in a tug-of-war. I felt edgy, as if I was on display, a Master of Ceremonies, although of what I couldn't say. Even the fact that we'd brought sandwiches seemed significant, somehow indicative of a need for self-sufficiency, a desire to remain apart. I tried to push the feeling away from me and enjoy the day for what it was. A picnic, after all, was an adventure; but Evie, for reasons of her own, became uncooperative, insolent, and would hardly move from the car. Suddenly Mum, who had been tapping ahead with her walking stick, turned on Evie.

'This isn't about you, this is Mummy's special place, and you are spoiling it!'

I looked at Mum. *Mummy's special place.* I was oddly thrilled to hear Mum fight my corner, even against my daughter. Even so, we couldn't get Evie out of the car park. She wrapped herself around one of the few trees planted to act as a windbreak. I was aware of the pressure inside my head. Eventually I snapped:

'Stop it! Stop it! Stop it!' while trying to recall if it was illegal to shout at your children in England, or just bad form. We glared at one another.

'This is a magic place,' I said, feeling as if I was falling down a hole. 'On the other side of the dunes is a portal to another world.' Evie looked unconvinced. At the edge of the boating lake signs the size of postcards read: *Beware of Blue Green Algae. Do Not Touch the Water. Danger.* About five hundred yards away – painted brightly and hedged in with shrubs to protect it from the wind – was a children's playground. It had snagged at the edge of Evie's vision and, I finally realised, was the cause of her dissent. Beyond stretched the dunes, characterless and dull, over which the calico sky was drawn down like a blind, a lighter area overhead denoting the position of the sun. We had to pass through the dunes to get to the beach. The playground was the only thing Evie could see that was of interest to her. But she had liked the word *portal*. I wasn't sure why I'd said it. I wondered if Evie knew what it meant, or if I did, for that matter. It had sounded vaguely sci-fi, indicative of travel.

'Look,' I said. 'Just come with me through that gap in the sand and you'll see. If you don't like it we can come back and go to the playground.'

'You promise?'

'I don't need to promise. You know it's true. In fact, we can go there anyway. Just come with me and Grannie first.'

A boardwalk led to the gap through the dunes. I wondered who swept it, who maintained the space, and how often they needed to do it.

Portal.

Evie let go of the tree, her eyes lingering briefly on the upright posts of the playground, the only brightness in the muted landscape, then looked towards the dunes with as much apprehension as though she were going for an injection. Mum was already half way there, the steadfast click of her walking stick on the wooden path a tortoise challenge to Evie's hare. Evie let go her breath then ran after her.

I walked behind them, aware of the push of the wind from the north, and caught up with them as they came to the gap. On either side of the pathway the dunes were fenced in, grown over with spiky grass and lilac sea holly. There were more signs saying: *Erosion, Keep Off*, which Evie ignored, running to the top of one dune and scudding down the other side. Mum and I walked through the gap, the three of us arriving at the same time, each of us surveying the beach.

Another Place is an installation of one hundred life-size casts of the artist Antony Gormley, although it took us a while to see them. Gradually the immobility of the figures intensified before the shift of the sea and the slowly revolving sky. The metal men became apparent, one by one, stretching into the distance. Their rows disappeared into the grey water, neither waving nor drowning. Mum, with a gentle smile, absorbed the fact of them. Evie saw one, pointed, and ran to it, and then another, and then quite suddenly became aware of the extent of them, realised that they were all around her, and that the beach was dominated by them. She stopped running, and turned back to me, her laughter breaking free.

When I first came here, the 'Antonys' were new, austere, automaton-like. I was surprised how little time it had taken to soften them, rust rising to the surface of their cast-iron skins in a patina that looked like lichen. Their extremities had eroded, were becoming vague. Some of them were buried knee-deep in sand while others stood on previously hidden plinths. There was an echo of the upright timbers of Spurn Point, although they lacked the physical function of the groins, and were entirely without altruism. Yet they seemed united by a resolution to remain between the sea and the land. I stood next to one of the metal men and tried to follow his gaze. Looking out to sea. My task this summer, the task I had set myself, was to look back. To turn my back on the sea, on what it might mean, and walk back on myself. Out there was another place, the whole of life not lived, and, at some point, although very distant, I hoped, was death. But I didn't want to look at the setting sun, or even the rising sun, as it dropped into or lifted out of the sea. I had unfinished business to attend to.

★

Taliesin was a poet whose story is told in *The Book of Taliesin*, one of the sacred texts of Wales. Before he was a poet he was an ordinary boy whose name was Gwion Bach. Late one night a great lady, who was also a witch, took Gwion from his parents' house. The witch had a son who was both dull-witted and ugly. She wanted wisdom for her child so that he might be made welcome at court, and also to compensate him for his appearance, about which she could do nothing. But she could do something about his stupidity, for there was a famous spell, which she made. The spell had to be stirred for a year and a day and the first three drops, when it was ready, would bestow the Grace of Inspiration. The rest would turn to poison. So because her son was lazy, as well as dull and ugly – and anyway grand people never do these things for themselves – she took Gwion from his parents' house so he might stir the cauldron night and day.

The witch told Gwion, in no uncertain terms, that he must never taste the spell. But on the last day, which was the first day of the second year, three drops of the boiling liquid spat onto Gwion's thumb, and burnt him. He was so hurt, so shocked, and so very, very tired that in his confusion he forgot about the witch's words and put his thumb straight into his mouth to soothe it, thereby tasting the spell intended for her son, and in one vast, eternal, tiny instant, Gwion became wise. He knew, without being told, everything there was to know. And the first thing he knew was that the witch would kill him.

He ran away from the castle as fast as he could, the cauldron exploding behind him. But the witch, who was gathering herbs, felt the betrayal as surely as though a great door had closed far beneath her. She came after him. When he saw her, Gwion turned into a hare, and ran. But she became a dog, a great grey long-limbed hunting dog, and she followed the hare and turned him until there was no land left for him to cover.

So Gwion became a fish, and he slipped through the reeds into a lake, where he hid from her. But the witch became a she-otter, all needle teeth and oily pelt, and she chased Gwion all around, until he jumped from her, became a bird, and flew.

She turned into a hawk. No sooner had Gwion gained the blue heights than he saw her beating over him. He caught sight of her curving talons, saw her wing feathers fanned like knives, and heard her *arr-wah* cry. He watched as she retracted her wings, the wind spiralling a tunnel around her, its voice caught humming and whirring through her feathers, and all the time she came falling, faster and faster still until the fear in his heart was so great that he felt it must burst. Yet at the moment that she reached him and righted herself, her wings releasing the song of the wind, her thorny toes clasped air.

Gwion was dropping away from her, a golden grain of wheat, too fine for her scissored feet to hold.

He came to rest in a barn, amid a heap of grain.

The witch became a black hen, high-crested, with yellow claws, and she scratched at the grain; Gwion's terror was so great, and at last she found him. Ate him. She could feel that he was inside her, and she was glad.

But Gwion wasn't dead, although he was at the end of his strength. He knew that he was inside the witch, and used all that he had left to make one final shift. He became a baby. He grew inside her into the most beautiful child the world would ever see. The witch determined to kill him as soon as he was born. But when her time came upon her, and she looked at the lovely little boy, she knew she couldn't do it. So she threw the baby into an old leather bag, and tossed it into the sea.

There was a poor man fishing at the mouth of a river. He had caught nothing all day long and had decided, very sadly, to go home. Just then he saw the leather sack, which had caught against a pole in the weir, and he fetched it, and opened it. He took the boy ashore, this special golden child, and lifted him gently onto the back of his horse, heaping up the blankets, all he had with him, to make a bed. And of course the man and his wife had no children of their own, so they kept him, and they loved him, and called him Taliesin. Which means: Radiant Brow.

As the child grew up he told astonishing tales. His voice was as pure as water, and he became a famous bard, singing at the court of King Arthur, and other things, which we don't need to know.

What matters for this story is that the life of Taliesin, the only life he knew, began at the mouth of a river.

The first time I came to this place was by accident. Or rather, the first time that I came here knowingly. I had been to the read-through of a play. I was tired and cramped from being indoors, my eyes sticky from staring at the page. I had longed to walk on a beach. As Liverpool is a port it seemed obvious that if I headed north then sooner or later I would find one. So I had left the writer, the cast and the director, with their curling sandwiches and their vending-machine coffee, and had driven from the City Centre, past the Cunard, East India and Exchange buildings until the seafront gave way to the fragmented, potholed road, cracked and meandering, which ran alongside the docks. My car hugged the walls and fences and the razor-wire security until finally the road opened out, the city became residential again, and I saw a sign: *Antony Gormley's* Another Place. And because I didn't know about the metal men, and had forgotten about wanting to be on a beach, I grew curious, and I followed the signpost, and it brought me here.

Now, I had been adopted as a small child and I knew little of the circumstances of my birth. Mum and Dad had told me that I was conceived as the result of an *indiscretion* during my mother's engagement, and that my mother had married her fiancé shortly after I was born. But — and there was always a *but* — the condition for this gesture, this saving from disgrace, had been the giving up of the evidence, the discarding of the cuckold's horns. I remembered asking if that meant I was a bastard, as I had been called the name at school, my cheeks more pink with worry over using a bad word before my parents than any possible revelation about what the word might mean, and then Mum saying that 'illegitimate' was the proper way of saying it, though I wasn't, not any more, because they had adopted me. That was the story that Mum and Dad told me, one night, when I was eleven years old, after I had finally plucked up the courage to ask. We never discussed it again. How, or where, it had all taken place, there was nothing written down, other than the district of my birth, unavoidably preserved on my birth certificate along with the name of my birth mother and a thin blue line, a hyphen, that represented my father.

So on that day I had come to the beach for what I presumed was the first time in my life and found it familiar. In fact I was overwhelmed by the idea — not just that I had been there before — but that I had been born there.

★

A few years ago salmon were found in the Mersey for the first time in two hundred years. The fisherman who found Taliesin hoped for salmon, which is why there was a pole in the weir. A net was strung across the river mouth, at the place where the river meets the sea, to catch them as they returned to their breeding grounds. Before they stopped coming, when the effluent pouring into the rivers made the water too dirty to sustain them, salmon were common. In *The Water-Babies*, Charles Kingsley tells of a petition from the children in an English workhouse begging not to be fed salmon more than twice a week. In days gone by this magnificent fish was considered food for the very poor. It still is: Alaskan tinned salmon even now cross the seas to Africa, complete with a book of recipes, the shelf-life of a can, six years.

In addition to being their breeding grounds the high pools to which salmon make their way are also, for the most part, their graves. As the disintegrating bodies of the parent fish fragment and float back towards the sea they sustain the tiny smolts. It is a curiously sacramental death. Birth. Dark there, under the sea, the cool fresh easing towards them, the late spring floods bringing a scent, a peaty memory, diverting them from their diet of prawns. How do they know when to respond? What calls them?

On that day, I'd had a sense. I'd felt a pull, a draw, as though something were listening. I'd felt it in the space around me. It was so strong that I had turned in my tracks, away from the shore and away from the Antonys, and walked back, towards the land. Later, I wondered if the cleaning up of the Mersey had contributed to my feelings on that day. I wondered if I was able, finally, to perceive something that until then the dirty water and chemical spill had smothered. Drowned. Or perhaps the time just happened to be right; everything in alignment, a coincidence.

So I had walked towards the children's playground, the one that had so captivated Evie. There was an ice-cream kiosk, and two ladies waddled towards it along the same boardwalk path, a young girl between them in a green crocheted dress, a matching hat, her eyes wobbling behind thick lenses. Above and behind them hundreds of knots whirred in their two-tone winter plumage. The knots vanished briefly, then reappeared, with the slight tilt of a Venetian blind as their underbellies, which were the colour of the sky, made them momentarily invisible, although the air still crackled with their passing.

'Excuse me,' I said, 'is there a hospital around here?'

'There used to be,' said one of the ladies, and pointed through a gap in the sea wall. 'It's just up there.' It was a convent, they told me, and the sisters still lived there, but it wasn't a hospital any more. Quite grand, it had been, a sort of private nursing home.

'I see. Thank you.'

I followed their directions and came to the house. Inside the hallway was a brass plaque dedicated to the Sisters of Mercy, *who have cared for the sick in this place for over one hundred years*. No longer a hospital, but a guest house with a reception, which was empty. There was a bell, which I chose not to ring. Behind the desk there was a door into the main house, with a Yale lock. But it was on the latch. I eased inside.

The house opened around me, and grew larger, or perhaps I grew small in relation to it. There was a rectangular stained-glass window above a staircase; I felt certain that I knew it, that I had seen it before. I found a chapel, and what I took to be a baptismal font although it could have been a holy water stoup. A grille divided the house from the nuns' residence, and a few aged sisters sat in the pews, white as doves, tucked into prayer. An electric candle stand illuminated a painted metal relief of Our Lady, and I thought of school and Physics, the simple circuits and fairy-light bulbs.

'Can we help you?' As I turned and walked back into the hall-way I almost knocked over two of the sisters.

'Oh! Yes. I'm sorry. There was no one in reception.' The sisters waited. One of them was about my own age, while the other was ancient, the crown of her veiled head barely reaching the shoulder of the younger nun. I found myself thinking of a pepper-pot.

'I was wondering if it might be possible that I was born here?' The nuns seemed unfazed by the question.

'Yes,' the younger one replied, 'it is. In fact, if you were born in a hospital, in this part of Liverpool, then there was nowhere else. What's your name?'

'We can look up your records,' said the older nun, 'though I'm sorry that they're not of the best.'

'Actually, I was adopted as a child, and my name has been changed, but I know the name on my birth certificate: Marie Therese', and I mentioned a surname. The two nuns lifted their arms in unison, white puppets acting surrender.

'Sister Marie Therese!' they both said. I looked over my shoulder, thought perhaps someone was standing there. There was nobody.

'Sister Marie Therese?' I asked.

'Yes,' the older sister said, and turned to the younger woman next to her.

'Could Sister Marie Therese help me?' I asked.

'Yes,' said the older nun.

'Can I meet her?'

'No,' said the younger sister. 'She's died, ten years ago. But we know who you are.'

And as we stood in the hallway they told me the story, finishing one another's sentences, of the midwife who had been left, quite literally, holding the baby and of the mother who had fled the hospital. The younger sister seemed to be as familiar with the details as the older nun who had witnessed them. The midwife's name was Sister Marie Therese and she had taken charge of me, and looked after me, and kept me until a home could be found for me. 'She baptised you and she gave you her name.'

Whether this was Sister Marie Therese's own name, or one that she had taken on entering the Convent, I didn't think to ask. There was no time for me to register any feelings about the discovery, and loss, in under a minute, of my namesake. The idea, the fact, that I had one.

The sisters were gentle, animated. They seemed to be not at all surprised by what was happening, no matter how unlikely. They took an almost childlike pleasure in the continuance of an inter-rupted narrative. They showed me the room where I had slept, the cupboard where my nappies were stored, and where the baby food was kept. They showed me the room where I was born, which was now an office. Grey-metal filing drawers belched disorganised paperwork. I noticed a heavy glass paperweight with the three-tiered crown and crossed keys of the papal coat of arms. A tree filled the window. 'It would have been here already on the day of your birth. It would have been the first green thing you saw.'

I had got the idea that this must have been a Catholic mother-and-baby home, and presumed my story to be a common one. But no! The sisters were even a little put out by the suggestion. It was a hospital, a private nursing home, just as the ladies on the beach had said it was. Why was I trying to reduce this extraordinary circumstance, to render it commonplace? The sisters would have none of it; I was the only one, Sister Marie Therese's baby.

There were more sisters now. They didn't stop what they were doing, the internal pathway of their lives adhering to a proscribed invisible order, but they looked, pausing briefly in their steps. Word had gone about: 'Tis Sister Marie Therese's baby, and she's come back to us!' I felt their curious eyes, their kindly faces, those who had joined the Convent in more recent years seemingly as familiar with the story as the older nuns. I had a sensation of being contained within a mechanism. My unveiled hair and dark clothes, which trapped the scent of the outdoors – of wet leaves, of sea, of woodsmoke – seemed brash among the detergent white of their habits. I felt hot, faint. A smell of bleach and polish, which I had noticed on entering, now felt pervasive, oppressive. I asked if there was a garden and yet I didn't want to be an inconvenience; but the sister who had become my guide said I wasn't disturbing her. She worked in the local hospice and her working day had ended. I found her at her leisure. A nun's leisure: I realised how little I knew about the working of this order, any order. But I understood, or thought I did, that she had come here at this moment to be of help. Some of the older nuns were well into their eighties, and it would be getting time to prepare the evening meal. I had the impression that she remained, on the pretext of being social, to share, and thereby lighten, their burden.

She opened a door into a garden, adjuring me to stay as long as I wished. We could have tea, if I liked, when I was finished.

A dream. Clouds, talc, soap, milk. A veiled woman dressed in white, turning slowly towards me. I always woke before I saw the woman's face and felt that, if I did see it, I would die. Yet here she was, the veiled woman, made of concrete and painted glossy white. Green-black moss covered one side of her nose. It frosted the beads of her rosary. Lichen bloomed about an enigmatic smile. Pots of shrivelled geraniums clustered around her feet and her dress was spattered in compost, displaced by a watering can. But there was another part to the dream, another fragment: a real woman, a blue coat over the whiteness, her hair a pale blonde flag. The flag of hair had blotted out the light as she bent down to lift me from my pram. Summer tar, cracking wood, the peppery scent of tomatoes. Glasshouses, row upon row of them. This woman, bending down to me, I had assumed she was my birth mother. The smell of washed linen and, beyond her shoulder, the glasshouses, and that green hot reek of tomatoes. I know exactly where I was the first time I articulated this memory, the only time I told it to somebody else. I was in Bluebell Wood catching minnows with my cousin, Susan, string handles tied about the necks of our jam-jars, the silver fishes jabbing at the thickened glass, jerky as compass needles. I thought perhaps my cousin might have known the lady. I thought the lady might have been my mother. I can't have been more than four because after that we moved away from the village, and never went back to Bluebell Wood.

But as I turned away from the concrete statue I found myself looking at the glasshouses, row after row of them, the wooden frames splintered, the panes all but gone, and I realised that the woman in my dream with the flag of pale hair was not my mother, but a sister, probably Sister Marie Therese, and that the beloved face, which had always eluded me, was hers. Not hair, then, but the veil; the crisp white cotton of the Augustinians.

'I've made some tea!' It was the sister who had become my friend, and I followed her back into the house, the sunlight folding as we entered the panelled hallway. Her name was Maria, but before she joined the order it had been Katherine. My name had been Marie, but had then been changed to Katharine. I was born in the Convent and had then gone out into the world. Sister Maria had given up the world in order to enter it. We laughed at the inverted symmetry of our lives, our names. Sister Marie Therese had been Maria's special friend, and had cared for her as a novice, had cared for both of us.

'She prayed for you every day of her life,' she said, and I had no idea what to do or say so simply sat there, the teacup slipping across the yellow saucer until the sounds of the kitchen and a smell of frying onions made me conscious that I should be on my way.

When I left we exchanged addresses. Sister Maria said that this was my first home, and that I would always be welcome here. Later she wrote to me with a photograph of Sister Marie Therese and a baby, although she couldn't be sure if it was me.

The newborn Taliesin had regarded his discovery in the river mouth by the poor man as a most propitious event. For the man. For though he was only one day old Taliesin miraculously spoke, chastising the man for being sad over his empty net, adding that in the time of need he, Taliesin, would be worth more than three hundred fish. Later he spoke to the poor man's father, and gave the most colourful account of his provenance:

> *Into a dark leathern bag I was thrown,*
> *And on a boundless sea I was sent adrift,*
> *Which to me was an omen of being tenderly nursed,*
> *And the Lord God then set me at liberty.*

Taliesin was one for whom the cup was decidedly half full. The wondrous story of his life, which – after all – he wrote himself, has survived for fifteen hundred years. He was without self-pity as he acknowledged, and slid over, his humble origin as Gwion. The pathway from lost boy to mighty bard was bright and packed with adventure, for which Taliesin took all of the responsibility and all of the credit, although he thanked God for his release.

I too began my life at the mouth of a river. I had found a missing piece in the broken vase of my history, accounting for the lost months of my babyhood. I had been born in this place and now, by chance, I had returned. It was as though I had been given a coat that turned out to be a perfect fit without ever having realised that I was cold. I found it hard to remember that the gift was new, and that yesterday, or even an hour ago, I didn't have it.

Yet, at the same time, I had stumbled on heartache. I had no recollection of a loving birth mother who had given me up against her will. I had no more fragments. The shard of memory I had conserved, of a woman looking into a pram, was not of her. When she married she became as carefully hidden as Gwion's grain of wheat, her husband's name as common to the Welsh as John Smith is to the English. I had never found her and no one, as far as I knew, had ever looked for me. The day of her wedding was the day of my adoption. I presumed she was aware of this. When Anne Boleyn was executed, upright, on her knees, with a fine French sword, her successor, Jane Seymour, was trying on her wedding dress. Which was yellow. Not quite the image of the English rose that has been so carefully handed down. Perhaps if she'd lived long enough she'd have shown her colours.

This sounds bitter. It is. Although I felt no ill will – the opposite in fact. I was thankful from the bottom of my heart for my existence, although not to her, the gift of life unintentional, abortion illegal. But in her desire for anonymity, be it conscious or feckless, my birth mother had also hidden me from my natural father, and I could not tell what hurt the most, the two things rushing against one another, noisy, confluent. All I could see, from looking in the glass, was that I was most likely of Celtic origin. And even that could not be certain, although I have always passed for such.

I was sorry not to have known my foster-mother, Sister Marie Therese, but it was her goodness, and an unexpected sense of my own completeness – or rather normalcy – that I took away with me that day. The rest I left on the shore; a life I could have known, but never did, its myriad possibilities suspended.

We walked along the beach, Evie making zigzag tracks in the sand, which I did my best to follow. Mum came behind us with her stick, her footsteps and the circular divots made by her cane running in a median line between our undulating ones, and I thought of sine waves and Aboriginal paintings. One of the Antonys was wearing a cardigan, another a scarf, one had a pair of socks on his hands, while another had a Tesco bag tied about his wrist. We sat on a concrete wall and ate our lunch, wind tickling the greaseproof paper. You had to chew the brown bread and crumbly Cheshire cheese for a while before it became something tasty, melded into something good, and Evie just munched the middle out of her sandwiches and discarded the crusts, impatient with the process. The tide was coming in. Some of the Antonys slipped below the waves, their clothes loosening.

Evie was the first to reach the playground.

'Grannie,' she called, 'there are four swings!' A man dressed wholly in red, including a prize-fighter's belt and a scarlet baseball hat from which stiff dreadlocks protruded, stalked past us in the direction of the shore. Two workmen in Day-Glo overalls ate ice cream. One photographed his 99 cornet with his mobile phone while the other, holding an ice-lolly, laughed. Two robust identical orange-haired boys scaled monkey bars. Their mother was pale, with dark smudges under her eyes, as though the twins had sucked the goodness from her. We stopped for ice cream at the kiosk by the playground: *Soft Ice-Cream Sold Here. Lolly Ices. Cold Cans. Slush. Hot Drinks. Popcorn. Candy Floss & More.* Then, ice creams in hand, we made our way back over to the swings. Mum laughed at the sign that said only children under the age of fourteen could use the playground, and then graciously, but firmly, ignored it. She used the hook of her walking stick to bring one of the swings within reach, and then Evie held the seat in place while Mum manoeuvred herself onto it. Evie and I then sat on the two swings flanking her, and the three of us rocked to and fro, gazing seaward, eating our ice creams. Mum wore a woolly hat to keep her hair from the wind. She laughed when she caught me looking at her.

Mum had always been an enigma to me. Throughout my childhood she had remained unfathomable. When I was Evie's age, possibly younger, Mum would bounce light from a compact mirror around the living room, swearing it was a fairy, and when I tried to touch the flickering image she snapped the compact shut and, laughing, dropped it into her handbag. It took me for ever to realise it was a trick. It was only now that Dad had died that Mum was starting to afford tightly angled views into herself, although she remained very difficult to read. She had an easy love of simple things, like swings, and ice cream, classic novels. Walking through wet leaves. Driving. She was uncomplicatedly happy. I had never seen her cry. It was her extraordinary engagement, her zest for life, that had drawn Dad to her, that drew all of us. I had always known that Mum wasn't my 'real mother' and, for a long time, as a child, I had tried to make sense of our relationship, the word *mother* connoting something both formal and alien to me. For some reason Dad had been exempt from this sense of 'otherness'. Perhaps because no one mentioned the possibility of my having another father, so for a long time he was the only candidate. It was only as an adult that I had grown curious about the man whose identity remained hidden, concealed behind the hyphen on my birth certificate.

Mum and Dad had met when they were children. Dad lived in a Cheshire village, defined by a Norman castle, in a community divided by Church and Chapel. Mum lived a couple of miles away, in the industrial township of Runcorn, but they had attended the same primary school. Mum left school at sixteen, and all I really knew about her early life was that she had once run a hundred yards in 11.4 seconds, that her mother was the District Nurse, and that her father had a car with white wall tyres. Most of the stories, although it was Mum who told them to me, were about Dad.

He had proposed to her when he was twenty-four, and Mum was twenty-two, at the top of Tryfan, in Snowdonia. On a clearer day the mountain might just be visible, across the estuary, from the playground where we now found ourselves. Certainly, if you look the other way – north-west from the summit of Tryfan – you can see Liverpool Bay. It is a deceptive and formidable mountain. Mum would tell how she and Dad had skipped up the Heather Terrace, a prettily named, if scant, footpath, through the eponymous heather, that was pocked with steep drops down to the valley. At the summit were two stone monoliths, about ten feet high, known as Adam and Eve. After agreeing to become husband and wife, Mum and Dad had held each other's hands, and then leapt from one rock to the other, a distance of just over a yard. Then, apparently, they got lost in mist and almost walked off a precipice on their way back down.

I followed Mum's gaze as she drifted with the swing, now moved only by the breeze. I wondered if she realised that Tryfan was across the estuary. A few summers earlier, at Mum's request, Rupert and I had carried Dad's ashes back to the mountain, passing them between us, taking it in turns, and then tipped them out and left them, blowing furiously between Adam and Eve.

When Evie was ready to leave the playground Mum asked if we might visit the Convent. When I first told her that I had found the place by chance, she had simply said, 'Well, we always knew you were a Catholic,' and this had silenced any further discussion. This trip to the beach, this picnic engineered by Mum, was something new, and unexpected. We set off in the direction of the house.

The sisters were welcoming, just as before. *You're the one that was born here? Marie Therese? Come in!* I glanced at Mum but she didn't react to the use of the discarded name. When Sister Maria explained to Evie that this was my first home, Evie suggested that we all move in. Mum seemed wholly at ease as she chatted and laughed with Sister Maria and the older nuns. They talked about recipes for fruit cake. When it was time for us to go Evie crammed her pockets with biscuits.

Careful directions from Sister Maria brought us to a cemetery. It was within a field, far enough from the sea to prevent the water from permeating the graves. A cluster of yew trees, poisonous to the cattle, creaked safely inside the walls. The sisters' plot was in the farthest corner, and marked by two large headstones. I scanned the memorial list of names and stopped at *S. Marie Therese Fay, Canoness of the Augustinian Order*. Evie made a shrine from things she had brought from the beach: bottle tops and razor shells, bladderwrack and sea cabbage. Stones. We planted sedum, careful not to crush its squashy leaves and winking suns. We hoped it took. Mum clapped her hands to bring warmth back to her fingers, then took Evie's hand in her own. The flat sky lightened marginally as the sun slipped beneath the cloud line. We told a decade of the rosary, and then went home.

Afon Geirch

Evie wiggled a forefinger through the widening gap at the top of the car window. She was striving to point something out to me and she couldn't express herself fast enough.

'Look, Mummy! Look!'

Three fox cubs bounced down the hillside, hot loaves knocked out of their tins. As I slowed the car to a stop they righted themselves. A wire fence, tufted with wool, acted as a buffer against a roll into the road. Their faces heaped together, as neat as party sandwiches. After appraising the car and the two of us inside it they circled back where they had come from, ululating, warbling, snout to brush, repeatedly glancing behind them, the next shunting tumble not far off. We marvelled till the cubs were lost – it was over before there had been time to steal a picture – and when they were gone there was just the Jew's harp buzz of the wind in the grass and the dropping notes of skylarks. We had stopped the car on the natural border to the Llŷn Peninsula in the midst of three peaks known as the Rivals, which gives a combative and brotherly ring to the Anglicisation of Yr Eifl, meaning the strides. Below us, at the bottom of the hill, was Nefyn Bay.

Evie called this place the Misty Moor, after a line in a children's prayer: *Matthew, Mark, Luke and John, hold my horse while I leap on, hold him steady, hold him sure, till I win o'er the misty moor*. She called it that because the Rivals were usually covered in cloud, even on the hottest days, though on this day the sky was clear but for the odd tugged wisp smoothed over the tops. The island of Anglesey was visible to the north, Cardigan Bay and the mountains of Mid-Wales to the south, and the Wicklow Mountains, across the sea in Ireland, stretched out like a knotted string on the western horizon. Behind us, to the east, the cantilever of Yr Eifl's peaks gated off Snowdonia. Ahead, the road spooled towards the volcanic cone of Garn Fadryn. Somewhere on Garn Fadryn's flank, very small, not yet visible, was our cottage. The Llŷn Peninsula floated before us, towing its islands with it, the sea and the sky continuous, indistinguishable one from another.

We pulled up outside the cottage, one of four houses on a crossroads. Tony, who lived in the house opposite to ours, waved from the armchair in his glass porch. He spent most of his days, and nights, in this armchair, a tank of oxygen at his side. I was about to speak to him when Evie clambered over the rendered wall on her way to our front door.

'Be careful!' The wall had a crack in it from top to bottom and had split into free-standing halves. The pieces gave perceptibly whenever anyone vaulted it. According to Tony it had been like that since the summer of 1984 when, thirteen miles beneath the mountain, the European Plate had eased its position relative to the Mid-Atlantic Ridge. The subsequent earthquake had measured 5.4 on the Richter Scale and remains the most significant seismic movement on record in the British Isles. It had rattled teacups and crumpled chimneys as far away as Liverpool. There was some debate about whether or not ours was one of them. When I first bought the cottage, which is a traditional two-room bothy, the inglenook fireplace was concreted in. I asked a local builder to try to reveal it and Tony had come over in his vest and slippers to watch the work and have a beer. There was no foundation to the house, only mud beneath black tiles. A few inches below the surface an underground stream ran out from the centre of the fireplace and on through the only bedroom. The stream was visible, outside, at either end of the cottage, where it ran clear beneath rusted grilles. The newly revealed inglenook and chimneybreast dominated the room.

'You want to watch that,' Tony had said. 'It started shifting after that last rumble. That's how come it was rendered in.' Tony leaned against the mantel and gently scratched his belly with the hand that wasn't holding the bottle. Geraint, the labourer, looked up from the hole that he had dug in the floor. It was filling up with water from the stream, which no longer ran clear. His spade hit something hard. Emlyn, the builder, climbed down into the hole and the two men eased up a pillow of granite from the centre of the fireplace. It belched free of the mud, they curled their arms beneath it, staggered with it, lurched and slipped towards the door, as though carrying a newborn calf. There was an uneasy moment.

'That's the foundation stone,' offered Tony.

'What?' asked Emlyn.

'It'll fall down now, for sure.' Tony shifted his footing to get a better look in the hole.

'You want to mind you don't fall in,' Emlyn said. 'My insurance won't cover it if you do because you're not supposed to be here.'

'Well, I'll come back when you've put the floor in. Thank you for the beer, flower, *Diolch yn fawr!*' and with that Tony shuffled out.

The men persevered. Over the next few days they dug a footing, more than two hundred years after the house was raised on the turf from *random rubble*, which is a technical term in the building trade meaning *anything that comes to hand*. They accommodated the stream within a layer of gravel, and a membrane, and covered it all in concrete. They built a wooden cabin bed for me, and a ladder up to the crog-loft for Evie. The chimney was restored and the stream, visible beneath the grilles at the sides of the house, regained its former clarity. The 'foundation stone' remains, where it was dropped, in the garden.

I lit a fire. Even though it was June there was a chill to the stones. The house had been empty since Easter. Over lunch we discussed our project, our plan to find the well at the world's end by following watercourses from the sea to their sources.

'Can we count the Mersey?' asked Evie.

'I think so,' I said. 'I don't think it has to be the same river that we follow, as long as we eventually get to an end.' Evie thought about this, then nodded her agreement. We could count the trip to the Mersey Estuary as an exploration of 'sea'. Evie wrote an account of the picnic in her journal. She drew a picture of the beach with the Antonys.

'What should we do next?' she asked.

'I think we should follow the river that comes out at Cable Bay,' I said. 'We could go now, and see how far we get.' Evie pressed her lips together. Having just arrived at the cottage she was loath to go out again, but after the two-hour drive from Mum's I wanted, dearly, to stretch my legs, uncoil my spine. I put some chocolate and water and a couple of apples in a rucksack. The purple-and-white wrapper caught her eye.

'Can we eat the chocolate now?' she asked.

'Let's have it when we get there.'

'Can we eat some on the way?'

I glanced at her. 'How about we open it when we get to the beach?'

Evie slipped down from the table. 'All right.'

Cable Bay is the nickname given to a curved beach near our home. Its name in Welsh is Abergeirch, which means the mouth of the River Geirch. A rusted metal pipe runs down to the sea, alongside the Afon Geirch, supported on concrete blocks. All kinds of local stories account for the function of the pipe. One of them involves a telephone cable running under the sea to Ireland and it is this that has given the bay its nickname. The place nearest our home where the road meets the sea is called the Bwlch, so that was where we headed for.

Bwlch means pass, or valley, and it is a natural cut through the sandy cliffs, a place where boats can be ferried from the beach on trailers tugged by tractors. The shelter it gives from the wind makes it a natural oasis and its banks were stacked with montbretia, the orange lilies dancing over pliant, strap-like leaves, racing along the paths like a Pentecost. Lanterns of green and blue hydrangea ballooned against red and purple tutus of fuchsia. Roses made a scaffold for the softer plants and gave them substance against the wind.

The beach was the reason I had bought the cottage in the first place — or rather, Rupert had bought the cottage. It was his extraordinary wedding gift, funded by a film deal from one of his books, *so I will know where to find you when you wander.*

I had first come to the beach when my father was dying. We had planned to come on a family holiday – everyone knew it would be the last – but at the last moment Dad felt he wasn't well enough. Evie was still a baby, and she and I came anyway. My brother and his family had gone ahead, and Dad had waved us off. His eyes, that were sometimes the colour of slate, on that day shone blue.

'Goodbye, my darlings!' He had stood on one leg outside their house, and raised his walking stick in a yogic salute, Mum standing anxiously behind him, her hands hovering at each side of his body. As I turned the car onto the main road I could still see him in the rear-view mirror, wobbling, happy, laughing. His smile seemed to say, *Go on, my darlings: anything is possible!* Yet the reverse had felt true. I had pushed my sunglasses up the bridge of my nose to cover my tears before glancing at Evie. Like Dad, she too was laughing, constricted by the baby seat, her blue anorak with pink roses rucked above the straps where she'd turned to keep his gaze.

When we had arrived in the Llŷn I was unable to settle. I could see no beauty in anything. The hills were too low, the sea was too grey and the sand was a characterless expanse. The cliffs were unstable. Two hours' drive away Dad was dying; in a few weeks I would never see him again. Yet I was on holiday, collecting shells.

But despite this the location drew me, and after Dad died I found myself returning. On some days the sea's surface wrinkled like elephant skin; on others it had the opacity of emulsion paint. Sometimes it was as clear as camomile tea, and Evie and I watched the hard ridges of sand below the water from the tops of the cliffs, pointing out the banks of bladderwrack, blue mussels and barnacle beds. The beach, too, rearranged itself, its skirts lifting to reveal clay, pebbles the size of tennis balls, shark's eggs, which were really dog-fish spawn, hard rectangular pouches with spiralling tentacles at the corners. Chips of red jasper, fists of granite, a cormorant's skull, smooth as a pen, a spider crab's pimpled shell, fishing floats, a knot of polyprop rope.

Once, when the tide was low, we found some big square stones. A fisherman said they were the foundations of a castle. A house, near the place, was known as Hen Blas, which means the old place, or perhaps the old palace, and this seemed to be all that was needed to verify the tale. The fisherman said that a minstrel, on his way to a feast, had been warned by a fairy that he met at Nefyn Fair not to sleep at the castle, so he'd slept under a hedge, had moaned all night, but by dawn all the guests had been murdered, and the minstrel was the only one who was saved. But a few weeks after the fisherman told the story the sand came back and the castle, or jetty, or harbour wall, or whatever it had been, vanished.

One icy March the beach was dotted with clams. They pulled themselves across the frosted sand with a single orange digit. Evie and I followed their monorail tracks, trying to remember the words to 'The Walrus and the Carpenter'; shouting sing song, over the wind. We'd picked them up, and taken them home, and then eaten them, every one.

The beach was a book that fell open. Each visit was a different page. I could not read it, neither could I leave it.

Cable Bay was on the north side of a finger of land, and the two beaches were back to back. 'Our beach', as Evie called it, Porth Dinllaen beach, was sheltered, but Cable Bay was hit by northerlies, and was rugged, and rocky. Porth Dinllaen had once been a contender for the location of the Dublin car ferry, but the contract had gone to Holyhead, on Anglesey. The beach, as might be supposed from this, edged a wide natural harbour. There was a pub at the water's edge, the Ty Coch, meaning the red house, and Evie tugged at my hand as we passed it – *Not now, Mummy!*

We looped around the headland, stopping to open the chocolate, and then clambered down onto a pebbled beach. In years gone by geologists had come from all over the world, as far away as Hawaii, wearing hard hats and dangling silver hammers, and specimen bags.

'Daddy says it's got some of the oldest rocks on earth,' Evie said, as though she had been reading my thoughts.

'Really?' I asked.

'I don't know. I think so. It might have been Daddy. Or it might have been somebody else.' I smiled, because I'd meant the stones. Folds of rock, red and blue, heaped like futons across the gravel, spilled in a stream from Garn Fadryn's cone, cooled into blocks by the sea. Or maybe the sea came later. A blue pebble caught my eye; I bent and picked it up. It looked like a beetle with red lines to mark its wings, as though it were crammed with fire; like the tadpoles of glass called Prince Rupert's drops that explode if you snap their tails. I closed my hand around the stone, its surface so smooth it felt soft. It nestled in my palm. *Basalt* is a satisfying word, glassy and seismic-sounding, and I wondered if it might be the right one. Other rocks rose like giant molars, umber and black, yawning from the beach. I thought about the tectonic plates and the rumble under the ground, 5.4 on the Richter Scale. I glanced in the direction of the hill, as though Garn Fadryn herself might answer.

I lay down on the pebbles and closed my eyes, lulled by the sound of the sea through the stones. Each retreating wave was an apnoeic gasp, gravel lungs filled with water, drowning without panic.

Time held me green and dying,
Though I sang in my chains like the sea.

The lines popped out of nowhere. They were by Dylan Thomas. I opened my eyes.

I must have fallen asleep. I raised myself onto my elbows and scanned the beach for Evie, my heart scrunching like a ball of baking foil.

There she was, at the edge of the sea, the yellow smudge of her blonde hair bright against the monochrome shore. She was throwing stones at a piece of driftwood. It was rotted and fragile. She pelted the driftwood until it broke, coming apart in pieces like bread on the water. A few yards beyond her charcoal birds, their blunt wings lifted, heads tilted back, vied for the shrouded sun on a rocky islet. The outline of the cormorants formed a mandorla around Evie; she was illuminated like a medieval saint. The sun was veiled behind a haze of cloud and showed as white as the moon, although the dark stones beneath me held the heat. I was confused by this, the warm stones, and the sun-moon, the time and the season slipping. But then Evie turned and looked for me, the driftwood crusts of no more interest to her, and I raised an arm, and could sense her smile, and suddenly she was running towards me, her head angled down, her arms straight at her sides, the small stones skittering at her feet.

A promontory crowned in sea pinks marked the edge of the beach. Cable Bay was the next inlet. The sea churned and gurgled through uneven channels. So we followed a footpath above a seam of grass in an oblique traverse across the cliff. From the top we were able to follow rough steps down to the river mouth.

At the back of the beach the sea had formed a bank of heaped-up pebbles, and the river pooled behind it, forming a kidney-shaped lagoon. Beyond the pool the Afon Geirch looped tightly between banks and beaches. It meandered through a deep wide gulley, back into the land, with sandy cliffs on either side. Montbretia lined the gulley walls, just as at the Bwlch, but where the sand ran to clay the orange flowers gave way to the first uncurling ferns, heads lifting uncertainly from their nests of bracken like hungry pterodactyl chicks. The rusted pipe, that may or may not have once held a cable, and was more likely to have carried sewerage, maintained a straight course towards the sea, the river winding under it.

At the place where the stream was widest there were stepping stones, although they were so steep, and so smooth, as to be unusable. They looked like tortoises. A few yards beyond them a thatch of phragmites reeds and bulrushes partially concealed the water. Between the rushes and the stepping stones was a wooden footbridge carrying the pilgrims' path that led to the tip of the peninsula. We stood on the bridge, and peered into the flow, shading our eyes with our hands.

'Look!' Evie said. 'Fishes!' And there in the darkness were the tails of trout, four of them, all in a row, their position sustained by a ripple of fins, and betrayed by the odd flick of a tail. I turned around and looked upstream and found myself staring at a heron. The fountain of white feathers springing from its breast seemed close enough to touch, its gold eye cold as glass. It was so still it could have been a decoy.

'Evie,' I whispered. 'Look!' And she gasped, we were all three taken aback, bird and people alike, but the heron had no intention of giving up its place, in thrall to the small fat trout.

We left the bridge and continued upstream. Partly because of the thick vegetation, and partly because of the marshy nature of the riverbed, there was no obvious way along the bank. Keeping the stream to the right, we followed it at a discreet distance, clambering to the top of the gulley, which formed a V-shaped cut in the land. On our side of the stream was a links golf course. Fields fringed the opposite bank. But the path across the golf course veered away from the water and into a sunken footway, a path from a time long before there was a golf course – a green lane, a holloway – spun around with gorse and blackthorn so that it formed a prickly tunnel adjacent to the stream. When we reached the end of the green lane the water was over to our right. At the edge of the golf course was a barbed-wire fence. We turned and went back to the footbridge and tried following the stream on its western bank. The western path went through a farmyard, towards the village of Edern, and again it bent away from the water, which now seemed to form a boundary to the farm, and was fenced in with barbed wire on both its banks. The houses of the village clumped ahead of us. I had read somewhere that Edern was the last village in Britain where fairies were seen. An old lady had apparently left a cake out for them, each week on baking day. She had done this until the 1950s. I started to tell Evie about it.

'Mummy?'

'Yes?' Evie was tired, her face smooth, pale despite the sun, the usual animation of her features still, folded away like birds' wings. 'Come on,' I said, 'let's go back.'

We retraced our steps, and broke out the remains of the chocolate, and resolved to try again. We would pick up the stream a bit closer to its source, somewhere on the shoulder of Garn Fadryn. But not today.

★

As the summer unfolded, this became something of a pattern. We would pick up a river along the coast of the Llŷn and follow it as far as we could. But there was always a fence, or a field, or someone's garden, private land, or a bull: something that could not be easily got around. Several of the rivers were enclosed, like this one, with barbed wire along both banks, so that the riverbed was the only pathway. In other places the fence might cross the stream itself. As the land rose higher water skipped through gullies, bouncing and slipping over rocks and stones, between banks that grew ever more deeply ferned. Occasionally we came across oases of vegetation, watercress and duckweed, nourished to frenzy by the fertilisers that washed off the land. The streambeds were difficult to ascend safely or with comfort. The enclosure of the land was constant, and uniform, and it forced us to go back, or around. It seemed impossible to trace a watercourse without wire-cutters and secateurs.

'What are they frightened of?' Evie asked, and I had no answer for her.

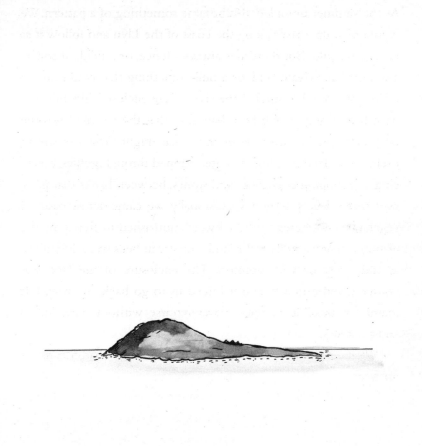

Ffynnon Fawr

At its western tip the Llŷn Peninsula is like a pointing hand; a solitary finger gesticulates a warning against the Irish Sea, at the place where the tides converge, and this place is known as the Swnd, or Sound. Sometimes the sea is calm, but when the tides turn the slabs of water heave alongside one another to create whirlpools and vortices, currents that are legendary. A hill crouches on the south side of the headland, cloaked by heather and stubby gorse that forms a pretty, but prickly, mantle. Below the hill, running to the edge of the land, is an apron of baize-like grass and this flourishes, protected from the worst of the weather, kept short and neat by sheep. In the centre of the green-baize apron is all that remains of St Mary's Church, now a rectangle of four low banks with a half-moon on one of the shorter walls, a ghost of the semicircular apse, although the whole thing has long since, centuries ago, grassed over. Occasional loose stones spill through the banks and people use them to write their names, or make symbols, or the sign of the cross — the round grey rocks on the short green grass encouraging a game as aimless yet seemingly addictive as the idle rearrangement of fridge magnets.

Each summer our family come to the headland for a picnic, and Evie and her cousins use the almost perfect rectangle for a slightly too large wicket, the natural ha-ha created by the grassed-over walls serving as their boundary. At the edges of the green apron, where the land meets the sea, there are cliffs, striated with red jasper and capped with a yellowish, ochre-coloured crystal, peculiar to this place. The children know to stay well back from the drops. There are no beaches in the immediate vicinity, and on clear days the children perch within the safety of the crags and watch the shifting currents below. Often they see seals. Sometimes they see fishermen checking lobster pots at the base of the cliff. And, almost always, they see the island, Ynys Enlli.

We have never been to the island although we've looked at it often. All we know of it is the fin of its mountain, the huddled ruins of its abbey. On rough days we have watched the waves break white as sail sheets against an inchoate shore. On clear days we have seen the sun fall full over its back, bleaching it pale as sea-glass. Once, when the haze was slight, we saw Jules Verne's green ray, were surprised by it, as a last curve of coloured light became visible in the sea air. It flared, acidic lime, almost fluorescent, for the smallest moment, before the sun dropped into the sea, leaving an unlikely crème de menthe afterglow.

A tree grows on the island – an extraordinary tree – seeded, it is said, from the pip of Merlin's apple. The apple that he discarded as he turned away from a wicked enchantress; growing hard, his power drawn from him, he was turned to stone by her, and only his bones remained. The bones are said to lie inside a cave and a child could reach for them, could feel for Merlin's bones, if only they knew where to look.

In our garden, pushed into the hedge, there is another tree, although it's more like a bush, being round like a spider's nest with no obvious trunk, just spindles of leaf-covered wands which in late summer are studded with lemony, pink-striped fruit. Our tree was propagated by a local horticulturist from this one twisted parent, the oldest apple in Europe, the oldest apple in the world, which has evolved beyond recognition into a clattering wooden net, as vigorous as a vine, braced against the thin soil and burnt salt winds of the island. Twenty thousand saints are buried alongside Merlin, and possibly also King Arthur, for Geoffrey of Monmouth maintained that it was Avalon, after *afal lon*, meaning lane of apples in Welsh.

But our business was not with the saints, or with the apples, or with the king and the wizard and his bones. We had come to the headland, to Anelog, and we were searching for St Mary's Well.

When Evie and I arrived we found everything enclosed, improbably, given the June day, in mist. The road was discernible, although only just, and when it ran to grass I stopped the car. There was nothing to see – no hill, no apron of land, no island. Cool and white, we inhabited a cloud; it was a curiously muted world. We left the car and began to walk in the direction of the cliffs. Our eyelashes and hair filled with beads of moisture that ran down our faces like tears, both delighting, and frightening, Evie. She was sure that a space had opened in the mist around us, and that this space was following us, which unnerved her. I tried to explain the idea of visibility, the idea of cloud density, and that we were able to see a little way ahead, and also a little way behind, but she could not comprehend it. Why were we able to see where we were going but not where we had come from?

'How do you know where we are?' she asked.

At first we had followed a drystone wall but after a while that came to an end. I heard the muffled sound of the stream that ran to the zawn, to the place in the cliffs where we might climb down to the well, though I could not see it. By moving fractionally to our left we would meet the mantle of heather and gorse that covered the hill, and this would also suffice as a guide, so I pointed it out to her.

The gorse and heather brought us almost to the edge of the zawn. It seemed to be an impenetrable chasm and Evie's eyes were wide with wonder. She had remembered an incident with a football the summer before, when her cousin Connor had kicked it over the cliff.

'You mustn't bring the other children here. It isn't safe, do you understand?'

'Your secret's safe with me,' she said, as though I had just told her I had robbed a bank. She could not believe she was going to climb down into the place where Connor had kicked his ball, and I had declared it lost.

At the edge of the cliff a pocket opened in the mist or, as was more likely, we were below it. Rising air currents from the sea maintained the space. We followed the trickle of water, which we had found again, and the path, which sloped steeply down. Below the cliff edge there was a moss-filled gully, skittering to stones, before the way ran to nothing over red and yellow rock. It looked, at first glance, as if there was no safe way down, a sheer drop into the sea. But by scrambling carefully sideways we were able to pick out handholds cut into the rock and reach the base. A narrow cleft led deep into the cliff face. We had to brace our feet on either side of it, because the sea rushed in beneath us, making bridges of our legs. At the end of this passage, almost inconsequential, and revealed by the ebbing tide, was a pool. A rope of water fed the pool from above and about this flow, by an odd trick of the light, the rainbow colours of the spectrum were gathered. The pool itself, the sacred well, was no bigger than an upturned hat.

St Mary's Well is known locally as Ffynnon Fawr which means the big well. It is said to have been consecrated by Mary herself when she visited the headland, presumably in the Dark Ages, because that's when all the indeterminate and exciting things seem to have happened. It is said to have been the last watering place for the medieval pilgrims before they made their way, or attempted to make their way, to the island, because for a long time three trips to the island netted the same number of indulgences as one return pilgrimage to Rome. This may all be true, although there are many other springs along the coast and it is much easier to launch a boat from the long sandy beach two miles away, in the village of Aberdaron. One of the reasons the well was deemed to be special – which sufficed as a miracle in the eyes of the medieval pilgrims – was because its salt water would turn, at certain times, to fresh. The poet R. S. Thomas, who was the Vicar at Aberdaron, described it in his poem 'Ffynnon Fair':

> They did not divine it, but
> bequeathed it to us:
> clear water, brackish at times,
> complicated by the white frosts
> of the sea, but thawing quickly.

The transformation is in fact no more than a conjuror's trick, a natural sleight of hand. The salt water of the pool, left full by the departing tide, is slowly displaced by spring water. Yet local legend has it that if you fill your mouth with well water, climb back up the cliff, and run three times around the ruins of St Mary's Church – and can do this without swallowing a drop – then your dreams, your wishes, will come true.

We looked down at the pool. I hadn't told Evie about the wish. The skeleton of a seagull, the odd feather clinging to its fanned and broken wing, pointed to the well. I thought about Allardyce, the rotted human compass in Robert Louis Stevenson's *Treasure Island*, its bony arm pointing dramatically, if no longer accurately, to the place where Flint's treasure might be found. A traveller called, appropriately, Ieuan Lleyn, who visited the Llŷn Peninsula in 1799, described entering 'St Mary's cave, in which is a well dedicated to Mary, and many other papal relics, such as the hooves of Mary's horse and the likes. As the place was steep and scary I tried to come up . . . as fast as my hands and feet, nay even my teeth would take me!' My own eyes were becoming accustomed to the milky half-light in the narrow space beneath the pulsing ceiling of mist. We were in a natural chapel whose walls of black stone rose sheer behind the pool. I made out what at first appeared to be a skull, but in its perfect roundness turned out to be a fishing float, one of the small buoys used to mark the lobster pots. There were bits of bone and driftwood, a plastic gallon container and a nylon orange net; all wedged deeply between tall wet splinters of rock. The rope of water, with its fans of gathered rainbows, spilt down into the pool. Any papal relics intended to remain here would have needed fixing in place with iron pins drilled into the rock, as securely as any mooring, if they were to withstand the twice daily onslaught of the sea which must entirely flood the passage. It seemed more likely that Lleyn had found the remains of an animal that had slipped over the cliff. Sheep droppings were visible on the ledge above our heads, over which the spring water splashed, the dark turds kept moist upon cushions of bright green moss and interspersed with tufts of wool. I had no desire to hold this water in my mouth, or anywhere else, my anxiety over hygiene interfering significantly with my capacity for wonder. I glanced around us. I felt certain that this couldn't be the right well. But if we were in the wrong place, so too had Ieuan Lleyn been, when he came here in 1799.

Evie, recognising by some unspoiled instinct holy water when she saw it, dipped her fingers into the triangular pool and dabbed her forehead with it, the water trickling down her nose, and this felt like a happy compromise, for although I seemed unable to free myself from a pervasive anxiety, almost nausea, I was relieved of the necessity of having to share it with her.

As we turned to begin the rocky climb back I was caught by a memory, raw as the day it retrieved. A spring afternoon in Barcelona. Three months earlier. Returning from the clinic. There had barely been time to collect Rupert from his office, for him to drive me home, and then for him to collect Evie from school. I had been adamant that I did not want to see anyone.

I'd heard them first, outside the front door. Green parrots were squabbling in the palm tree on the other side of the road. I couldn't make out what Rupert and Evie were saying above the parrots' squeaky-toy din. I had no idea what to expect, no idea what he had told her. When the door opened Evie spilled in with the sunlight, her face half full of wonder.

'Can I see the picture, Mummy? Of the baby?'

I could not believe he had not told her. I was absolutely unprepared for this, particular, moment. 'There is no picture, my darling. You see, the baby's died.' Her face. His half-turned body. Not looking at me; looking instead at the keys in his hand, the edge of his anger, the heat of his shame. I could not believe what we were doing.

'Where is it?' she asked.

'It's here.' My fingers touched my swollen belly.

'And it's died?'

'That's right.' She paused, still assimilating. 'Does this mean I'm not going to have a baby brother or sister?' I had tried to think of a decent lie, a euphemism, something that would make it all right. I was unprepared, defenceless before the truth. We all were.

It was dark in the hall after the door had closed.

'Can I watch TV?' she asked.

'Of course.' Evie slipped past and I could not be bothered even to recriminate. The damage, for what it was worth, was done.

I tried to fold the memory, reduce it. But it clung to me, sticky, insistent.

We made our way out of the channel on stepping stones while seawater funnelled beneath us. The waves hissed and foamed like the froth that slips over the rim of a beer glass. It was a cushioned world, opaque as cataracts, and the mist, when we reached it, was as dense as before. We pulled ourselves up the rocks towards the path. I followed Evie, remaining behind her in case she slipped. I pointed out handholds to her across the red and yellow stone, and helped her to place her feet in footholds, until I heard the crunch of little stones beneath her shoes and knew she had regained the path. I heard a sibilant trickle, a mischievous chatter as the stream spattered over gravel, and the white cloud once again pressed around us. The only colour was in the bright moss, visible once more at our feet.

Evie was delighted as the stream became apparent and then dumbfounded as it disappeared again. I pointed out to her the path, made plain by thick vegetation, of watercress, thistles, spiky marsh grass and sphagnum moss that indicated the water's journey. She listened: the mist was thicker and whiter now; the silence seemed to stop up our mouths. And then a sound, quiet as an indrawn breath. The water. She didn't want to talk. She was intent, like a spaniel, following a scent.

And then she saw it.

A round pool, a bowl of clear water, as wide as her arm's length, as deep as her knees. At first it appeared still and we saw fine sandy gravel on the bottom, the occasional green weed. Tightly coiled water snails, small as seeds, bright as jewels, encrusted the straight walls and heaped against the stems of weeds. Somewhere below the surface where the spring fed the well these images bent, the refraction attesting to the pulsed movement. Around the pool were signs of pilgrimage. Flat stones marked its edge and at one point they were drawn into a lip, the run-off that formed the stream. The grass around the well was flattened, muddied by many feet, and the stones had been grouted in to keep them stable. On either side were long sticks where someone had lifted green algae from the surface, and this was now browning in the air. Evie noticed and peered for more pea-green discs. She tried to pull a young fern, to act as a scoop, but the fronds came off in her hand, leaving the stem bent, but still attached.

'Will you help me, Mummy?'

There was a bluff, hardly that, a winged mound behind the water, where we counted pink saxifrage, primroses – no longer flowering – a yellow flower – tormentil – and purple foxgloves, whose tall rods screened the well. Beyond the bluff the heather and gorse and new ferns led back towards the drystone wall where we had begun our journey. I told Evie about the legend – the running round the church, the wishes. A veil seemed to pass across her eyes. The white mist pressed closely all around us, and I saw that she had no need for the miracle. All she wanted, she had before her. She took her water bottle, emptied it out, and then filled it from the silent well. She studied the contents, held them up, and asked me to reaffix the lid. Then, suddenly a child again, she put out her hand for me to hold, and we left.

I no longer knew what to wish for.

Health and happiness, I think. Nothing more.

Traeth Porth Dinllaen

Two weeks after the Spanish school holidays started, in an explosion of fireworks for the Feast of St John, the British school holidays began. The first to arrive on the beach at Porth Dinllaen, in early July, were a handful of Scottish children. They were closely followed, a week or so later, by children from the British independent schools. Finally, almost a month after we had got here, the state educated Welsh and English children joined the beach party. Now, in early August, the rock pools which had been Evie's exclusive domain became, at low tide, cluttered with warriors armed with plastic buckets and Day-Glo fishing nets. The older children carried spools and lines. Bits of bacon or gooey winkles served for bait.

Evie's preferred method for luring crabs was with a nylon drawstring bag, one that had come in a box of washing powder, and was intended for use with the detergent. She placed a boiled potato, soaked in bacon fat, inside the bag, then attached this to a hook and line. I had snapped the barb off the hook with a pair of pliers and now watched as a brick-red crab, a pointillist crown etched onto its shell, nipped the potato with a bone-coloured claw. Evie transferred the crab into a bucket of seawater with a careful sweep of her arm. A number of children clustered about; they exuded a mixture of excitement and awe, curiosity and envy as Evie tried to shake the crab free of the bait with determined, jerky movements, finally taking it between finger and thumb and slowly twisting it until it released the potato, its nut-cracker pincers open, pointing skyward.

The rock pools formed a narrow peninsula that bisected the curve of the bay like an arrow drawn over a bow. At its sea-facing tip the stones were caramel-coloured and smooth, the barnacles and seaweed polished away and stopped from coming back by scores of feet and bottoms, giving easy access, a slide if you were brave enough, to a plunge pool that opened, in its turn, onto the bay. Evie and the crab were surrounded by admirers. I watched her for a while. She looked up at me, and smiled, and I pointed at the bay, and then at the rock pool and mouthed *You stay here!* She nodded, widening her eyes in an *as if!* gesture, her hands opening like flowers, and I slipped into the mermaid pool. I swam between two rocky islets known as the Oysters, then pushed into the open water, registering the drop in temperature as a spiral around my body, the cold digging into my arms and neck like cheese-wire. I swam a tentative breaststroke until I located a ribbon of warmth, then stretched out into freestyle. The surface of the water was criss-crossed with these warmer paths, as wide as carpet runners, a reminder that the Gulf Stream ran near by.

We were waiting on the beach for Rupert, who was coming to join us for a week. The previous night, while Evie brushed her teeth, I had told her of the visit. She stood in front of the bathroom mirror, singing 'I Don't Care if the Sun Don't Shine' by Mack David. Toothpaste foamed over her chin, and dropped onto her foot. I was glad I hadn't told her sooner. Later, she had gone to the swing at the end of the area of trimmed field that was our garden, because it was the only place near the cottage that had any cover, and she had phoned Rupert. She twirled around with her arms about the ropes, the phone pressed to her ear. Behind her was Garn Fadryn's triangular cone, the first of the heather glowing like coal. Rupert must have said something about wanting to catch mackerel because she'd laughed, and said: 'Actually, Daddy, we're all a bit mackerelled out.'

The mackerel had arrived a couple of weeks ago. Our friend, Mike, had bought an old fishing boat, and he and his friend Anthony took us to the edge of the bay. A family of seals balanced on exposed rocks, their bodies curved like smiles, their heads and flippers raised to catch the sun. Evie had drawn fish after fish with a line and spool, no bait, just a spinner. She held the line between her thumb and forefinger and knew at once when she had a bite. A cheeky herring gull, following the boat, swooped down and nipped one of Evie's mackerel behind the gills as she drew it from the water, and she had handed me the spool, saying: 'Faster, Mummy!' She was determined not to give up her prize. Anthony was a surgeon, and he showed her how to lift the fish heads through ninety degrees, killing them softly with a quiet 'pop', and Evie was fascinated, and solemn. She wasn't comfortable about removing the hook. Later Anthony showed her how to gut them, placing the tip of his knife at the opening in the belly, pushing out the insides with his thumb, and washing the fish in seawater.

One evening I had a phone call from Endaf, a local builder. He had caught more than he could eat and asked if we would like some of them. I drove down to his house with a carrier bag to find him sitting on a deckchair in the garden, a plastic crate at his feet. A monkey-puzzle tree towered over us.

'How many do you want?' he asked me.

'Oh, just enough for supper. Two.' He frowned. 'Three?'

'Ah, take more than that. You can freeze them.'

'I don't know, Endaf, that's very kind. Twelve?' and he had nodded as I started to pick up the fish one by one.

'Oh for God's sake don't count them!' he said, and disappeared into the house. When he came back he held a black refuse sack, and he filled it with handfuls of fish. When I got home I waved to my neighbour, Joan, and she took half of them. The rest I stuffed into our little box freezer.

As the days rolled by we barbecued mackerel in salt, pan-fried them in custard powder, poached them in milk and wild dill collected from the shore. Evie stuck fish heads into a stargazy pie that neither of us felt like eating, and we smoked them on shavings of apple wood and then whipped them into paste, with crème fraiche, and lemon, and pepper. Even hearing the word *mackerel* now made me queasy. We were at the *sleek and glossy* phase of our holiday, it happened every year, when our blood became more fish oil than iron, our hair and skin soft and shiny despite the constant exposure to salt.

Later, after the phone call, we read *Swallows and Amazons* together. Evie squealed with delight at the part where the boy Roger swam with one foot on the bottom, because she too 'swam' with one foot on the bottom, and I could sense her, in that moment, resolving not to. We were curled up in the big cabin bed, and I had said that she could sleep there, for tonight, although tomorrow she must go back to the crog-loft, to her futon nest of cushions and pillows, to the place where adults never went, because the ceiling height precluded it. At some point in the night her hand reached out, her palm flat against my neck. And then she shifted and pushed both feet into my solar plexus, to the place under my ribs where she had grown. She smelled, mysteriously, of peaches.

Evie kept asking when we were going to the airport. She seemed unable to retain the information that we weren't. My friend Bronwen was arriving at Liverpool at the same time as Rupert, on her way to visit her parents in North Wales. She had offered to give Rupert a lift, and would stop over for one night.

Keeping to my warm ribbon, I swam across the harbour. A flat tender was moving towards the beach. Ken, who owned two fishing boats, which made him important in the life of the village, stood in the middle of the tender, his hands on his hips, while another fisherman sat at the back of the boat with his hand on the tiller. I stopped by one of the mooring buoys, treading water, and lifted my arms so they could see me.

'You want a lift?' asked Ken.

'No, I'm all right. I just didn't want you to run me over.' I held onto the side of the boat with both arms. My legs drifted beneath it. I was trying to remember what Dad had told me about the fluid mechanics of flat-bottomed boats, and vortices in shallow water. Dad had been an engineer. Dad would have known what was happening. A cloud covered the sun and a breeze lifted the hairs on my forearms into barbs, wet hair flicking across my mouth. Ken allowed me a head start before re-engaging the motor. A current had wrapped about me, or the tender had drifted into it, and for a moment I appeared to be going nowhere. When I reached the far side of the harbour I touched the sea wall. My hand was splayed like a starfish. I noticed the way the orange lichen spread like rust over the rocks above the water, and how the stones beneath the waterline were indigo. And then I noticed the white band where my wedding ring should have been. I put the hand quickly back into the water, took it out again, and re-examined it.

The ring had gone.

I didn't allow any thoughts to form about this discovery but turned quickly and went back the way I had come, including the detour through the current where Ken's boat had been. The ring had come from Tiffany's in New York. It was made of twenty-two princess-cut diamonds and weighed about four and a half carats. Rupert had given it to me when Evie was baptised. We didn't get married until Evie was five, when we found ourselves travelling through Las Vegas. We had used the ring as a wedding ring because we had forgotten to buy another. And anyway, I didn't want another ring.

Rupert would be here in a matter of hours.

When I reached the rock pools I stood in the shallow water by the place where I had entered the pool. I looked again at the white band around my finger. The noise of the children, the waves and the wind was shut out by a growing anxiety. Rupert would read this as a sign, I was sure of it. An indication of how I valued our relationship.

I had lost the first ring he ever gave me within a few hours of receiving it – also, as it happened, on a beach – in Mexico. We had searched for that ring for over an hour, but the shell-white sand had swallowed it. I stared at the toffee-coloured Welsh beach, unable to believe what I had done. At the rock pool a group of children was gathered around a young girl in a sarong, who was covered head-to-foot in wet clay, her hair dreadlocked into ropes. It was Evie. She was pointing to a place beyond the rock pool where a squashy seam had been revealed by the tide. The sun broke through a tear in the cloud and a movement on the sea floor distracted me. I bent down, my chin just below the water. Dancing rays and spots of light were bouncing around a barely discernible shadow-circle, like a child's illustration of the sun. It was the ring! It must have come off my finger as I entered the water. I would never have seen it, against the sand, without this coincidental, actual sunburst, that bounced white light through the stones. I reached for the ring and the sea filled my ears, covered my head. It was as hard as a drawer full of knives. I stood up, looked at the ring, brushed away the sand. Then I pushed it over my fattest, middle, finger.

When Evie noticed me standing in the shallow water she grinned, and the clay, which had dried into a ghostly mask, crackled like the face of Methuselah, and I was incredibly happy, and yet also afraid, although I couldn't, in that moment, have said why.

At four o'clock the fishermen began stacking crates of blond whelks onto acrid, flat bed trailers. There were spider crabs for the Chinese restaurants in Manchester. Some lobsters nosed about beneath a net, litmus blue and lively. The fishermen dragged the trailers off the beach behind rusted Massey Ferguson tractors that hummed with a metallic riff. Evie spotted Rupert and Bronwen almost as soon as they passed through the Bwlch, tall figures in urban travel clothes, their city shoes incongruous on the sand. I imagined the trapped, reconstituted air of the plane escaping as their coats flapped in the breeze. Evie had already tucked in her chin and was running as fast as she could towards them.

When I reached them, Rupert and Bronwen were laughing. Behind them, at the Bwlch, a crowd of people were clustered around a Land-Rover. Gulls hopped and shuffled inquisitively along the ridge-tiles of the nearest cottage. Evie's eyes were round and two little waves at the top of her nose indicated a frown, despite her joy at seeing her father. Bronwen was holding a plastic carrier bag.

'They were four for a pound,' said Rupert. Of course, of course, today had been the Mackerel Race to raise money for the RNLI, when anyone who had a boat set off at the crack of a starting pistol to catch as many mackerel as they could in just three hours. Evie was staring into the pungent, slippery bag as though it contained the head of a seal.

Later, we all lay on a woollen blanket in the garden, our eight legs making a star-shape, our heads clumped together on cushions. The charcoal on the barbecue was turning to powder, although it gave off more heat than ever. White wine knocked the edge off the night. Cold blades of grass tickled my ankles and feet.

A solitary flash caught my eye. As though someone had drawn a chalk line then erased it. I looked at the place where it had been, and saw a second streak, fading, even as it passed. Soon they were coming every few seconds, the Perseids, they happened every

August. High above, behind the shooting stars, was the Milky Way, and it really did look like a glass of spilled milk, thrown across the sky, and sinking into velvet. We stayed outside as long as we could, laughing and pointing at the stars, until the blanket and cushions grew damp with condensation, and the cold drove us indoors. We made up the cabin bed for Bronwen. Evie disappeared into the crog-loft, into her tangled den of pillows and toys, and arranged herself so she could see the fire. Rupert and I slept in a wooden shepherd's hut in the garden.

The next morning I woke before dawn. I pulled on a sweater and a pair of jeans and sat on the steps of the shepherd's hut, aware of the shift as the darkness began to fade, my eyes adjusting from night to day vision. Because we were in the west, the sun was up a good while before it finally appeared over Snowdon. It was cold in Garn Fadryn's shadow. The stars dimmed, then disappeared, till only Venus, the morning star, was left. I liked to watch the sky brighten behind the Garn although I could not see the summit, still enclosed in its envelope of mist. Locally the hill is known as Madryn, from *modron*, meaning mother.

I had tried to prepare for this visit by Rupert. I felt soft, closed, like a soap bubble. Before Rupert arrived my friend Mike had lent us a wooden dinghy. It was painted Baden-Powell blue and was called the Mirror. Whether Mirror was its name, or described the kind of boat, I didn't know, and hadn't wanted to show my ignorance by asking. I had been fascinated by the noise the water made as we cut through the waves, the ripple of the wind against her blood-red sail. I had become accustomed to small sounds, to not talking, and not touching, or being touched, other than in my day-to-day contact with Evie, and now Rupert was here. Over the next two weeks we would laugh, love, and argue. There would be a chink of glasses. A rectangle of light stretching over the garden as we kept ever later nights. I would become a half of something, or rather, a third. For some reason I was unsettled by this. The arguments that had railed over the baby, the possibility of the baby, the things that had been said, that could not now be unsaid lay between us like a badly made rope bridge upon which I dared not trust my weight.

The realisation that our baby should now be in my arms spilled and stuck to the surface of my mind, garish as white paint flung across a road, as difficult to remove. I felt more fiercely alone, perched on the wooden steps, Rupert sleeping behind me, Bronwen and Evie in the cottage, than I had ever felt when I was actually alone.

There was a hip flask full of damson gin in the shepherd's hut. I reached for it and removed the lid, took a sip of the clear liquid, garnet red, flecked with fragments of blue-black fruit skin, which were ticklish on my palate, like tea leaves. I had made it with my brother, John, three years ago on my birthday. We had gathered the damsons from a tree in his garden that is no longer there.

I tiptoed into the cottage, heard a movement.

'Bronwen, are you awake?'

Her voice came from the other side of the wooden panel that separated the bedroom from the living room: 'I am.'

'Shall we go for a swim? It's high tide in less than an hour.'

'Brilliant!'

We left a note and headed for Lifeboat Bay, a secluded beach at the tip of the headland. As we walked the sun lifted behind us, and the mist over Garn Fadryn grew lacy. In front of us the sea and the sky were merged into a single sheet. Blue as smoke, soft as silk. Lifeboat

Bay was exactly what it said it was: home to the RNLI station. The water looked still, although warning signs discouraged swimmers, advising them to keep off the concrete ramp. Strong currents pulled just off the point. We ignored the signs and dived from the ramp, into sea that was as limpid as oil, and as cool as the light. The earless wet-dog head of a seal peered at us from beyond the current.

A radio was playing. And there was litter on the beach. It was still only five o'clock. I was about to say something when Bronwen caught my eye and pointed, bright water falling from her outstretched arm. An untidy head had lifted from the foreshore and a young man stared at us, incredulous. I watched him trying to assimilate the populated nature of his wilderness experience: two women and a seal eyeing him from the middle of the bay. He started to pick up beer cans and discarded clothes, watching us as though we were the police. I felt for him; my own experience at Spurn Point was still fresh and perplexing to me.

As the sun lifted higher we could see through the water to sand-coloured crabs betrayed by their shadows and squid-like pulsing seaweed. A darting shoal of little fish, camouflaged against the sand, was momentarily visible as it changed direction. The surface of the water had seemed sheer when we entered it – but I could now see that it was speckled with flies, leaves and dust motes caught in a vast meniscus.

The night before Rupert returned to Barcelona we visited our friends Peter and Jackie in their cottage on the beach. We ate lobsters, caught by Ken the fisherman. The usual debate about how best to kill the lobsters had fizzed around the beach like gunpowder. For the most part we were all agreed on the 'freezer method', which meant putting the lobsters in the deep freeze until they were drowsy and then dropping them, dribbling, into boiling water, which we believed to be 'humane'. My friend Lucy had trained as a chef in France and she advocated stabbing them in the back of the head with a knife, but Peter had tried this and missed the spot, or maybe he hadn't, but the lobster had clattered to the floor, and then set off in an erratic dance, the knife waving like a metronome, frightening the children and dissipating the appetites of the guests. But in time the shells had turned from dusty blue to scarlet, and now lay empty, as did several bottles of wine. Evie had fallen asleep, and was tucked up in a bunk bed with her cousin, Lauren. After Rupert and Peter crashed through a chair, their high spirits reducing it to kindling, the three of us set out in Peter's rib for the middle of Nefyn Bay, so we could see the phosphorescence in the water. Jackie was visible as a bright point on the sand, a funnel of light from her torch reminding us where the shore was. Every so often I looked back at her. She must have been walking up and down the beach, because the tiny funnel moved first one way, and then the other, with tiny erratic jumps indicating her footsteps. We were all so drunk I was amazed she'd had the foresight to think of this. Beyond the bay were some of the most treacherous waters in the British Isles. Both the sky and the sea were black. But in the bay, tonight, the water was calm. Rupert and I trailed our arms in the inky sea, the cold fit like opera gloves. The glow of phosphorescence illuminated us, our arms and fingers were green. It lit up Peter's face above the tiller and frothed behind the propeller in ghostly, cheerleader pom-poms. Beyond the little boat, the starless darkness pressed about us.

The next day Evie and I waved Rupert off from Liverpool Airport, his smile disappearing as he passed through to Security, leaving an imprint fading in the air, a moment of brightness, an impression of light, and then he was gone. People swarmed around us, holding plastic zip-lock bags and their hand luggage. Walking back to the car we picked our way through the holidaymakers as they surged about us, arriving – tanned and tired, or departing – pale and anxious. As Evie and I began the two-hour drive back to the cottage I found myself thinking of the Canadian pianist, Glenn Gould, whose recording of Bach's Prelude and Fugue from *The Well-tempered Clavier* is on a satellite headed for the end of the galaxy. Gould believed that there was a ratio between the time one could spend in company, and the time it subsequently took to recover from it. Our days in the Llŷn had, ordinarily, a sequestered quality about them. But the recent weeks had been packed with company. This was a good thing, we were cushioned in friendship – but suddenly I too had a yearning to travel, to move on, to go somewhere else. It was a sensation that I knew well. It was the same hankering after remoteness that had brought me to the Llŷn Peninsula in the first place.

Caherdaniel

Our departure from the Llŷn Peninsula happened almost straight away. Less than a week after Rupert had returned to Barcelona, I received a phone call. Evie and I were walking along the sand, Evie scouting for skimmers, when the phone buzzed and I recognised an Irish prefix, although not the number. It was my friend Sean:

'It's Pamela.'

'What's the matter?' Pamela had often been unwell; she'd had a string of operations. Evie had found a stone. She held it up to show me, then threw it, and it skipped in lively arcs across the waves.

'It's serious, man. She's on life support. They're turning it off tomorrow.' I looked at the phone in my hand, and then put it back to my ear.

'Are you in Belfast?'

'I'm in Tralee. Can you get here?' I stared at Evie; the sea stretched behind her like tarpaulin. A black-and-white collie-dog was dancing alongside her; he clearly thought the stones were for his benefit.

'Yes,' I said, 'I hope to be ... I'll be there when I can.'

I wasn't quite sure how I got Evie off the beach, but suddenly we were driving back to Mum's house, two hastily packed overnight bags behind us. I tried to book a flight from Liverpool or Manchester but neither Mum nor I had a computer. It was almost impossible by phone. Sean rang again and I realised I wasn't going to make it to Tralee. I focused my energies on the funeral, which was to be held in Limavady, County Derry. Mum took Evie to her cousins' house, and I booked a morning flight to Belfast.

I had first met Pamela the day that I turned thirty. I had held a birthday party, and over a hundred people came to a sunlit ballroom in Earls Court Square. I had been due to leave in a couple of weeks for a new job, in Belfast. Senator Mitchell's Peace Process was just about to begin, and I was going to play my part developing grassroots drama among the divided communities, as a script editor with BBC Northern Ireland. The party was a send-off as well as a celebration. There had been an enormous table covered in tea-lights that joined the dots between vases stuffed with cow parsley, which Rupert and I had gathered that afternoon from Brompton Cemetery. An armada of half-filled glasses floated, bubbles blinking between the fingers of gesticulating hands. At a certain moment the voices rose, and then relaxed, becoming a part of something whole, and the room filled with a sudden expansive loudness. I had never really had a party before, certainly not one on this scale, and I watched with wonder as the glow-worm constellations of tea-lights asserted themselves before a slow, but eventual, sunset. There were some unexpected faces, friends, I supposed, of friends, and one in particular caught my eye, or rather my ear, because it was the sound of laughter that made me turn my head.

In the 1990s London people always wore black, occasionally white, although there was a season they'd all worn brown, and while this undoubtedly widened the palette, it hadn't left much of an impression. Pamela was wearing an aquamarine linen shift, her red hair smooth as a helmet. She was like something from antiquity, classical and rare, and when our eyes met she began to move across the room, pulling her companion by the arm.

'I know, I know —' I caught her voice, the sing-song, soon-to-be-loved Limavady tilt. 'I hope you don't mind but I *had* to come, I was talking to Jackie here and it all just sounded ... so *lovely*.'

On my first Thursday in Belfast Pamela telephoned me: *Just pack a bag and take it with you tomorrow, then come up to the house after work.* I had been wary as I set out from the new city. The Union flags and the tricolour kerbs of the different tribes perplexed me, and the fortified police station at Dundalk unnerved me, with its razor-wire fence and bulletproof glass. I had driven over the Glenshane Pass, and wondered at the heather beginning to shine against the dark, underlying peat. From Limavady I followed Pamela's directions: *Find the low bridge and then continue up the lane, you can't miss the house.*

No, I couldn't miss the house. I turned into a driveway between crenellated turrets to gaze, at the end of a long lawn, into rows of windows that reflected the evening back to me. Walworth was a large, fortified plantation house. I had heard of such a thing but never troubled to imagine it. The façade was grand and appeared to be Georgian, but turning the corner into a yard I found a cluster of other dwellings, including a cottage that stuck out in an L-shape. Clearly those who the house had been built to protect, who had come to 'plant' the land, had not ventured very far from its cover. In spite of the unquestionably Protestant nature of the estate an Ulster flag waved from a pole on the lawn.

When I walked into the kitchen I had found a small, wiry woman, muscularly building a fire in an enormous grate. I assumed this was Pamela's mother, and held out the flowers I had brought with me. The woman took them and put them in a vase and called: *Mrs Brown, there's someone here for you*, and an elegant woman of indeterminate age appeared in the kitchen, holding out both her hands in greeting. *Hello, I'm Noreen, you must be Kate; Pamela said you were coming.* We had eaten supper in a long panelled dining room where I counted eight grown-up children including Pamela, some with lovers and children of their own. I was trying to figure out who they all were when Noreen caught me looking.

'Brian is my second husband,' she said. 'We have four children each, well, Brian also has a fifth, Felicity, but she isn't here tonight. Actually, she grew up in England,' Noreen nodded. 'She's got young children.' As the wine spilled, and the night yawned, a story began to come together. Noreen and Brian had been lovers for years. Both of them had young families, both had despaired of their marriages. One night, Noreen's husband Arthur had appeared at the door of the house and set about Brian with a blackthorn walking stick, beating him to the ground and cracking two ribs.

'You had to hand it to him,' Brian said. 'She was a woman worth fighting for, and I dare say I deserved it!'

Noreen wore a large emerald ring and I asked her how she came by it. She had been holidaying with her family in the Far East and Brian – unable to part from her – had followed them and even stayed in the same hotel. He had bought the stone and given it to Noreen when Arthur's back was turned. Of course she couldn't wear it or even declare it at Customs, so she re-entered the country with the emerald hidden. She smiled at the recollection, and glanced at the ring as she talked: deep as sea-glass, and spilling dark light, it was clustered around with diamonds.

They had both divorced and eventually married when Noreen's youngest child turned eighteen.

I began to spend most of my weekends at the house. Even my parents and an aunt came to visit. Brian always seemed especially interested in me. We had something in common, he had rapidly gleaned: I was an adopted child. He had given his firstborn up, although the decision had been both against his wishes and out of his hands. A few years ago he had paid a private detective to find his daughter. She had been born to his first wife, but before they were married, and convention or scandal didn't allow them to keep her. The baby had been given in adoption to an English vicar and his wife, and they had called her Felicity. As it happened the vicar had recently died and Brian appeared at just the right moment. He brought Felicity to Walworth, with her husband and little daughter, and she met the unruly family that were her kin.

This was the dream that I had never dared acknowledge, and for Felicity it had come true. I glowed in the warmth from Pamela's family, like a stray dog drawn to a fire. To me they were beautiful, wild, generous, hilarious, glamorous, and good.

Noreen told me one night of a home movie that had gone missing at the height of the Troubles, when Brian was a leading defence lawyer representing various Protestant paramilitaries, despite his Catholic business interests. The film was of the family playing Cowboys and Indians. Brian had worn a feathered chieftain's headdress and stripes across his cheekbones. Noreen was a squaw. The children were everything in between and at one point Brian's eldest son had surfed down the kitchen staircase on an ironing board, devastating both the ironing board and the stairs. Brian roared at the thought of MI6 or the IRA or the Army or whoever had pinched the film scratching their heads at the tomfoolery.

I had longed to be a part of it – and in a way, of course, I was. But I also longed for such a story to open – for me. In part, this yearning stopped me from revisiting the house when I left my job in Ireland. I had driven away from Walworth, for what turned out to be the last time, the morning after the 1997 General Election. The Labour Party had taken power in a landslide victory with a majority of over two hundred seats. Brian had placed a rollover bet. He was especially interested in proportional representation, and he won fifty thousand pounds that night. I drove past him in the grey first light. I was due to be in Belfast at nine, and Brian was asleep. He was sitting very straight on a wooden bench beneath a tree, and a soft rain was falling. His glasses had misted over, and his two Irish wolfhounds lay at his feet, the fine rain sticking to his hair and their coats so that all three figures seemed adorned with pearl hairnets. For me, in the years that followed, other things came up: Evie was born, my own adopted father fell mortally ill, and I didn't return to Ireland until Evie was almost two years old, when we came for Pamela's wedding. And now, seven years later, I had come again, and this time it was because Pamela had died.

She had been swimming in the sea off Caherdaniel in Kerry with some friends. It was in a river mouth, as it happened, where the Atlantic breakers surged against the downward stream, and at high tide you could bodysurf through a channel into the shallow water of the river. Pamela was struck by a headache and had come out of the water, walking to a house above the beach. She was staying with the same friend who had introduced us to one another, all those years ago. Pamela had said something about going to make the lunch. But her headache grew worse until soon she could not speak. Her husband, John, was with her, and she lost consciousness looking into his eyes. An ambulance brought her to Tralee. Noreen took a taxi from Limavady. As many of Pamela's friends as could get there in time gathered around her bedside, and then her life support was switched off. The cause of death had been an aneurysm. That, at any rate, was the story that I pieced together when I eventually got to the house.

I missed the funeral. I had missed my flight from Liverpool to Belfast because I fell asleep in the bath, and the next flight wasn't until noon. By the time I got to Walworth the mourners were streaming home. The family and Pamela's closest friends were gathered at the house. I passed Arthur standing in the yard behind the house, a glass, half empty, in his hand. He was talking with someone who was inside the kitchen, but he made no move to enter. In the living room of the cottage where Pamela had lived were two wooden trestles where her body had lain in an open coffin. The room was filled with flowers, many of them cut from the garden, hydrangeas, roses, marguerites, lilies. They surrounded the place where Pamela had been. Her husband John was sleeping, and the voices in the cottage were subdued. Towards evening someone commented that the room felt cold. People supposed that it would be all right to light a fire, but felt they'd better wait till John woke up. I went back into the big house where Noreen was moving among the mourners, gracious, outwardly calm. The emerald glinted on her finger, there were more at her throat and wrist. She held a cut-glass tumbler of dark liquid, which I supposed to be brandy. I grew vaguely anxious at the thought of meeting Brian. I still hadn't seen him, and I wasn't sure what my reception would be. But when he saw me, his face opened into the same wild smile, and he said:

'Did you ever find your father?'

'No,' and it was my turn to smile. More than ten years had passed since Brian had first asked me that question, but I had never even learned my natural father's name or, as Brian saw it, my own.

'I'm so sorry,' I said.

'What about?' asked Brian.

'Well, Pamela —'

'Ah. Death slides off me like water,' he said. 'I've seen enough of it to last a lifetime. What have you been doing with yourself?' I told him about my summer plan to follow a Scottish river from the sea to its source and how I had so far failed to get off a beach in Wales. Until now.

'Book Five!' he roared.

'I'm sorry?' I said.

'Of *The Odyssey*. "But Hermes did not find great-hearted Odysseus indoors but he was sitting out on the beach, crying, breaking his heart in tears." Odysseus spent nine years crying on a beach before the gods remembered where they'd left him. Only then could he fulfil his destiny.'

'And what was that, Brian?' asked a passing mourner, a glass of wine in each of her hands.

'To go home, to his family, to his sheep and his pigs.' Brian's hand came down on the mourner's arm, the ash from his cigarette toppling. 'What else is there?' The question didn't seem to need an

99

answer and the young woman smiled and moved on. 'Kate, where are you staying tonight?'

'Oh, I have an early flight from Belfast,' I started, but Brian patted my shoulder.

'You must stay here, of course.'

Later, when the wine and spirits had been replaced by tea, and the sad tales by poetry and song, I slept on a long leather couch in Brian's study, where the housekeeper made up a bed for me, protesting that she could find me *a proper bed* if I wanted one. But I was where I wanted to be, behind the sign on the door that said: *Piss off I'm busy*. I watched the fire burn to nothing as the sun diluted the darkness and I felt something, some spirit, flow through the house, binding us, and holding us all together.

When I got back to Wales I was disconsolate. Evie was still at her cousins' house; she'd been invited to stay for the week. I was alone at the cottage. I thought about a conversation I had had with my friend, Liz, who lived near Berwick-upon-Tweed.

'If Evie's in Chester why don't you come over? I mean, you're just on your own down there.'

If I were to visit Liz in Berwick, as she had suggested, then I would have reached Scotland. The journey I had told Brian about, the abandoned trip to find the source of the Dunbeath Water, re-presented itself, shadowy, but real. I walked down to the beach. The wind was blowing in a cool flat block, and I pressed my back into the harbour wall for shelter. A man was also leaning on the wall and I didn't notice him until he spoke to me.

'You love it here, don't you?' he said. I realised that he was one of the fishermen, and that I had never actually heard him speak before.

'Yes,' I replied, and I found myself trying to explain the feeling that just being there gave me; and the odd sense of breathlessness whenever I thought of it, like an ache underneath my ribcage.

'It's love,' said the fisherman, 'I feel it myself.' I was amazed. In part because I hadn't thought one could feel such a thing for a place, and in part because I hadn't recognised the symptoms. Which seemed a tragedy. As I walked back along the beach I picked over the unexpected conversation.

Love. I wasn't sure about it. But the feeling of longing, or yearning, for something not quite discernible that could almost be nostalgia. A sense that was as acute as hunger, or homesickness, but not necessarily for a place that one knew. Something elusive, unquantifiable, and yet – in its very depth and poignancy – as compelling as desire.

When I got back to the cottage I telephoned Rupert, who agreed that there didn't seem to be a word for it in English. But Rupert spoke German. He said:

'Try *Sehnsucht*.'

'But what does it mean?' I asked, and Rupert found it difficult to reply. It's made from *Sehnen*, he said, meaning yearning, and *Sucht*, which means addiction, but *Sehnsucht* conveyed more than simply an addictive yearning. I waited on the telephone while he tried to find a better meaning. He said: 'C. S. Lewis describes it as: "That unnameable something, desire for which pierces us like a rapier at the smell of a bonfire, the sound of wild ducks flying overhead, the title of *The Well at the World's End* . . ." '

'You're joking,' I said. 'Did he really say *The Well at the World's End?*'

'Yes. It's a book.'

'I know what it is . . . Look, I've got to go.'

I called Liz straight away. I packed a sleeping bag and a thermos flask, as well as a hip flask, *just in case*, and carried them out to the car. I then turned the car round so that it faced downhill. In the morning, before the sun had reached around the Garn, or pushed aside the blanket of mist, I closed up the cottage. Liz lived just the other side of the Scottish border; I could be there by the end of the afternoon.

Skell

I retraced my route over the Pennines from the early days of
the holiday – this time in daylight – under the warm August
sun. The moors looked hazy, the heather at the cusp of
flowering, with a promise of lilac fire. When I reached Yorkshire,
I headed north. The previous day Liz, on whose coat-tails I was
following, sent me a text: *Just passing the Angel of the North, he is
so big and strong!* And he was. I gasped when I saw him, another
Antony Gormley metal man, part Titan, part spitfire, dark as
mahogany. The Angel stood on a smooth mound between two
carriageways of the A1 and I pulled up the car in a lay-by-cum-
car park next to him. Oddly, like the metal men at Crosby
Beach, the Angel faced the opposite direction to the one in
which I was travelling. Children gathered around his feet and
perched on them, eating sandwiches, or having their photographs taken.

The mound reminded me of Silbury Hill, the so-called
Neolithic burial mound in which no burial chamber has ever
been found. A well at its base, called Swallowhead Spring, floods

the River Kennet – at certain times – around the hill, to form the shape of a pregnant woman made of water. Much has been made of this, not least by me. On the winter solstice before Evie was conceived I made my way across the monochrome plains of Wiltshire. I ignored the barbed wire and the warnings to keep out and passed through a gap in the fence. When I reached the top I crouched beneath a tearing wind and shelterless sky, and as the white sun rolled into soft clay, I emptied my heart:

Give me a child!

But on this northern mound, between the two carriageways of the A1, there stood an angel, and he resembled nothing so much as the angel standing guard outside the gates of Eden – now a blasted wilderness – to keep prying eyes away from all that remained of the tree of life. Which would make the garden, now a wilderness, Scotland.

The Irish *Metrical Dindshenchas* are packed with stories about our relationship to the land. They tell how certain features of the landscape were called, or forced, into being and describe how they came to be named.

There was once a High King, a god, called the Dagda. Strong and tall, he was a warrior, and a hunter, a skilled musician, a storyteller, a lover.

A lover.

In *The Well at the World's End* Neil Gunn tells of a goddess who went to seek a well in the land beyond our own. It is called the Well of Elcmar, after its guardian, a water god. Boand, the goddess, was Elcmar's wife. Everyone was forbidden from approaching the well except those who were charged with its care. It was said to be impossible even to move before the water without incurring injury, and that the eyes of anyone attempting to look into it would burst. So what was Boand, *fair and white-limbed* – according to the *Metrical Dindshenchas* – *soft-blooming, and with perfect eyes*, doing there?

> *Hither came on a day white Boand*
> *(her noble pride uplifted her),*
> *to the well, without being thirsty*
> *to make trial of its power.*

Another version of Boand's story says she approached the well in the hope of finding knowledge, so she could learn how to conceal her infidelity. For that most capable god the Dagda was her lover, and she wanted to know how to hide this, as well as the child she had borne him, from her husband.

The Dagda did everything he could. When he and Boand began to make love, before dawn, on that first lovely day, he held the sun in the sky for nine whole months, so that in the space of their coupling their child was conceived, grew full-term inside her, and was born before sunset. And while this great feat of love-making continued, throughout the whole of this very long day, Elcmar was diverted by the most ludicrous of errands. Aengus, the love child, was magnificent – of course – and grew up to become the god of love himself. The affair was not so easy to conceal.

Or perhaps Boand was just curious. It was, after all, the fountain of knowledge. Yet even as she walked about the well, *heedlessly,* according to the legend, *three waves roared out of it*, one for each circuit that she made. One can more or less put money that she walked anticlockwise, or wicken way. The first wave *broke off her foot*, the second *took out her eye*, and the third *shattered her hand*. Boand rushed to the sea, in order to escape further blemish, and so that none might see her mutilation. But the waves followed her and drowned her. The water kept flowing from the well. And this water, this river, was named after her, and we now know it as the Boyne. Yet, while the River Boyne preserves Boand's name, fourteen other rivers – including the Euphrates, the Tiber, the Jordan and the Severn – were all said to have come into being when Boand upset the well. Even the River Tigris, which flows through paradise itself.

> *Every way the woman went*
> *The cold white water followed*
> *From the Sid to the sea (not weak it was),*
> *So that thence it is called Boand.*
> *Boand from the bosom of our mighty river-bank,*
> *Was the mother of great and goodly Aengus,*
> *The son she bore to the Dagda – bright honour!*
> *In spite of the man of this Sid.*

With thoughts of the Dagda and poor drowned Boand nudging at one another inside me, I got back into the car.

I continued on my way, the Angel receding in the mirror. I found him wonderful and saw in him a good omen, if any omen were needed. I felt as though I'd passed through a gateway, and that my journey had begun for real. I found myself thinking about *Another Place*. The Angel was made of iron, as were the Antonys at Liverpool. In the old tales iron is said to be abhorrent to the fairies, the people *of this Sid, aes sidhe*, meaning the hill dwellers. According to the fairy tales this is because the nails of the cross were made of iron. A more prosaic reason might be because the Celtic people brought it with them, or rather, brought the skill to work it. It represented, in the plough, and the sword, and the horseshoe, the displacement of a different way of life.

The Celts believed that the Otherworld was parallel to our own, and that you could step into it, or through it, at certain times. Only particular things, like a tree half covered in leaves, or a field full of black-and-white sheep, indicated that you were there at all. You had to look out for the signs. You had to know them.

The lay-by had been on a slip road, and I discovered that I couldn't get back to the A1. Somehow I had made an error, and was running parallel to my route. While I was wondering how to rectify this I saw a sign for Fountains Abbey. Many years ago I had worked on a film in which the abbey had been used as a location. I had been in the cutting room, in London, and was enthralled by the film rushes as they came in from the lab. I had held the 16mm film up to the window, saw the replicated images of green grass, a golden river, the lacy ruin of the church itself, each cube of sunlight separated by a frame bar, like dozens of emerald cut stones. So I followed the sign, and drove towards Ripon, presuming the abbey to be near by. But it wasn't. After half an hour travelling through undulating fields, I still didn't seem to be moving. The thickly clouded sky was silver, with the very high contrast of a black-and-white print. Hand-tinted. Bruised. The mustard stubble of the fields looked brittle. The road, which was featureless, seemed to absorb, rather than reflect, the sky, its surface flat, and suit-grey. I couldn't see anything ahead except an isolated copse and cylindrical wheels of baled hay where the wheat had been recently harvested. I began to consider turning back, but the road wasn't wide enough.

Just as I was feeling that I must have taken a second wrong turn, I entered the town of Ripon. After meandering for a few more miles, a sign for the abbey appeared. A perimeter wall bound an estate, and there were signs for Studley Royal Water Gardens. The abbey and the gardens seemed inseparable. I followed signs to a National Trust car park and entered, without paying. Doing my best to remember where I'd parked, I followed more signs to the abbey. I was hungry. I hadn't eaten since breakfast, and it was now early afternoon. I had an apple in my bag, and some chocolate, but I didn't want to stop and get them out. I ached from driving and needed to keep moving to ease the stiffness in my spine and hips. I was aware that I was on my way to visit Liz, and that I had told her I would be with her mid-afternoon. I missed Evie. We were probably together for three-hundred and fifty-five days of the year, and this unexpected week was feeling like an eternity. I was halfway through the third day.

The night before we had left the cottage Evie had been reading in her bed in the crog-loft. She crept down the ladder. Her eyes had a storm-washed look. Something tragic had happened.

'*Pony Club*?' I asked – her book: one of the ponies had been ill – and she nodded. I put down what I was reading. She climbed into the bed. I turned off the light, and opened my hand on the pillow. Evie eased her face into it. We lay there, her face resting in my hand, my palm slowly filling with hot tears, until her breathing changed, and she fell asleep.

Something seemed to pass through the room. There was a tightening among the shadows, a splintered movement in the fire. I must live a long, long time, and stay well, remain strong, until this passionate creature can find her feet. Perhaps some of Rupert's unyielding hardness – his brilliance, his discipline, his ability to focus on his work – might balance the tidal nature I had given her.

Lighthouse. Storm. Love.

I found the entrance. It was inside an eco-spacecraft welcome centre full of pencils with rubbers on the end, postcards, fudge, and CDs of wild birdsong. There was a fast track painted onto the floor – like an IKEA showroom – for Trust members. I followed the arrows, but the guardian of the gate, a sour-looking lady in a Barbour coat and Wellingtons, stopped me. She embodied what Wilkie Collins called 'that state of highly respectful sulkiness which is peculiar to English servants'.

'This is for members,' she said.

'Yes. Of course.' I showed her my green card. She peered at it. Hard.

Unable to find anything wrong with the card, the woman handed it back, then sucked in her cheeks and flicked her eyes towards the gate. I felt that she was disappointed not to be able to send me to the end of the extensive queue meandering towards the ticket desk.

I spent most of my year in Barcelona, where I communicated in the most basic Spanish. The rest of the time I lived in the Llŷn Peninsula where Welsh was spoken by seventy-five per cent of the community, but I was, so far, unable to follow it. I was protected from day-to-day grumpiness because all nuances passed me by. It was like living in a religious order that had taken a vow of silence. I was cushioned. If I did wish to communicate with any level of sophistication, it tended to be with friends or family. All other human interactions were pared to a minimum; Ockham's Razor had become a way of life. The downside of this was that when I found myself surrounded by my increasingly abrasive countrymen, and understanding every word of it, I felt as though I was missing a layer of skin.

'Thank you,' I said, smiling, and pocketed the card.

I set out across open ground, still following the IKEA-style footpath, and feeling oddly coerced, as though my freedom had been curtailed. There were more notices, they were everywhere, making suggestions regarding route or destination: *The Banquet House is now open*, and an arrow. My phone rang. Liz was in Newcastle – where was I? She was going to be another couple of hours. Time was suddenly on my side and I no longer felt obliged to hurry. But a sense of anxiety had accompanied me since I left the car. It had begun to emerge as I crossed the yellow fields, growing out of the feeling that I was lost. And now I felt put out by my interaction with the gate-keeper, who was the first person I had spoken to on this journey. It had been an interchange bereft of human kindness, and quite without welcome. It was the third time I had been alone, entirely alone, since my miscarriage. The trips to Spurn Point and to Pamela's funeral had been the others. I felt empty, my arms long and elastic. I had no one to look after, nothing to hold.

I followed the footpath downwards through a wood. Tall trees closed over me, wrapping me in green light. The air was cool. There was a quality of stillness about the place. A wood is usually crisp with sound, a place of constant movement: the gentle oscillation of the trees, the card-pack shuffle of leaves, the dry voices of twigs as they mutter and grate. There should have been a lifting cry of birds, the klaxon *haw!* of rooks, the snap and skitter of squirrels through the canopy – something to indicate the presence of the countless creatures that I knew were there. Yet there was nothing. I felt as though I were in an empty hall. The leaves rested against one another like papers on a desk. They could have been that way for years.

The footpath persisted, directing my steps. It descended to a valley and opened onto a vast manicured lawn. The River Skell curled through the lawn and past a water mill. The silence gave way to a murmur of voices, the vibrant hum of a souk. Before me was the shell of Fountains Abbey, out of all proportion to the trees among which it stood. It was like an emaciated creature trying to stand, but without enough muscle left on its bones to enable it to complete the action. The empty window at the end of the nave yawned out of the valley floor. Broken walls were capped in sky. It was something from another age – another perception – but it could as easily have been from the future as the past. I tried to imagine the abbey rising from the forest floor. The original church would have been made of timber – hand-hewn blocks of stone fitted around it, facilitated by a wooden scaffold. I wondered who had dreamed the building. How many generations of how many families had made this church their whole life's work?

A few years ago, while driving from Las Vegas to Denver, Rupert, Evie and I had stumbled across a ghost town, called

Bannack, in Montana. It had been founded in 1862. The school desks with their cast-iron fittings remained in the abandoned classroom, a blackboard was still affixed to the wall. A fragile roundabout, made of wood and metal, tilted in the playground, and we played on it. There was a grand hotel in the French style, with wood-burning stoves and a bread oven. There was a Wild West saloon bar with louvred swing-doors. Yet grass poked through the gaps in the boardwalk and filled the main street to knee height. The only sound was the ruffle of wind as it tested the blades and tousled the seed heads. The jail was a rough log cabin. The only people ever to have been executed were the Sheriff – a notorious outlaw who hoodwinked the people into electing him – and his deputies. They were hanged without trial from a gallows pole built especially for the purpose. We found this pole, lying in pieces, partially hidden amid the long grass. At first I mistook it for a telegraph pole. In its first five months Bannack was said to have produced $500,000 of gold that was ninety-five per cent pure – the equivalent of over $10,000,000 today – with a population that grew from four hundred to three thousand in the same span. But when the gold ran out the town was abandoned, almost overnight, the whorehouse and saloon silent.

Fountains Abbey was abandoned when Henry VIII dissolved the monasteries, its abbot, prior and thirty monks paid off with handsome pensions. But now it was part of a curiously polished theme park, with cafés and facilities and the heavily signposted footpath. It swarmed with people. One couple, holding hands, stared up at the carcass of the church. Then, quite suddenly, they embraced, sobbing into one another's arms, the rough bark of their cries flat against the stillness of the trees. I pulled my sunglasses down onto the bridge of my nose, conscious that I was staring. I wondered if they were descended from one of the masons who had built the church. Perhaps they were going to get married. Maybe someone had died.

There is a children's film about an articulated bin that saves the planet after pollution forces the Earth's inhabitants to go into space. In the spaceship the people become obese and diabetic, and develop osteoporosis while eating junk. But the bin, which has found a plant, brings them back, so that they can go forth and multiply, and fill up the planet once more. Only this time, one has the impression, they will be a bit more ecologically aware.

Fountains Abbey felt like a stepping stone towards such a future. The manicured footpath ensured wheelchair access and an easy passage for baby buggies. Yet its primary purpose felt like the fulfilment of a Health and Safety directive, an attempt to reduce the risk of litigation. I had never seen so many super-sized people. A young girl walked towards me, her face as glorious as an angel's. In the middle of her brow was a ridge of flesh, her smile disappearing into dimples. I imagined the size of her heart. Visitors were encouraged to shuffle along the neat path, and to stop for cake, or ice cream. None of us were encouraged – or even free – to wander at our leisure, to poke about, or climb. To sleep overnight, or to have an adventure, to camp among the cold old stones.

A tour was about to begin. A group clustered about a man who held a shepherd's crook over his head. I watched, perplexed, neither in nor out, the guide's words thrown like a net.

The community at Fountains was established in 1132. Thirteen rebellious monks, longing to live a simple life, were taken into the protection of

Archbishop Thurston of York. He granted them this valley, uninhabited, thickly overgrown and 'Fit, rather,' as the Revd. A. W. Oxford put it, 'to be the lair of wild beasts than the home of human beings.' It is a perfect place for a community – remote and secluded – protected in its wooded valley from the winds of the Yorkshire Dales. The valley was formerly known as Skelldale, from the Saxon skel, *meaning spring, and Old English* dael, *for valley, and refers to the many springs that rise in the woods. This woodland, and the steep sandstone cliffs of the valley walls, also provided the raw materials for construction. It seems likely that the Skelldale springs originally gave the abbey its name: St Mary of Fountains. The name 'Mary' derives originally from the Hebrew, Myriam, which itself means strong water. Or it may be an allusion to the 'fountains of living water' promised by Christ to the Woman of Samaria. Three years after they arrived, in 1135, the Yorkshire monks were embraced by the Cistercian order. The abbot of the great abbey at Clairvaux at that time was called St Bernard de Fontaines, so Fountains might have been named after him, as the monks doubtless received much help from Clairvaux. The coarse white habit of the Cistercians is made from undyed fleece and, with time, and the assistance of a community of lay brothers, the monks became wool merchants, and fabulously rich, as seems to be the way with austere orders, the Franciscans being another obviously wealthy example, despite being founded on a rule of poverty. The lands of the monks at Fountains extended to the Lake District on one side, to Teesside on the other . . .*

It occurred to me that if I stayed I might learn something helpful, something about the nature of sacred wells. I had been interested to learn that Myriam meant strong water. Mary, Maria, Marie, would seem to come from the Latin *mare*, meaning sea. The lines on my palms form the shape of an M and as a child I used to look at my hands, and wonder at the mystery locked in the letter. The secret reminder of my name before my adoption: *Marie*

Therese, permanent as a tattoo. But I couldn't keep still, or bear the proximity of so many people. I made my way, alone, through the ruins of the church. High up, at the apex of a window, was an angel. On the external face, in the reverse position, was a carving of a Green Man. He seemed surprised by the foliage issuing from his mouth and encircling his furrowed brow. It was as though he had meant to speak, but the alacritous vine prevented it. On the surface the message seemed clear enough. The Christian angel was on the inside of the church while the pagan deity was out in the cold. It was surprising he had survived at all. And yet the ancient gods are often near at hand. The Dagda was said to be the father of St Brigid of Kildare. Characters change their names and shift their histories, but their archetypes remain, dense with lived experience. They rise up like grains of gold, glittering, from the silt.

The guide, and his group, wandered back into earshot.

One of the first poems written in English – found carved into an Anglo-Saxon cross – is called 'The Dream of the Rood', meaning rod, or upright post. In the poem, the Rood tells how it came to be felled, separated from its fellow trees, and forced to play its part in the crucifixion. The Rood is an object of veneration because, without it, the Passion could not have taken place. The tree sang: 'They drove me through with dark nails. On me are the marks, Wide-mouthed hate dents.'

Iron into wood. A tree that sang. I wondered, vaguely, about the relationship between mystical Christianity and trees. There was an early medieval Irish/Welsh alphabet known as the ogham script, whereby each letter corresponded to a tree. St Joseph was a carpenter. And the Rood, yes, well, that was a tree. Books were made of paper. I felt I had bitten off more than I could chew, although the idea of a mutually beneficial relationship between woodland and people didn't seem far-fetched as a place to start. A very holy priest

I once knew, Father Tony Storey, planted over four thousand trees during his lifetime – rowan, hazel, oak and birch – the trees of the English forest. 'The two most important things in life,' he maintained, 'are to love, and to plant trees.'

I walked beneath the Green Man, moved beyond him. I was back on the lawn, which was clipped, like shearling fleece, for as far as the eye could see. The river had been diverted in this section of the valley and ran as straight as a zipper. The footpath passed on either side of the Skell. There was a bridge next to a ruined house. Beyond that, like a selvedge, neat woodland hemmed the valley. I crossed the river and turned back on myself, facing the way I had come, but on the opposite bank.

And then I saw it.

The prissy path, which had so irritated me, was in fact a garden footpath. The grass had been clipped because it was indeed a lawn, and the crumbling abbey a giant folly. The whole valley had been landscaped into a surreal vision: the Studley Royal Water Garden.

The river ran in a liquid avenue down the centre of a formal garden in the neoclassical style. At the end of the valley it was dammed into a bean-shaped pool. I felt like a pantomime character to whom the audience had been shouting: *It's behind you!* The cupola of a temple was visible above the trees. I abandoned the church and the abbey buildings and followed the river – or rather the canal – downstream. It was swollen and brown, spotted like a seal. On either bank a tidemark of sweet wrappers, bottles, cans, leaves and grass cuttings marked the place where the river had flooded – a Hansel and Gretel trail – parallel to the water's edge. The greensward, which ordinarily should have been the bank, veered out of sight beneath the water. A slow-moving scum covered the surface and I thought of Maxpax hot chocolate, a powdered drink popular in the 1980s that always came out watery, the dried milk never quite dissolving but floating in viscous bubbles. The footpath on my side curved away from the river, passing into woodland. People crowded the opposite bank. I contemplated cutting through the wood to the furthest extent of the garden, where I might be able to cross the river, and then walk back, on the other side, beyond the surging people. But I seemed incapable of leaving the Skell. I hugged its shore, as though following an invalid, waiting for someone to fall. Two blond children played on the far side. They threw sticks into the water. One of the sticks was sucked under the surface, disappearing into a scummy whirlpool. My anxiety followed it, dipping like a mallard, and reappeared, all but unseen, downstream.

When the river opened out onto the bean-shaped lake, it became apparent I was in the wrong place. The bank was wet, and slippery. I made muddy prints as I circumvented the water, windmilling my arms in an attempt to remain upright, the soft mud beneath the grass deceitful as ice. After a while I came to a bridge, and joined the proper path. The river-canal, as it left the lake, was ruler-straight. A right-angled bend afforded a glimpse of further pools, but the footpath again forsook the bank for the trees, and this time I followed it. A bird, as big as a pheasant, but bald-looking, crossed my path. And then two more – the first wildlife I had seen – but they weren't like any bird I knew. A tree rose above me, tall, very tall, a Scots Pine. I thought of Winnie-the-Pooh, and Christopher Robin, and the bees.

I had met a man over the summer, on Porth Dinllaen beach, who told me his father once had an affair, and that a child had been born of it. This child had been adopted. It was a little boy, and he was never named. The man and his brothers and sisters knew him only as Christopher Robin. The man's sister had left a message on the Adoption Contact Register and this said, quite simply: *Searching for Christopher Robin*. But if he had never been named, how would he know that it was him?

In Ireland Brian had asked me if I had ever found my natural father. All I knew him by was the hyphen on my birth certificate. In order to learn his name I needed first to locate my mother. Over many years my searches had turned up nothing, beyond the date and place of her wedding. I had made that discovery after hours spent riffling though the marriage records in St Catherine's House, in London. But after that initial, hasty victory, the trail ran cold. My searches were sporadic. For the most part I didn't think of it, but from time to time I would find myself looking. In the 1980s I leafed through phone books, in later years I scanned the electoral register. For a while I had been employed as a professional researcher, and had access to a number of databases. But there was never a note for me, or a message from a private detective, although I left messages for her, in all the obvious places – the Adoption Contact Register, and also in some of the less obvious ones – with the current owners of the farm that had been given on her marriage certificate as her home address. In 1792 Georgiana, Duchess of Devonshire, was forced by protocol – for which she didn't much care – and her husband, who told her that he'd prevent her from setting eyes on her legitimate children ever again if she didn't cooperate with his demands, to give up the baby daughter she had borne to the future Prime Minister, Charles Gray. The child, Eliza, was raised by Charles Gray's family. Georgiana visited her daughter in secret whenever she could, and gave her small gifts, although she never revealed her identity or was able to give her money. The Cavendish family later destroyed many of Georgiana's letters, embarrassed by the scandal confirmed in them. But a poem made its way into Eliza's effects. It ended:

> *. . . should th' ungenerous world upbraid thee*
> *For mine and for thy father's ill*
> *A nameless mother oft shall assist thee*
> *A hand unseen protect thee still.*

I reached my own hand towards the tree, aware of a pain between my eyebrows, an aching heat behind my eyes. A flat weight, hard as a coin, pushed into my sternum. It is a common theme in the stories of displaced children that their absent parent thinks of them, that they somehow continue to care for them, and keep a flame burning through the years of separation. The Greek myths are full of tales of gods who softened the paths of their demi-god children, who in turn grew into heroes: Theseus, Perseus, Achilles, Helen of Troy. When I was a child Mum told me that my birth mother had been unable to keep me, but that she loved me, and that she had done the very best she could by me. In which case, why had she never contacted me? I was fighting to control my breath, to smooth the contours of my face, but I couldn't. So I sat on a low wall at the edge of the manicured path, and wept for all that Christopher Robin means.

On the other side of the wood, the footpath rejoined the canal. Ahead was a sort of aquatic ha-ha, which must once have been a waterfall, but about ten yards short of it the river had been diverted.

The naked mechanism of the man-made watercourse was visible, the paved and slimy riverbed, the sluice gates, and the iron wheel that moved them. I thought momentarily of a mechanic's garage, a car raised up, the unexpected aspect of the vehicle's workings, and was taken aback by the crack in the façade, the realisation of impermanence, and artifice.

I crossed the empty riverbed at the place where the waterfall had been. A lake was to my left, inhabited by nodding swans; there was a café, but I wanted nothing. I continued to follow the riverbank and passed beneath a bough of yellow honeysuckle, shot with indigo, the petals curled like fingers or little traps, the glossy stamens sore. They were the first flowers I had seen in the garden, but I didn't stop. I regretted it immediately, and went back. The scent was hardly discernible in the dying flowers, but the piquant rot of an early autumn gave an unexpected subtlety. The impression of colour, of lightness, was instant.

Suddenly I saw beauty. A child shook his bag of sweets for the sheer pleasure of hearing the sound. And because it confirmed that the contents were still there. And still his. I stopped worrying about why the English ate so much, and acknowledged that I was starving. The footpath opened onto a round pool, separated by a pea-green walkway from other, crescent-shaped pools. The water was tea-coloured. A pink temple, fronted by Doric columns, knelt above its own immaculate reflection in the gold August sunlight. A statue of Neptune rose before the temple, trident in hand, his face turned away, his gaze angled along his cheekbones. I felt as though I had stumbled upon some intimacy, that my appearance had somehow disturbed the god. I imagined those who were here before me, long ago, now long dead. This was a place for laughter, lovers, whispered trysts.

There was a shifting movement through the trees, a blown warmth, soft as a kiss. I stood still, and looked about me, not sure what I expected to see. The surface of the tea-coloured lake wrinkled; the immaculate reflection scattered. But just as quickly as it had appeared, the pocket of warm air passed by. The water settled. The reflection began to piece itself together. A hush rolled over the woodland.

Tummel

Ten-year-old Dexter sat on the floor outside the bathroom while I lay in a claw-footed bath. My big toe was wedged inside the tap, hot water funnelled round it. I twirled a champagne flute between finger and thumb, and watched it mist and clear. Steam rolled in bales about the panelled walls, the wood forming a buffer against the cold stone beneath.

'Kate?' The voice came from the other side of the bathroom door, below the level of the doorknob.

'Hello, Dexter.'

'Are you all right?'

'I'm fine, darling. Are you?'

'Is there anything I can get you?'

'No. Thank you. You don't have to sit outside, Dex. I'll come down very soon.'

'You're all right ... I'm OK here.'

Later the three boys quizzed me while their father, Chris, made supper. Liz and I sat opposite one another at the kitchen table, working our way down the rest of the bottle of champagne.

'Where are you going?' asked Angus.

'I'm going to follow a river.'

'Which river?' said Elliot.

'It's called the Dunbeath Water.'

'Will we see you again?' asked Dexter.

'Yes. I'll come back this way.'

In spite of living just inside the Scottish border, none of the boys had been to the Interior, as they called it. They told me it was full of mountains, forests and lochs. There was a lot of golf. And it rained – all the time.

'Where are you going to sleep?'

The next morning Liz and the boys heaped me with gifts. There was a well on their land and Elliot, the oldest boy, brought me eighteen litres of spring water. Dexter and Angus made me sandwiches. I didn't see Chris. He was up at the farm, harvesting. As I got into the car Liz leaned in with a half-full bottle of Rioja that we had opened the night before.

'You might want this in your hip flask,' she said. At the end of the drive I turned and looked back at the house. The three boys waved to me from the upstairs windows, their bare feet dangling beneath blond sandstone sills.

The Forth Bridge was exciting. The fields and hills of Scotland unrolled like a rope of silken handkerchiefs tugged from a magician's sleeve. I had reached the A9 that wound from Perth to Wick. All I had to do was follow it and I would come to Dunbeath. After a couple of hours the road, which had been hugging a river, took me through a town. A sign read: *Pitlochry Welcomes You In Blood*. It seemed very visceral. And then I realised that the sign said: *In*

Bloom, and referred to the baskets of flowers that lined the streets and hung from lamp-posts along the riverbank. There was a Fish Ladder marked on my map. Incongruous images flourished in the space between the otherwise familiar words. I parked the car and walked down to the riverbank.

The water was fast-flowing, shallow, pebbled. Dark trees reached from either bank as though attempting to touch. The air smelled of wet leaves. I could taste malt. A distillery was on the other side of the river. I was slightly hung-over from the champagne and Rioja that I had drunk with Liz the previous night, and the fumes from the distillery triggered waves of nausea. I began to walk in the direction of the fish ladder. I had an image in my head of utilitarian tanks, rising in even steps, industrialised and smooth, each filled with glittering salmon, bright as aluminium. I envisaged the fish leaping up through perfect waterfalls alongside a shining dam.

The reality was different. The fish ladder was indeed comprised of concrete tanks, thirty-four of them, and they did rise in uniform shallow steps. But they were blackened with moss and slime. The water screamed and boiled. Signs warned of: *Strong undercurrents, Danger of drowning, Water level may increase significantly at any time.* Some of the tanks were larger than others, resting places for the fish. One of the tanks contained a viewing chamber. It was a dingy room, dripping and cold. I thought of submarines. The sound of the water was all around me. A wall of thickened glass opened into the tank but it was grimed over on the inside, the interior difficult to make out. A chute about the width of a barrel funnelled water from the tank above. A second chute exited on the other side. A fallen branch turned and span, buffeted by the flow; trapped in a cycle, it would remain there until the waters broke it. I felt sick. There were no fish in the chamber.

Dad had been an engineer. If he had been here today he would have explained what we were looking at, described the fluid mechanics of the tank. He could have lifted away the fear that clung to me in wisps. Dad would have found the viewing chamber wonderful. And also the dam that was behind it. I imagined him chuckling at the simplicity of a vision that gave electricity to thousands of homes by the simple act of bricking up a stream. It was like a halter thrown over the head of a horse. As for the fish, displaced by the illumination of the Highlands? Well, of course, they must be helped. The fish ladder was an engineer's dream.

I turned away from the viewing chamber. The hydro-electric power station was between the fish ladder and the dam. In front of me a section of the river had been fenced across to stop debris from being drawn into the turbines. A man with iron-grey hair in a blue woolly jumper was looking over the metal rail, and he was pointing to something in the water. I realised he was speaking to me.

'Sorry?' I said.

'They'll not turn against the flow.' He was talking about the salmon. 'If they slip through these rails they get trapped.' They were young fish, mostly, he told me, coming back after just one winter at sea. Or cock fish, slimmer than the spawn-packed hens.

I looked down. There was a salmon. Every so often it jumped, its head black against the slate-coloured water, its grey eye cold as a pearl.

'Why's it black?' I asked him.

'The longer the salmon are in fresh water, the darker they get. The silver colour you get at the supermarket is caused by something called guanine; crystals laid down beneath their scales. It protects them while they're at sea.' The salmon also had a breeding livery, he told me, of russet and gold. The few that survived and returned to the sea were known as black salmon, or kelts, yet they began to change colour as soon as they left the breeding grounds, swiftly rebuilding the armour that would shield them from the corrosion of the salt. It was mostly females who survived; as soon as they had spawned they turned, ravenous. Salmon rarely ate on their upward journey. Even so, only around one in five of them would return to the sea. But the males stayed in the high pools, fighting among themselves, seeking out fresh females until their lives were spent.

The man told me that his job today was to free the fish that were caught in the turbine pool, to open the gates in the metal grille, and try to flush them out. The thin black salmon leapt again. I studied it for a while.

The Celts believed the salmon had all come from a well. The same well Boand provoked by walking around it widdershins. Nine hazel trees encircled it; their fruit contained all knowledge. As the hazelnuts ripened and dropped into the water the salmon that lived there ate them. As a result of this they embodied all the wisdom of the world.

When the well rose up, and Boand drowned, the salmon were washed out to sea. Not one of them remained. To this day they are trying to return. The spots on a salmon's back tell the number of hazelnuts it has eaten. Not all salmon are wise. But if you can catch one, and roast it, then the first three drops of spitting fat will confer all the knowledge in the fish. The rest, alas, is poison. One of the best-known versions of the story is that of the Irish hero, Fionn mac Cumhaill.

Fionn, which means the Fair One, was a young man, and hungry, and wandering in the forests near the River Boyne. A Druid, called Finegas, known as Finn the Seer, had waited seven years to catch a salmon. That afternoon he had succeeded, and was roasting it on a spit. He saw Fionn, and asked him to oversee the cooking, making sure not to eat any of it, while he went to attend to something else. But three drops of fat spat from under the crispy skin and landed on Fionn's thumb. He put the injured digit into his mouth, and acquired all the knowledge of the world. He carried the salmon to Finegas who immediately noticed something different. There was a brightness to the boy, an alacrity, that hadn't been there before.

'Have you eaten of the fish? the Druid asked.

'Well, no,' said Fionn, 'but I did burn my thumb and I put it straight away into my mouth.'

'Ah,' said the bard, 'then the knowledge is yours.' He handed the fish back. From that time on, if Fionn had a problem, all he had to do was suck his thumb and the answer would present itself. The Druid explained to Fionn that the knowledge always found its way to the one most deserving of it. For his own part, he would wait another seven years, and try again.

I walked towards the power station. There was a museum that told the story of the fish ladder, and a cool humming room that housed the turbines. The first fish ladder had been designed, and patented, by a miller called Richard McFarlan, in New Brunswick, in 1837. He had designed the ladder to circumvent the dam at his water mill. The museum also told the story of the electrification of the Highlands. I tried to picture the workers, the men who had come from all over Europe, in the strange, disjointed months and years after the Second World War had ended, to dam the River Tummel and raise the loch behind it. I sensed the caress of rough cotton shirts, and fabric stiff with sweat. The blistering pinch of hobnailed boots. Scratchy trousers, lice and wool, dirt and ice, the cracked-bell ring of a pickaxe.

On the tiled exterior wall was a bronze memorial relief of a kindly, but sad-looking man. The portrait was executed in profile and the artist had shown no mercy in depicting both the softness beneath his chin and the almost monastic severity of his pate. An unpunctuated script read:

SIR EDWARD MACCOLL 1882–1951
ENGINEER AND PIONEER HYDRO-ELECTRICITY
SCOTLAND

It was a muted dedication: nine words, two dates, no frills. But the dam spoke. The nine dams of the Tummel Valley Hydro-Electric Scheme. One for each word of his epitaph. It seemed that MacColl had died just before the opening of the Pitlochry Station, and instead of a party with bunting, and a band, and tea and cakes, there had been the respectful unveiling of this monument.

I felt I should move on. I walked back through nodding trees to the car. After a very few miles I saw a sign for the village of Killecrankie. We used to come to Scotland, Mum, Dad and my brother, for two weeks every summer, when we met up with my grandparents, aunts, uncles and cousins. One year we had visited the grave of one of Dad's graduate students. I seemed to recall this being in Killecrankie; but when I got to the village the cemetery was unfamiliar, so I called at the local Heritage Centre, thinking I might ask if there was a second cemetery. But the staff all came from Eastern Europe. Not one of them knew the village, other than as a bus stop on their way to work. I passed a café. A conversation in the kitchen caught my attention. Two ladies, well into their middle years, were in loud and animated discourse with a young man. He was tall, and slim, with black hair and liquid eyes. Neither of the women reached higher than his shoulder. From a string about his neck hung a spiral-bound notepad with a pen pushed through the wire. His hands moved with grace and precision creating pictures, like charades. I realised that he could not hear, although he could lip-read, and that they could not sign. When the women were unable to understand his mime the young man wrote, instead, and the ladies, one at each of his elbows, peered down at the notepad. He caught me looking, and I felt invasive but he grinned, curling his fingers around the idea of a cup and then lifting it briefly towards his mouth. I nodded.

When he came over to my table I told him I was looking for a cemetery, and I described the jigsaw bits of memory I had retained. The cemetery was down a long straight track. It formed a perfect square, and was flanked by trees. I couldn't remember if there was a church. The young man nodded and opened the notepad, and put it next to me on the table. He drew a square, filled it with crosses, then drew two huge trees and a straight road that ran up the centre. 'Yes, that's it.' He wrote: *Blair Atholl*.

In less than half an hour I had found it.

I walked along the track, which separated fields full of bullocks. I passed beneath the sheltering trees, which had now grown vast. The track had been grass in my memory, but had now been tarmacked over. A stream chirruped along one wall, a wood closed off the back. I hadn't remembered the cemetery being so close to the road.

Iain MacMartin was killed, very early one morning, in a motor-cycle accident, while returning to the university after the Easter holiday. He was working towards the completion of his doctoral thesis. Although it was over thirty years ago his sister, Miss MacMartin, still wrote to Mum each Christmas. I knew I was in the right place. I remembered Miss MacMartin telling us that the coffin had been carried on a grocer's cart. This detail had seemed important at the time, as though the young man had been transported on a gun carriage. There had been a piper. It was only a small place, and I began systematically to search the headstones. But, try as I might, I could not find his name.

A fine rain began to fall, and I was aware of the lightness of its touch. I recalled having my face washed as a child, the softness of the cloth, the gentleness of the hands, yet here was no kindness, no unkindness; the caress without feeling or intention. A brown buzzard eyed me from the adjacent field. It shifted from a gatepost to the grass, before lifting away, peevish.

Iain MacMartin. I looked everywhere, searched every head-stone, searched again. There were Robertses, Robertsons, McFarlanes, Macfarlanes, Shantos. I observed how connected many of the names were. I thought of Robert Macfarlane, and his book, *The Wild Places*. It was Robert who first told me of *The Well at the World's End* and introduced me to the writing of Neil Gunn. I thought about Richard McFarlan of New Brunswick, who had patented a fish ladder in 1837. I became intrigued by the idea that one might come from somewhere. Or perhaps, rather, that one might know where that somewhere is. All around me, lying side by side, were kinsmen. A field of them.

★

Rupert and I had been together for twelve years before Evie was born. A surgical investigation revealed the architecture of my Fallopian tubes to be imperfect. I might fall pregnant naturally, but it was really very unlikely. If I were to have *in vitro* fertilisation, then the obstacle presented by the damaged tubes would be bypassed. We met with a fertility specialist. The benefits of IVF were obvious: we might have a child. But the disadvantages, too, were concrete: it was expensive both financially and emotionally. It would take up a lot of our time, possibly over several years. There was a significantly increased risk of cancer in women who received the treatment relative to those who did not. Whether this increased risk was connected to the reasons for referral in the first place, or whether it increased as a result of the treatment itself, was not clear. After a while the doctor asked us if we would consider adoption. Well, yes, I said, adoption was a possibility. But I was an adopted child myself. Whenever a baby was born, or a family idiosyncrasy discussed, or if an old photograph came to light, then I had always stepped back – by which I meant that I would get up and move – deliberately maintaining a respectful distance from what I perceived to be the genetic hum in the room. I had done it since my earliest childhood. If I didn't move fast enough then there would always be someone who could, and generally did, point out the impossibility of the baby, or great-aunt, or whoever it was, ever looking like me, or me like them. What for others might be a moment of shared history was, for me, an ongoing reminder of my charity status.

My grandmother used to fascinate me with the stories of Dad's ancestors. Of Faithful Norbury, the sixteenth-century groom, who was 'elevated beyond his station to his mistress's bed', which gave a whole new slant to the family motto: *Regi Et*

Patriae Fidelis. Of William Norbury, converted from the liquor to Methodism by John Wesley himself, who then paced the county for the next forty years with a suitcase of sermons written in minute cursive script and carried by a 'half-wit lad', who had never been known to leave his side. Or of Roger de Bulkeley who had changed his name to that of his Shropshire land: *Norbury*, meaning a northern town or fortification. Genealogy allows us to construct our identities from our own myths and legends, to know who we are, and where we have come from. Or we can use the stories as a starting point for where we might like to go, a legacy to be built on or rebelled against. Sara Maitland describes the tradition of storytelling as 'a very fundamental human attribute, to the extent that psychiatry now often treats "narrative loss" – the inability to construct a story of one's own life – as a loss of identity or personhood.' The stories I had inherited were fascinating, but they weren't mine. I had never met anyone who shared my blood, or who looked like me. There was no genetic starting point from which I could begin my narrative. I didn't even know my nationality.

In answer to the doctor's question, then: I didn't, in the first instance, want to adopt a child, because I was lonely. Not superficially so, not lacking in friends or loved ones. Cosmically. I felt, I had always felt, dizzyingly adrift. I realised that this might be regarded as a poetic conceit, or even a form of vanity, but it also happened to be true.

The doctor then told us that when he was a little boy his own father – a GP – had abandoned his mother, abandoned both of them. The word *divorce* was never mentioned, at any rate he had no recollection of hearing it, and his mother did not remarry. Each birthday and Christmas a present arrived, purporting to be from his father, but the doctor recognised the writing on the package to be that of his mother. Even as an adult he could not bring himself to discuss the subject with her. Shortly after his mother died an aunt had contacted him. She told him that his father was buried in the graveyard of St Mary's Priory in Abergavenny. The doctor was unable to describe his feelings in that place. He realised that he had followed in his father's footsteps, and had clung to what little he knew of him – his profession. Our doctor had facilitated the conception of hundreds of children – their photographs covered the wall behind him. He had four daughters of his own, and several grandchildren. He said: 'I am personally acquainted with the loneliness of which you speak. In my own way, I have sought to fill the void.' He had noticed that a disproportionately large number of people who were adopted, relative to the normal population, presented themselves for fertility treatment. In other words, either adoptees with impaired fertility had a greater desire to create a child of their own than non-adopted people in the same circumstance, or adopted people were proportionally more likely to encounter difficulties conceiving than the non-adopted population. He had even written a paper on the relationship between unexplained infertility and shame, in which shame might be defined as the sense that one is different from other people and therefore, at some level, *not right*, and not worthy to continue one's line, in a very literal, physical, way. This perception, of being different, was sufficient, he believed, to explain infertility. The American psychologist Nancy Verrier has written about the way in which the brains of children who have suffered separation trauma might differ from those of children who have not. Others refer to 'attachment disorders' and these are both, perhaps, ways of describing what the fertility doctor had observed. Adoptees inherit a complex legacy.

Returning to this graveyard, to this wet afternoon, it seemed fitting, or at least ironic, that I who came from nowhere that I knew of – before the Convent – was unable to find the one person I was looking for, and even that was someone – no longer living – who I'd never known in life. I wondered if I had misremembered his name, Iain MacMartin, and if it was an Anglicisation from the Gaelic. Or if it perhaps referred to the little blue bird, the martin, the one with such a long migratory path.

> *Where trouble melts like lemon drops*
> *High above the chimney tops*
> *That's where you'll find me . . .*

The words of 'Over The Rainbow' began to revolve, in unexpected spirals, inside my head. They were accompanied, like the hiss of an old 45, by the drip and crackle of the rain.

> *And the dreams that you dare to . . .*
> *Why, oh why, can't I?*

One of the graves was marked by a wedge of granite. There was no name. It was flanked by two jam-jars of freshly pulled heather, tight clusters of magenta bells. It was a wild place, made tame. I stopped and crouched down next to it and for those few moments drew my dead about me, my own lovely darlings, those whose arms had enfolded me, those small enough to hold in the palm of my hand – Dad, Pamela, my lost baby. Neither Dad nor my miscarried child had a grave that I might visit. Pamela had been buried, but I arrived too late to visit the churchyard. The following morning I had left, in a rainstorm, and though I had driven past the cemetery where Pamela was lying, I had been too afraid to stop. I didn't want to look at the flowers, and the mud, and know that she was under them.

The rain in this Highland cemetery was becoming heavier. It found a way inside my collar, down my sleeves, it flattened my hair against my skull and in wet curls against my neck. I carried my dead in a net, a clattering catch of bones, of promise, of might-have-been. I knew that I had to leave them, free them, free myself. Yet something was interfering with the resolution of my grief, complicating it. Dad had been dead for almost eight years. I felt as I had the day I accidentally found the Convent where I had been born, as though there was a truth, close by, if I could but see it. But the beginner's luck that graced me then had gone. I could perceive this truth in the flickering landscape, like watching television without an aerial, an incandescent image beneath the cloak of rain; but I was either looking too hard, or not hard enough. In part I had not been honest. I did not begin this journey on behalf of Sofia, the girlfriend to whom I gave my copy of *The Well at the World's End*. I came here because I wanted to. There was no other reason. But I couldn't understand what motivated me on my not quite random, yet only loosely guided, path. I turned away from the unmarked granite and as I did so four words, cut into a nearby stone, caught my eye: *Glad did I live*. I was puzzled by the brevity, the baldness of the statement. The inscription felt like a gauntlet, a challenge, requiring something from me.

Early on the last day of Dad's life, I had gone into the room where he was lying. Outside, a Japanese maple tree flapped, ragged, in the wind. I had looked at the scarlet, tenacious leaves, wanting to point them out to Dad. Then realised it was too late. There would be no more trees. I rested my head on his chest. He appeared to be unconscious, and yet I could sense his anxiety, a steady fizzing below his skin, beneath his ribs, at his core.

'Dad?' I ran my fingers over his, put my mouth close to his ear. 'Remember . . . The first law of thermodynamics states that energy cannot be destroyed. Or created. It can only change its form.' I watched his face: it was opaque as alabaster in an unlit room, the deep cold already separating us, drawing us further apart. For all intents and purposes, Dad was in a coma. And yet, in spite of this, he smiled.

Glad did I live.

Newton's first law, of which Dad was also fond, states that an object will remain in a state either of rest, or of uniform motion in a straight line, unless compelled to change by the action of an external force. For me to be able to look back on my life, and to know those four words to have been true, I had to alter my course.

Garry

For the rest of the afternoon I travelled ahead of the weather, the A9 before me, companioned by the River Garry. The dark sleepers of a railway line were laid out as neat as pickets. All three paths – road, rail and river – ran in parallel across the plain that divided the Am Monadh Liath, the grey hills, from the Am Monadh Ruadh, the red hills – the Cairngorms.

The previous night, at Liz's house, I had toyed with the idea of abandoning the journey to Dunbeath. It was still a day's drive away. I had lingered over a map of this plain, looking for a river that might replace the Dunbeath Water. The River Garry was a tributary of the Tummel, which was itself a tributary of the Tay. It had its source in Loch Garry, which in turn was fed by three other rivers. Strictly speaking the Garry didn't run from the sea to a source, but rather it formed a part of such a journey. The River Spey did travel from the sea to its source, Loch Spey in the Corrieyairack Forest, and it also ran across this plain. This new idea was tempting. I had a connection with the River Spey, because we used to holiday next to it when I was a child. I had even caught my first fish in it. However, I was already many miles inland, the Spey ran alongside a road for much of its length, and I wanted to walk from a river mouth. Also, the idea of actually reaching Dunbeath was becoming concrete. I found I couldn't even look at the surrounding hills because I did not wish, as the result of an accidental glance, to develop an idea that might divert me from my intention. I was well aware that I could spend happy hours, if not days, in the Cairngorms. So I kept my eyes at the level of the road, and glanced only occasionally at the river. But at the turn-off to the village of Dalwhinnie, I noticed some buildings, small as matchboxes. Beyond them the mountains rose in lilac slopes.

I stopped the car in a lay-by and got out. I leaned on the boot and listened to the *clatter-clatter-clatter* of a magpie. I watched it lift up and then alight behind each car that passed, picking at something red and furry that was mashed into the tarmac. Overhead, clouds were combed out like wet hair. Rain covered the western side of the plain like plastic sheeting, sealing off the direction I had come from. The weather front that encompassed me in Blair Atholl was getting nearer. I had no map and no adequate protection from the elements.

I had another reason for wanting to continue my journey, beyond these practical considerations. I wanted, just for once, to complete something I had started. My life was cluttered with abandoned projects: degree courses, film scripts, houses, journeys. My head was noisy with unanswered, or only half-formed, questions.

I had made a reservation at a hotel in Grantown-on-Spey. From Grantown it was a just few hours' drive to Dunbeath. I got back into the car.

Spey

A buzzard perched on the *Welcome* sign in the small Highland town of Grantown-on-Spey, its head angled down and sideways. Its eye peered into my own, a bright pulse of contact as I drove by. My reservation was at the same hotel where our family used to holiday each summer, although it was decades since I had been there. We had first returned to Grantown because my brother John, aged fifteen, had won a local golf tournament, and Dad thought he should have the chance to defend his title. After that we just came back because we liked it. After meandering up and down the side roads, running parallel to the main street, I eventually found the Springfield Lodge Hotel.

Its wide gravel drive had given way to a car park, with white lines painted onto pitted asphalt. There had been a croquet lawn at the back of the hotel, with bent rusted hoops, but this, too, had disappeared, beneath a development of executive homes. Previously the grounds had felt exotic, in a *Secret Garden* kind of way, with clipped yew hedges and rhododendrons. Now the place had a hunched, suburban feel, and the word *conference* formed in my mind. But for the most part the house was familiar to me. I walked through a set of double doors to see a walnut writing desk. I recognised the Victorian glass display case that still housed a – possibly depleted – collection of hand-tied fishing flies. Watery sunshine reached the lobby through the open doors of adjoining rooms, and the half-lit fishing flies bristled, iridescent, over their hooks.

I had often wondered how fishing flies worked. The man I had met at the power station in Pitlochry had told me that returning salmon starved themselves, sustained only by the fat of their sea-years. So why then would they be attracted by a fly? Perhaps it was a reflex that made them snap at the disturbed water surface. Or maybe the flies that fell into the river didn't count as eating, too few and far between to constitute a meal. Perhaps the fishing fly was the salmons' last temptation, a pretty feathered demon with a curved steel tail, complete with a vicious barb. Its sole purpose to distract them, perhaps fatally, from their journey upstream. As a child I used to watch the goldfish in our garden pond use their mouths like hands, to examine anything that was of interest to them. Possibly salmon took the fly in order to discover what it was. I had placed my own hands on the glass case but lifted them, suddenly conscious of my fingerprints, when I realised that a woman was staring at me.

'Can I help you?' she asked.

'Yes, thank you, I have a reservation,' and I gave her my name. The woman peered at the computer screen in front of her. She seemed slightly puzzled.

'Is everything all right?'

'I'm not sure,' she said. 'I have you down for tonight and for two days hence but not tomorrow. Is that right?'

'Yes,' I said, 'I will be spending tomorrow night outside.' I told her about my plan to follow the Dunbeath Water to its source.

'My goodness! Do you want me to hold the room for you? It's forecast rain.'

'No. Thank you.' I would need to check out early though. I asked the woman if I could have breakfast at seven. She smiled, and held a key towards me.

'You can. Good luck if I don't see you in the morning. Callum will take your bag to your room.'

I couldn't see anyone who might have been Callum so I picked up my holdall and made for the stairs. I thought about asking the woman if she knew who had made the fishing flies, but she was peering closely at the computer screen. Its milky reflection shone in her spectacles.

The hotel had seemed vast in my recollection, but was in fact no more than two floors of rather grand rooms beneath an attic of smaller bedrooms which our extended family of grandparents, parents, aunts, uncles and cousins, together with me and my brother, must pretty well have filled. The only other guest I remembered was Mr Kenneth Yields, an angler who always took his holiday in the same fortnight as us. Mr Yields had helped me land my first brown trout, when I was eight, which the kitchen staff had cooked for breakfast. My brother had eaten it while I watched on, preferring the hotel's thin, brittle toast and hand-curled butter.

The staircase ascended between landings of polished wood with well-worn carpet runners. A row of heavy white-painted doors, the numbers stencilled in black gloss, opened onto the stairwell on each of the first two floors. My own room was at the top of the house. I put my bag inside the door and went back down the stairs. I still hadn't bought an Ordnance Survey map for tomorrow's journey. I also wanted a bivouac bag, which was a weatherproof cover for my sleeping bag. The shops would be closing in less than an hour.

There was nowhere in Grantown that had what I wanted, so I drove back to Aviemore, fifteen minutes away. In Blacks they had not heard of a bivouac bag, *a what?* And I was surprised, and also worried by this, because I hadn't brought a tent. But in the last shop I entered, pushing past the proprietor as he turned the card in the window, I found what I was looking for. The man didn't seem to mind about the time.

'Now,' I asked, 'do you sell maps?'

'I do,' he said. 'Where are you looking for?'

'Dunbeath, in Caithness. I want to follow the river there to its source, so I need a map with all of it on.' He found a map of Dunbeath and opened it out so we could check it had the river on it. I had been driving all day, and I needed glasses, but my first impression was that most of the page was blank. I thought perhaps some of the colours hadn't come out.

'Do you mind if we move it closer to the window?' I asked. The shopkeeper carried it as though it were an origami swan's nest and laid it in a rectangle of sunlight. This initially bleached the paper further, but my eyes were becoming accustomed to the whiteness. It was the right map.

At one corner of the sheet was a wedge of blue: the sea. Along the coast ran the A9, long and lovely, and pink as bitten candyfloss. The fishing town of Dunbeath was there, and the knotty blue squiggle of the river. To begin with there were woods on either side of the strath, a few buildings, some ruins – *Old Sheilings, Burnt Mound, Standing Stone*. But that was all. Much further north there was a forest, in green, and some terracotta web-like contours. The white areas must have been moorland, and yes, there were blue tufts, hard to see and discreet as fallen eyelashes. It was a bog. As the contours snagged together where the land began to rise I made out clusters of blue spots, half the size of sequins and as random as spattered ink, and the words *dubh lochs*.

'What are dubh lochs?' I asked.

'Black water,' said the shopkeeper. I had no idea what he was talking about. 'Sometimes they are only a few feet across but the waterhead is like a sponge, it's full of holes. Stay away from them, and use a stick to measure depth, even if it looks like a puddle.'

I felt a flicker of fear behind my pubic bone as though an oil-lamp, containing my essence, had been knocked.

'It's all right,' I said, 'I'm going to be following the river.'

I traced the blue line as it coiled and bent over the folds in the page, through the slowly rising landscape. As it wound higher it was joined by tributaries. When that happened its pathway grew deceptive, labyrinthine, the lines of water as evenly balanced as fingers on hands, so that it was not clear which stream led to the source. There was no loch, no thumbnail oval, just a petering out among the scattered pools in a frightening lonely emptiness. Had I seen the map two months ago, when I began my journey north, I would never have come this far. I wasn't certain whether the new knowledge was an advantage, or if I would have been better driving to Dunbeath without a map and simply following the water. I hoped that when I found the place where the tributaries joined the river that the right path would become apparent to me. The shopkeeper had been kind, but he wanted to go home. I thanked him and left with the map and the survival bag, and headed back to Grantown-on-Spey.

Woodland pressed almost to the heart of Grantown. Beyond these woods was the river. As there were still a couple of hours before supper I decided to walk down to the Spey. A sign directed me to a footpath, curtained on either side in green-black firs, so that I had the sense of being in a corridor. After a while the trees became more spaced and in the lighter places the needle-deep ground choked into life. The summer bilberries had gone, the blackberries were not yet ripe. Gold lichen tufted quartz boulders stained to copper by the peaty soil. Toadstools pushed through moss. The forest scent was pungent; a soft sweet churchy resin over mushroom over mulch. Falling leaves drifted like confetti through the trees, the first messengers of a change in air pressure, the front that I had remained ahead of, yet had followed me all day long.

My memory of the river was of smooth black water travelling between green banks, the fish clearing the water in deep pools below the bridge. There had been occasional sandy coves, child-sized beaches, where I had constructed dams and captured elvers to use as bait. My eel-trap had been a wine bottle with a hole drilled in the bottom, a piece of Mum's nylon stocking stretched over the neck. I would lay the bottle among the gravel of the shallows in the path taken by the elvers. A piece of bacon fat lured them through the hole in the base and, because they only swam in one direction, they became trapped against the stocking at the top. I never did have the heart to put a hook through them. Each one was returned to the river, but not before I had stared at them for the longest time. The smoky bottle of undulating eels was as fascinating and mysterious as Aladdin's magic lamp. But as I came out of the woods on this August afternoon I was greeted by a swollen, opaque, drowning river, matted with daisy-filled weeds. It was an Ophelia river that heaved against heavy, muddied banks. I remembered the debris that had littered the submerged banks of the River Skell, and the water churning through the tanks of the fish ladder at Pitlochry. I realised, finally, that I was looking at the work of weeks of rain. It was so strange, after spending the summer in the sun, on the Llŷn Peninsula, which had been safe within its own microclimate. Tales of floods throughout the country, and newspapers showing ducks swimming under deckchairs had reached us, on our Welsh beach, but had felt unlikely, queer as fairy tales.

I tried to find the place where I had caught my first trout. I was seven years younger than my brother, and was often left behind when he and my cousins, who were all of a similar age, went on expeditions. Sometimes, Mr Yields would take me fishing. I recalled, at the end of one such afternoon, my auntie Marge making her way towards the water's edge in a PVC cream mac, approaching warily, yet sassily, in inappropriate heels, her smile a vermilion streak, her unnecessary sunglasses glinting in the pale light. Mum and her sister Marge shared Scottish/Welsh descent. Mum was the Scot, with the light brown hair and soft blue eyes of her grandmother. Mum was gentle, her features delicate, finely boned. She was at home on the moors, in the mountains, outside. My aunt was tall, yet voluptuous, with raven hair, and took after her great-grandfather, a Welshman called Ifan Evans. I felt certain I had seen a photograph of Marge as a young girl wearing a tall Welsh hat, a wool shawl pulled tight around her shoulders. But by the 1970s she was most at ease with a cocktail in her hand, fingers curved around a highball glass, her nails signalling red for danger. For the very first time it struck me that this occurrence might have been unusual, Auntie Marge coming down to the river, and she and Mr Yields wandering off, leaving me to oversee the rods. *Now you watch the lines ... Keep your eye on the float ...* and then they would come back a while later. I remembered sheltering from the rain in a wooden fisherman's hut, alone. Alone! A few days before the fishing trip with Mr Yields, my grandfather – who always carried a pearl-handled knife, ostensibly for cutting apples – had carved our initials and closed them in a heart on one of the upright posts of the hut. I had occupied myself, while I waited for Auntie Marge and Mr Yields to come back, by inking in our initials with a biro. Spots of rain had dropped through the water's surface, making circles as big as my head. Each round band had merged with the next, forming patterns as dense as chrysanthemums. The river hadn't felt dangerous to me then, not like now. It would never have occurred to me to go in, or to follow the adults. I had made a prop from a forked twig, to support my fishing rod, and devoted myself to my cave art, my private act of vandalism.

At a bend in the river I came upon a wooden shelter. It had been extensively patched and repaired. There was no sign of a heart and arrow. I turned the memory, questioned it, for in truth it seemed unlikely. But I was cold, the rain was coming fast behind the wind, which was rising, so I left the river, and hurried through the skittering forest.

By the time I got back to the hotel I was soaked. I walked up the wax-polished staircase, feeling the burnt-caramel oak of the banister rail, its textured grain sticky beneath my wet hand, and at a right-angled bend met another splintered recollection, bright and translucent as film. I had a sudden clear image of myself crouching on this first-floor landing, my hair unkempt, the laces of my damp pumps dirty as worms, and watching in fascination through the wooden rails while my uncle, who was a jazz musician, and had the floppy hair and angular cheekbones of Chet Baker, raised one hand in warning, and argued vehemently across the stairwell – presumably in full hearing of everyone, because the space would have amplified the sound – with the waistcoated and tweedy figure of Mr Yields, who blinked, and polished his spectacles, but nonetheless stood his ground. *I don't need you to teach my wife how to fish!*

The first time we came here Mr Yields had Mrs Yields with him, but in subsequent years he always came alone. On that first occasion I had assumed Mrs Yields was his mother because their children hadn't come with them. Possibly they didn't have any. Her lilac-tinted hair billowed in a wispy cloud over an apricot twinset and pinkish pearls, the colour matching the plastic arms of Mrs Yields' spectacles. My only memory is of her reading in the drawing room one evening, and folding a soft leather bookmark into the spine of her novel, adjusting the glasses on her nose, as my uncle and cousin appeared laughing in front of her, resplendent – as they saw it – in chest waders. They were going out to fish, beneath the bridge, at night. Mrs Yields didn't seem to find anything funny about a man and a boy wearing waders in a drawing room, and this had made them laugh even more.

In subsequent years, Mr Yields had told us, his wife went to stay with her sister because she claimed that the Highlands didn't agree with her. I developed the idea that Mrs Yields was an invalid, a word that meant nothing to me, but sounded exotic, although of limited interest. I imagined it involved having breakfast in bed, only all the time. I had seen *Rear Window* by Alfred Hitchcock in which the invalid wife is chopped up and put in a trunk. But I think I may have made the invalid part up because I couldn't see why anyone would want to stay behind when they could have been on holiday in Scotland. With us.

I tried to make sense of the memories. I searched the numbered doors for clues. As I did so one of them opened and a woman stepped out. Before the door closed again I glimpsed a double bed and behind it a casement window. A man was sitting on the bed, pulling on a pair of socks. The bed and the casement were familiar to me. I was sure that I had a recollection of Mr Yields sitting on the edge of my aunt's bed, framed by this same casement window, or, at any rate, one very like it. Auntie Marge often suffered with her lungs, but why would Mr Yields be sitting on her bed? Yet I remembered standing in the doorway, looking at them both, my aunt beneath a gold-coloured eiderdown, her fever spent, drifting in and out of sleep, but still wearing lipstick. Mr Yields had been engrossed in the newspaper crossword and had remained perfectly motionless, his pipe tucked into the corner of his mouth, although he raised his eyebrows in greeting when he saw me standing there, the pipe momentarily slipping.

One of the reasons we know so much about the Celts is that the Romans wrote about them when they came to Britain. Cassius Dio, a Roman chronicler, noted a British woman's response to an acerbic remark made by the Empress Julia Augusta: 'We fulfil the demands of nature in a much better way than do you Roman women; for we consort openly with the best men, whereas you let yourselves be debauched in secret by the vilest.' It occurred to me that my aunt, for whom I would have flown to the moon had I been able, may well, in her prime, have been a fine example of her race. Although they are both now deep into their eighties my uncle remains devoted to Marge, and she in her way to him, despite a slightly hysterical decade of divorce when it was never really clear who the wronged party was. They never remarried, but grew slowly back together, in the same way that bark heals around initials carved in a tree. A stroke, some years ago, slowed Marge down, softened her. But she still sees no reason to elucidate the myths that have grown with her, shrouding her like brambles. I commented recently on a photograph of her youngest son, taken when he was a little boy, struck by his bright blue eyes and Viking looks in such contrast with the black hair of his siblings.

'Where on earth did he get that hair?' I said, realising, only as the words left my mouth, what I'd done. But her eyes crinkled mischievously.

'Do you think the time has come to tell the truth?'

I stared hard at the photograph. Observed the Chet Baker cheekbones and the mop of unkempt hair. It was a different colour, but that apart, my cousin was the image of my uncle. 'Do you?' I asked, and she had pealed into laughter, saying:

'Now, are we going to have another gin and tonic or will you go and open a bottle of wine?'

I shivered as I turned the key in the door to my room. I put the bivouac bag and the map of Caithness on the bed. The map looked innocuous in its orange and silver covers with a photograph of a lone cyclist. Yet somewhere among its creases was the place where I would be sleeping the following night. Given how cold I was feeling the idea seemed at best unlikely, at worst foolish. I decided to have a bath. Going back into the corridor, I found a bathroom tucked beneath the eaves. I brought the towels from the bedroom and placed them on a Lloyd Loom basket; the cracked floor was ancient lino. I ran the bath using only the hot water tap because a granite chill permeated everything, even though it was August. An art deco mirror above the sink, which was flanked with engravings of angular sea creatures, steamed over quickly. Condensation trickled down flaking tongue-and-groove walls. The water in the bath cooled as rapidly as it filled, the cast iron stealing the heat. I ran the hot tap constantly, the water gurgling into the overflow, until I felt warm enough to turn it off, whereon a protest broke out in the pipes. The rain, which seemed to have set in for the night, rustled at the window, slipped across the slates, and I seemed to lose my grip on time, in this space beneath the roof, the old house becoming a memory box, where recollections matted with dreams.

An hour later I pulled on a pair of jeans and a sweater. I tried to call Rupert, and then Evie at her cousins' house, but there was no cover for my mobile and the rooms didn't have telephones. I took Neil M. Gunn's *Highland River* from my holdall. It described, in the form of a novel, the exact journey I hoped to make the following day.

A table had been set for me in the dining room, silver service, a crisp white damask tablecloth, but I had been alone all day. I suddenly craved the intimacy of the bar. There was a deep Knole sofa, next to an oak coffee table, in front of the fire, so I sat down and ordered a venison salad, followed by salmon. I watched the young barman talking to a German couple about whisky. He was tall, fair and blue-eyed, and exhibited an authority beyond his years. I wondered if he was the absent Callum who the reception-ist had referred to earlier, the one who had failed to collect my bag. The German couple wanted to know if a single malt whisky was better than a blend, and if age was an indication of quality. He answered them knowledgeably, yet evenly, exhibiting no personal preference, nor implying any hint of stigma or qualitative judge-ment, so that while being very well informed about whisky – in the abstract – they did not seem any the wiser, with regard to making a decision, by the time he had finished. His face was as unreadable as a poker player's.

I opened *Highland River*. It had been my intention to read the novel months ago, and yet a part of me wanted to experience the river first hand, rather than seeing it through the filter of the book. As a result of this I still hadn't got beyond the opening chapters. But the Ordnance Survey map had set anxiety fizzing around inside me like a toy train on a loop track. The rain that still landed against the windows in handfuls, now as hard as grain, only served to increase my unease.

The book told how a boy was sent by his mother, early one morning, to fetch water from the well-pool. The well-pool was close to the river mouth, and he disturbed an enormous salmon there, silver and blue-backed. He wrestled with it, and brought it to land.

A curious mood of fatalism comes upon a salmon that has committed its life to a pool. Up and down it will go, round this boulder, by the side of that, turning here, turning back again there, but never making any attempt to leave the known ground. No barrage of stones will drive it forth, however successfully timed. The dangers of the shallows are the dangers of the unknown, of death. If the pool be just deep enough a salmon will pass between swimming human legs rather than be driven forth, and in this restless fashion will ultimately tire out its enemies.

Although drawn by the narrative, I was aware of a subtext, and at some level I was distracted by it, as though I was straining to hear a radio playing in another room. When I glanced up, it was to see the barman removing my plate and asking me if I wanted anything else. He was standing in the space between me and the coffee table. Our feet were almost touching. As if in response to my unspoken discomfiture, he glanced behind him and down at the table, which was heavy, and pressed into the backs of his calves. He shrugged, creating an impression of a vague but deliberate insolence. Well, surely it would have been more orthodox to lean across from the side to clear the table? I put down the book.

'I'd like whisky,' I said, 'but I'll come and see what you have.' I eased past him and walked over to the bar. He was attentive, professional. As before, he gave nothing away. I made my selection, Glenfarclas, large, no ice, but he had several bottles of various ages, and I allowed him to guide me through this second stage. Another young man appeared. The two of them exchanged a few words. The second man was offering to make up my order, and I understood that the shift had changed. My barman placed the heavy tumbler on a tray, accompanied by a jug of water. I slipped down from the bar stool in order to move back to my seat by the fire, but in that moment a couple from the dining room entered. He and I watched as they sat down on the sofa, filling it. The tray was suspended between us. The barman looked from it to me, and his eyes darkened, a momentary flaring of the pupil, as he said:

'Would you like me to bring this to your room?'

Not quite sure that I'd heard him right, I focused on the button that secured his white shirt, the top button remaining unfastened. The skin of his throat was pale and this, combined with the white of the cotton and the fairness of his hair, gave him a slightly studious look, although he exuded a butterscotch warmth. The shirt seemed tight across his shoulders, which were wide, and arched as taut as a bow. His waist was narrow, he was probably a climber, or perhaps a rower, the deltoid muscles pulling a ruck across the line of his shirt, the hand that held the whisky strong. The distance between us seemed to expand, and then shrink, very quickly, back to nothing. I was aware of the planes of his body that were facing mine, and sensed a movement as silent, yet frenetic, as Brownian motion filling the space between us.

I lifted my eyes and met his look, causeway to an unknown land. I was aware of the exquisitely finite nature of the moment.

'I'll take the whisky here,' I said, 'thank you,' and as I lifted the glass the stones of my wedding ring glittered under the halogen lights of the bar. But I kept his gaze, was held by it, and for a few moments felt the promise implied there, the feckless possibility of sudden joy, ephemeral as the smell of hot bread. But then I dipped my head, and turned away, and when I looked again he had gone.

Dunbeath

The A9 curved out above the village of Dunbeath, dwarfing the harbour town beneath it. The road looked like a boomerang placed across an architect's model, and at first I missed the turning, and had to turn back and try again, to find the spiral slip road that curled down to the village. I stopped at the Dunbeath Heritage Centre and collected a tourist map, to complement my OS map, before parking the car close to the river. Above me, the traffic buzzed in a whining Doppler along the seaboard of the Eastern Highlands. Until this moment the A9 had been my path, since leaving Liz's house it had formed my route, yet suddenly it was veering away from me. I stood beneath the road at the edge of a deep crease in the land. In front of me was the sea.

I walked down to the harbour. The sea was blue and silver, striped like a mackerel, and the moorland that skittered into it over sandstone cliffs had the colour and appearance of deer hide. Crimson heather glinted on the wind-burned moor, iron oxide under gold leaf, the mineral pigments pure. Heaped-up pearly clouds covered the sun. I could make out occasional townships, slipped like love-notes into cracks along the coast. There was an almost mythological cleanness about the place, as though I were standing on a stage, these things just props, and a drama was about to begin.

The river mouth was held open, on the southern side, by concrete ballast. On the other side was a jetty wall, and both the ballast and the wall reached into the sea like the arms of a flamenco dancer. Scrubby detritus – a rubber float, gull feathers, old bits of rope, a one-gallon plastic container – garlanded the shore on either side of the dancing arms. A single lonely fishing boat rocked in their embrace. I walked to the tip of the wall, to the very end of the jetty, and looked down into the water. It was almost black. I watched the tide as it pushed into the river, and I found it difficult to focus, to judge distance, or depth, amid the waters' shifting pattern. This was the place, the beginning, or the end, where the identity of the river was lost, or discovered, depending on how you looked at it. I stood quite still following the movement of the water, the movement of my breath, and the sound of my heart and the blood in my ears drowned out the sound of the water. And then the moment passed, and the sky, which had seemed to grow suddenly very close, became once again impervious, a canopy, the sea was before me, the river behind me, the sense of dissolution gone.

I turned to face upstream.

On the opposite shore a man in chest waders, with a black-and-white dog, was tying a feather fly to his fishing line. On my side of the river was a bronze statue showing young Kenn, the protagonist of *Highland River*, resolute, determined, his fingers knotted through the gills of his fish, which was almost as big as he was. A cool breeze pulled at me, returning me, reminding me that the time had come to choose my path. The fisherman and the collie were on the southern bank, accessible by a footbridge. The bronze statue of the boy and the fish were on the other. I chose the statue. I would remain on the northern shore.

In his novel *Christ Recrucified*, the Cretan writer Nikos Kazantzakis describes a group of villagers as they prepare to take part in a Mystery Play. As the weeks slide by the amateur actors make the ancient lines their own, and gradually the villagers begin to exhibit the attributes of the characters they have assumed. As I passed beyond the metal figure, and past neat stacks of lobster pots, I felt as though I, too, was taking part in something, fulfilling a role.

I passed back beneath the viaduct. On the tourist map I had found at the Heritage Centre there was a black dot marked at the edge of the river that indicated the well-pool where Kenn caught his salmon in *Highland River*. I could see an inlet with some stepping stones, but I couldn't be sure if that was it. Maybe the recent floods had concealed the pool. A way-marked footpath crossed under a second, older road bridge that pulled the two sides of the village together. The footpath was clearly in regular use, and the first few hundred yards of the bank were littered with dog turds in every stage of decomposition, which gave this section of the pathway the urban feel of a city park. The fashion for notices that had been so evident at the River Mersey, at Fountains Abbey and at Pitlochry was also a feature at Dunbeath. While the English signs had been full of direction, and even instruction, about what one might − or might not − do, the Scottish signs concentrated on avoiding mishap: *Danger of Death: Keep Off, Danger − Overhead Electric Power Lines − No Fishing, You Cross This Bridge at Your Own Risk. Cast with Care.* Drawings of stick-men in different forms of extremis, hit by lightning bolts, falling into water, illustrated the hazards.

After a few hundred yards a wall appeared, reaching almost to the water's edge. It emanated from a ruin on a raised mound above the riverbank. According to the map this was the site of an ancient monastery and was known as the House of Peace. The stones were green and covered in moss; there was a farmhouse near by, called Ballachly, meaning cemetery. One night, according to the notes on the tourist map, a tributary of the Dunbeath Water had flooded, and the dead had been raised, and then lowered, although not quite in the same place where they had started. The farmer had ploughed the displaced remains back into this field, and was said to have had ill luck from that day on.

A wooden footbridge crossed the tributary burn and a path led to the Dun Beath Broch, marked on both of my maps. I walked on, beyond it, not wanting to be diverted, but the riverbank crackled with reminders of human habitation. A few more yards revealed a hut circle, the remains of a field system was visible on the higher ground. My OS map was dotted with clues: *Chambered Cairn, Quarry (dis), Settlement, Standing Stone, Broch.*

A long wall was bent in a right angle close by the river's edge. Behind the wall was a beech wood, framed in a perfect rectangle. The trees were huge, and their dry leaves chittered and clattered above the sibilant rowans and rustling birch on my side of the wall. A second right-angled bend marked the end of the enclosed beech wood, and small trees pressed closely on both banks of the river. Sunlight was filtered through the tissue-paper discs of hazel leaves. Lichen, ghostly pale, bloomed in the shape of oak leaves, garlanding and silvering the hazels. I pulled a sprig of green nuts from a branch and put them in my mouth, splitting the pliant shells between my teeth. A milky juice spilt from a soft core, tasting of grass, with a hint of wood, and it was like sucking an ice-lolly stick, but without having had the benefit of the ice cream. I reached for another sprig, snapped it off, and was about to repeat the process, but instead dropped it into my pocket. The green nuts, rather than providing a snack, were actually making me feel hungrier than I had been before I started eating them.

The land had been rising gently, and the river bubbled wide and shallow. But now a gorge opened in front of me, its sandstone walls tall as a church. The river opened into a peat-coloured pool, in the middle of which was an island of heaped-up pebbles. The banks on either side were smooth and grassy, but beyond the pool the gorge looked impassable, the red stone rising sheer above the river. I would have to leave the bank, for a while, and follow along the top of the cliff. I sat down and took an apple from my bag. The place was like a cloister, warm and green. The soft banks and quiet pool invited sleep. Brightness bounced off the water as it was whipped into peaks by a passing breeze, before flattening again, smooth as a new-made bed.

A dark fin broke the surface, a black back sliding through sunlight. A salmon! I longed to let my arm trail in the water, to feel the salmon move against my hand. But I was captivated by its appearance of indolence, in awe of its explosive power, and I couldn't move. I found myself wondering about Finan Cam of Kinitty, a sixth-century Irish saint, who was said to have been conceived when his mother went swimming in a salmon pool at night. Both Finan Cam's acuity and his great wisdom were attributed to his aquatic parent. Every so often the fish broke the surface and picked off a fly, leaving ripples as round as plates.

A Scottish tale, from Jocelyn of Furness's *Life of St Kentigern*, tells the story of a Highland queen:

who turned her eyes onto a certain young soldier,
who seemed to her spring-like, with a beautiful appearance . . .
And as a man who was sufficiently ready and inclined for such homage,
he was easily made to sleep with her.

She gave the spring-like soldier a ring, of great value, one that had been a gift from her husband. The young man was not at all discreet, and wore the jewel openly. An informer told the king about the lovers, and the king invited the soldier to escort him on a hunting trip. In the afternoon, when they had eaten, the king suggested they might rest awhile on the riverbank, and so the two of them lay down. The unsuspecting soldier fell immediately asleep. The king saw the ring in his open hand and, although he was sorely tempted to kill the soldier there and then, he removed the ring instead, and cast it into the water.

When the king came home, he asked the queen what had become of the ring he had given her on their wedding day. The queen said she thought that it was in a certain chest, and went off and made as if to look for it. Instead, she dispatched a messenger to the soldier, who sent word back that he had lost the ring. He then remained in hiding. Consumed with jealousy, the king accused his wife of adultery, and had her held under guard. He let it be known that, if she could not produce the ring within three days, he would kill her.

The queen sent a message to St Kentigern, who was living as a hermit on the banks of the River Clyde, begging him to help her. St Kentigern, who had already heard the story, ordered his servant to take a fish-hook to the river and bring him the first fish that he caught. When the servant brought the fish – which was a salmon – the saint opened it and found the ring inside its belly, and he immediately sent the jewel, with his servant, to the queen. Humbled by this quite extraordinary proof of his wife's innocence, and the apparent falseness of his accusation, the king knelt before the queen, begging, publicly, for her forgiveness, and swearing that he would put her accuser to death. But the queen wisely maintained that it was her deepest wish that the king should not harden his heart against the man, but forgive him. She then went to visit the hermit-saint, and made her full confession. She amended her life according to his counsel, *restraining her feet from another such fall.* While her husband lived, the queen never revealed the means by which mercy had been shown to her, but after his death she let the story be known to anyone who wished to hear it.

It seemed natural that St Kentigern should be kindly disposed towards the queen. His own mother, who was also the daughter of a queen, had been thrown from a cliff for conceiving outside wedlock. When that failed to kill her, her father took her to the deepest part of the ocean and set her adrift in a leather coracle beyond the Firth of Forth, without oars, and commended her to the mercy of the sea. She washed up on a shore, near Culross, and made her way to the embers of a fire, which she stacked up with driftwood, and then gave birth to her son. The light from the fire attracted some shepherds, and they brought meat to the mother and clothing for her and her child, and brought them both to the home of St Servanus, who named them, and cared for them, as though they were his own.*

* As it happened, Saints Servanus and Kentigern lived a hundred years apart, and would never have had the opportunity to meet.

With regard to the unknown paternity of the saint, his biographer Jocelyn of Furness simply remarked:

Truly we think the matter absurd to inquire further as to who the sower was and in what manner he ploughed or even planted the earth when, by the Lord's goodness, this earth produced good and abundant fruit.

Kentigern had lived over fifteen hundred years ago. He was also known affectionately as Mungo, meaning the dear one, or darling. In spite of being a hermit he attracted a great community around him, and this came to be known as *glas cu* meaning the dear green place. His community still thrives on the banks of the River Clyde.

Glas cu.

Glasgow.

Good and abundant fruit.

The salmon tilted in the pool next to me. My eye caught the curve of its back as it broke the surface, and I heard a *clock* as it slipped away.

I climbed up a steep bank clustered in hazels. Below me was the sequestered pool in its chapel. The riverbank had been protected from the wind, but now I could feel a cool damp breeze on my face, although there was no sense of rain. Two red grouse flapped up in front of me, *crack-crack-crack*, their voices like the hinge of a gate.

I stepped out onto a flat, wide world. I couldn't see the sun. The river was tucked away inside the gorge. At the northern and southern edges of the flatness were low rumpled hills. At the peak of one of them a monolith leaned into the wind, as though it were trying to walk. Beyond that, and some way north, were the twirling blades of a wind farm. The gold and chamois peat flows lifted in front of me. Two thin black lines, a Land-Rover track, ran parallel with the hidden river. Occasional low walls split the land into sections. These few features, like delineations on a board game, created an illusion of emptiness more intense than if there had been nothing there at all.

I approached a five-barred gate. According to a sign the land ahead was private. But *pedestrians visiting the cemetery* were welcome. In spite of the word *welcome* there was something off-putting about the notice. Possibly the inclusion of the word *cemetery*. Looking behind me I could make out a large low hunting lodge on one of the hills above Dunbeath. I wondered, belatedly, if I should have asked permission before coming here. But pedestrians were welcome. I climbed over the gate and took out the Ordnance Survey map.

I was standing at the edge of that same area of whiteness, that vast empty page, which had so unnerved me when I saw the map in the camping store at Aviemore. Three towns, Dunbeath, Latheron and Latheronwheel, were linked by the candy-stripe A9. Rivers, hemmed in green, bisected the towns, passing beneath the road and wriggling towards the sea. An intricate patchworked field system skipped along the coast, a lacy trim along the edge of the page. Inland, the map was minimalist. It seemed more so in daylight, and the occasional contours, blue lines, spots and tufts of grass were as mute and inexplicable to me now as when I last looked at them. There was no forest, or anything that might be thought of as a mountain, and no loch beyond the boggy clusters of dubh lochs.

The next feature marked on my map was the cemetery to which the wooden signpost referred, although I couldn't see it yet.

Beyond it was a farm, and these two things were the last signs of human habitation, if a cemetery could be called a habitation, on this side of the river. The only other building was on the opposite bank, about eight miles away, and there was no track to it. It was simply called Poll Roy. On my side of the river, at the far boundary of the farm, there was a footbridge across a tributary, and there, I believed, I could rejoin the river.

I came to a boggy pool at the side of the path. In the centre was a cushion of sphagnum moss and in the middle of the cushion sat a rabbit. It started when it heard my footstep but otherwise did not move. Its nearside eye bulged. It was blind. I thought of the glossy hare at Spurn Point that had loped sparkly-eyed from the shore: my wise and lucky sea-hare. Why do we read good omens into pretty things but are so quick to dismiss ugliness as fancy? With difficulty I ignored the rabbit, and tried not to develop the idea that my spirit guide had left me.

I longed to pass the enclosed land, and be alone. Of course I was alone, I had been all day, but the Land-Rover track, the cemetery and the farm buildings ahead of me were all indicative of regular human visitation. I felt vulnerable, and visible, in much the same way that I had at Spurn Point. Some way ahead of me a wall crossed the path and to the right of it was a chambered cairn that I had seen marked on the map. There was a gate across the track and an animal pressed its face through the bars. From a distance it looked like a goat, all devil horns and slanting eyes, but as I drew closer I could see it was a sheep. More sheep came to the gate and I was not sure if this was a response to my approach, or if they were expecting a visit from the shepherd. By the time I reached them, they were thickly clustered and showed no sign of moving. So I climbed over the gate and pushed my way between them, their sticky wool and unexpectedly bony frames rubbing against my legs. Looking up, I could see the cemetery. It had whitewashed stucco walls and was situated towards the edge of the gorge, overlooking the river below. The cemetery was filled with elegant black and ochre monuments. As the path curved, and my angle of approach altered, the monuments appeared to rearrange themselves, like the figures on a Bavarian clock. A padlock and chain coiled around iron gates. Below, in the gorge, the river glittered. I felt happy to see it again, as though I had been reunited with a friend.

Sheep pressed into the whitewashed walls, grubby against the pristine brightness. To the sixth-century icon painters sheep represented thoughts. A good shepherd was someone who had control of their thoughts, who could corral them, stop them from wandering. Orpheus had been a shepherd. It was shepherds who first saw the divine light of the Nativity. Evie's favourite character in the Catalan Nativity is called the *Caganet*, that is, the Shitter. In addition to the Shepherds, the Three Kings, the Angel and the Holy Family, the animals in the byre and the lambs, the Caganet squats, his eyes fixed on the manger, his skirts hoisted around his waist, while he drops an astonishing turd.

According to legend the *Caganet* was one of the shepherds to whom the Angel first announced the Good News, but unfortunately he was taken short. Anxious not to miss anything, he positioned himself discreetly at an appropriate distance from the Holy Family and relieved himself, while remaining in a state of wonder and contemplation. The field where he was squatting became fertile from that day forth, and so he has come to embody a number of ideas: the importance of a reciprocal relationship between mankind and the earth – for even as he receives he is giving back – and enlightenment, both physical and spiritual.

Ahead of me were the farm buildings. They were still so far away they looked like Lego blocks. Slowly they grew bigger until the track brought me to the farmyard. The moors lifted away on every side. The house and outhouses were well maintained. I peered through a kitchen window. I thought I might see a mug and a kettle, perhaps a packet of biscuits, or a chair. But there was nothing, the house was quite unfurnished, although there had been fresh hay and animal feed in the barn.

I passed quickly through the farm and after climbing over a stile set into the farthest wall, I was at last on the open moor. The Land-Rover track continued a little way beyond the last field, and then formed a neat loop back on itself, as precise as a surgeon's thread. There were more scattered remains of earlier dwellings, an old cistern filled with farm equipment, and then the footbridge. I had regained the river, and it was smoother now, a curving ribbon, fed by a single tributary. I crossed the tributary with a sense of elation, and was surprised by quite how much my heart warmed at the sight of the water. The river was gently and visibly rising, held in a gentle V in the land. The fear that I had felt when I first saw the map had quite dissipated. While I followed the river I could not get lost. It was as constant and as concrete as a ball of flax. I folded the map away and put it at the bottom of my bag.

Water always takes the easiest path. So, too, do deer, although they are not keen on getting their feet wet. Clear tracks followed the bank of the river, avoiding areas of moss and mud. Smiling, I noticed that the deer also preferred the northern bank. I caught a sudden movement at the edge of my vision, and turned as a vast herd of young stags rustled along the horizon, their antlers drifting like Shakespeare's Birnam Wood.

On the other side of the river was a stone house – I had reached Poll Roy. A waterfall, a low step, was the last of the river's features to be recorded on my map and I had been looking forward to reaching this place. I liked the name – it sounded heroic, like Rob Roy. Poll Roy seemed to be a conventional – if abandoned – farmhouse, but the fact that there was no road to the house felt wrong. It was like Dorothy's home landing out of nowhere on the Wicked Witch of the East, but without the ruby slippers. Glancing down I saw a rusted wire loop encased in plastic. A trap. It was old, and abandoned, but I narrowly missed stepping in a second. I came across two more, the metal nooses shiny. New traps. There was no real danger, although I might have turned an ankle. But the idea that someone might come here unnerved me. I was at least two miles beyond the end of the Land-Rover track. Behind the abandoned house ran a ridge of low hills. I sat down, retrieved the map Unfolded it. Beyond the hills was a second river, the Berriedale Water, and an unpaved track ran along the side of it. Later the track turned north-east, away from the new river, past a lochan, and then crossed the Dunbeath Water, about three miles upstream from where I was now. I don't know why I hadn't noticed it earlier. It hadn't occurred to me, on my linear trajectory, that one might cut across the hills to get here, and that I was not as remote from other people as I had supposed.

Evening was refracting all around me. I was aware of the cool air in the shadows of the house, the darkness pooling to one side of it. I was affected by its stillness and sense of uncertain abandonment, like that of the farm below. I wondered how it came to be empty, conscious of the legacy of the Clearances, when tenant farmers throughout the Highlands were turned out of their cottages by their landlords, driven to poorer lands, driven to the coast, or to the cities, to America, Canada and Australia, while their homesteads became vast sheep farms. I found that I was afraid, as I had been when I saw the madman at Spurn Point. I had walked about half the length of the river and although I intended to sleep on the moor, I didn't want to meet anyone, certainly not the setter of the traps. Although I was as much unnerved by the spirit of this house as by the thought of any human encounter. I decided to try and reach the track – the one on the map that bridged the river – as quickly as the path allowed. Beyond the crossroads I felt sure I would be alone.

The land was rising, and the river was narrowing, winding and curving between broken peat hags that curled down over me, two or three times my height. I was still following the split hoof marks of the deer that speckled the water's edge. White stones appeared at the bends in the river; other than that the earth was black, the roots of heather forming a ragged fringe along the top of the bank. Traps still appeared, sporadically, along the deer path, so I climbed up to the top of the peat. I could see in every direction, but there was nothing except the moor and the sky, which was as soft and white as the underbelly of a goose. There was no sound; the river, quiet at best, was inaudible from the slight elevation. No feature broke the horizon – either rock or stone or tree. How quickly I might get lost if I were to wander even a short distance from the water! My senses were alternately flooded and starved by the uncompromising austerity of the moor. The dry heather didn't make for easy walking, being rough and uneven, and the peat was deeply cracked. I was aware how frightening the place might appear if one were unable to trust one's senses.

When I was twenty-two years old I met a fortune-teller in Brighton. I had travelled there with a girlfriend, Emma, who had come from Nigeria to begin her Ph.D. in London, and we had taken the rattling train from London's Victoria Station, the grey-green landscape of south-east England obscured by the rivulets that meandered across the window glass. It was November. When we arrived at Brighton the rain had stopped. The sun was like a torch beneath a bed-sheet. A zigzag wind, vigorous as elvers, burrowed into our clothing. There were very few places that offered shelter. We ate fish and chips, and walked along the pier. We sipped afternoon tea from white china cups, and grew dissatisfied as it cooled too fast. We hunched into Lloyd Loom chairs behind chattering conservatory glass. The glass reminded me of garden cloches and I had an incongruous flash of Beatrix Potter's Peter Rabbit, naked and sorrowful, squeezing chubbily beneath Mr McGregor's gate. Simply being there filled me with panic, the desire to run tempered by enervation – it would be ten years before Brighton became fashionable and we seemed little removed, in our wicker chairs, from the old people gazing from the double-glazed care homes that bandaged the seafront like wraparound sunglasses covering the eyes of the blind.

Emma didn't appear to have noticed, or perhaps the newness of the monochromatic landscape filled her with wonder. Most of what I knew about Africa had been gleaned from a trip to Morocco. It had been an unmitigated disaster, and I was in and out of Africa in less than two days, my girlfriend and I with our inappropriate clothing and short, bleached hair attracting more attention than we either wished for or could cope with. We had spent a miserable night in a cheap hotel in Tétouan, where I saw my first cockroach, heard my first muezzin, and where strange voices muttered outside the door all night, knocking, and calling, *M'm'selles! M'm'selles! Would you like to see the souk?* In the morning we found the very same taxi driver who had brought us there and begged him to take us back to the port. I thought it unlikely that Brighton was having the same impact on Emma. She seemed enchanted by its gentleness, or perhaps its shabby genteelness, her brows arched with laughter, delighting in the fact that we two were there at all. And so I had tried to temper my anxiety, my longing to shrug off the fug of central heating and the cinnamon plastic aftertaste of teacakes. Later we made our way to the slick wet beach where a mêlée of traders struggled against the low season, recessed into the arches beneath the promenade, like cave dwellers, or bees. I wanted to stamp down to the water's edge, to stand before the flinty sea, fill my ears with the sound of the waves, and touch the spattering spray. It was the non-human element of the town that attracted me. But Emma was drawn to the life that hugged the shore, and she wanted to see everything, stop at every stall, and I felt it graceless to suggest that we might part. We passed purveyors of smoked fish, mussels, prawns, jellied eels. Fish and chip shops, with mushy peas, and gift shops with postcards bent into curves by the damp winter air, animals made from glued-together shells and imported from Taiwan. Finally we came across a sign above a door that said: *Professor Mirza, Famous Mystic of the East.* Outside was a sandwich board bearing a large delineated hand. We had stumbled across a palmist.

There was a price for one hand, double for two. The hand you have been dealt, and what you will make of it. The professor seemed ancient, yet his face was unlined. His skin was a warm mahogany, although it had the chalky bloom that an English winter's day gives to everyone. He wore a grey woollen astrakhan hat. I think in part it was a desire to look at the hat that kept me there. Also, it was warm in Professor Mirza's room, and the knowledge that cold legs scurried overhead lent a *Wind in the Willows* riverbank feel to the place. It had the same addictive cosiness that Ratty had shared with Mole. Letters lined the walls. While Emma chatted to the famous clairvoyant I studied the framed and often ebullient commendations from his clients. They included a short, polite note from Lady Antonia Fraser.

I don't remember what the left hand said, other than that I was naturally impulsive and had done little to temper this. But I do remember what he found in the right. I would become a writer − a detail that, oddly, I have only recalled as I write this account. I would live with more than one man. I would have a child in my mid-thirties who would compensate me for the loss of a loved one. I should beware of mental illness at around the same time. I don't recall the rest. I might have listened more, and argued less. I told him I was going to be a filmmaker, I had already met a good man, and I wanted to have many children. Professor Mirza asked for the birthday of my lover. When I gave it to him he began to laugh, for this was not the one − oh goodness, not at all. Beneath the laughter the professor conveyed a firm yet gentle authority. If I would but accept the knowledge, he seemed to be saying, it would be easier for me in the long run, and I could prepare better for the road ahead. After all, why else was I here?

I dismissed the professor's vision, because it wasn't what I wanted to hear. I had wanted to hear about romance and roses, success and plenty, and I was ill-tempered for the rest of the day. I have sometimes wondered if things might have turned out differently had I paid closer attention. Or if they turned out the way they did *because* of what I learned, so that my life became a self-fulfilling prophecy.

Many times in the years that followed I tried to forget what I had heard that day. It had amounted to a fifteen-year forecast. Shortly afterwards I had met Rupert, but the years slipped by and no baby came, and the *child born in your mid-thirties who would compensate you for the loss of a loved one* began to glow, ephemeral, persistent. Sometimes I tried to ignore it. If it was my lot to be childless then I should accept this fact, get on with it, and try to live a different sort of life. Because waiting interferes with living. I hoped, and I feared. I reached for her – I knew it was a she, I even knew what she looked like, down to the blue vein that curled like the tip of a vine from the outer edge of her eye. The prophecy became a hope that both sustained me and controlled me.

Twelve years later, when I was about to begin the IVF treatment that would result in my pregnancy with Evie, Dad told me that he had cancer. It was early one morning, still dark, in November, and he was sitting on my bed, holding a cup of tea that he had brought for me. My lovely father. He said: 'Everything is going to be all right.'

Suddenly it was me who had a vision of the future, of the set of scales in which Dad was balanced next to my longed-for baby. Cassandra was blessed with foresight by the sun god Apollo, and then later cursed by him, so that no one believed a word she said. I didn't want to be believed. There was no one I could tell. And yet

I didn't want to stop it; because I feared, at some level, I had agreed to it. The past grew insubstantial, the present began to seem unlikely, blotted out by a vision of a future in which that which I most desired, and that which I most feared, were – if Professor Mirza's prophecy was correct – about to coincide.

One day, standing in our kitchen, Dad – uncharacteristically, for he was always warm, but not especially tactile in the way in which he articulated affection – wrapped his arms around me, and held me close to him, burying his face in my hair, as though through the act of inhalation he could somehow conserve my essence, imprint it on his soul. I could feel the boniness of his frame, pared by illness, and no matter how close we stood, or how tightly we embraced, the gap between us seemed to be widening, the pockets of air expanding, and then acquiring the solidity of Perspex. Dad felt like a fairy's child that disappears when seen for what it is. I held in my arms a bundle of twigs and feathers, already splintering into dust.

There was a grace period.

The cancer metastasized into Dad's bones when Evie was three months old. He lived another seventeen months during which the two became the closest friends, so that she still speaks of him with affection, even today.

Eight days before Dad died, the day an ambulance brought him home from the hospital, I watched a plane bank into a building. It was on a television in a shop. I was getting a few last provisions before Dad's arrival. The fact that a portable television had been set down next to the cash till was unusual. The staff were clustered round it. I saw matchstick people, clothes fluttering, jump from a collapsing tower. I realised, dimly, that something terrible had occurred, although my only thought was: I mustn't tell Dad – he

175

was such an *Americophile*. He had taught at the University of Princeton, and had charmed us with his tales, of Professor Einstein, and of John Nash, the brilliant mathematician who became quite mad, who wandered the quadrangle, his arms heaped with papers, and whose story was told in the Oscar-winning film *A Beautiful Mind*, which had just been released that summer.

My own beautiful mind was beginning to shift. It was a tent in the desert, full of lovely things, but the sand was getting in as the wind tore at the pegs, loosening the ropes.

After Dad died I had found a torn-off piece of lined A4 paper. It was in a file marked *Kate*, among the school concert programmes and a lock of my baby hair tied with a turquoise ribbon. There were a few lines of poetry, written in blue ink in Dad's beloved, looping hand, and they told of a dream he'd once had. Of how that dream had now come true, and was here, beside him. At first I thought he'd written it himself. Later I discovered it to be a misquotation of some lyrics of a song called 'Long Ago And Far Away' by Ira Gershwin.

In the weeks following the funeral my life began to come apart. We had been living in a cottage that belonged to my brother, John. He had told me that we would be doing him a favour by living in it, through I suspected he had lent it to us so we could all be close to Dad. After Dad's death Rupert and I had intended to move back to our own flat, in London, but the days slipped by.

I had always found solace in walking. It was something Dad and I did together. We had probably, over twenty-five years, followed every single footpath throughout the hills and woodland around our family home. As Dad became sicker I began to walk these paths alone, or with Evie carried in a backpack. But an outbreak of foot-and-mouth disease stamped out all my wanderings. On the day after

Dad's death I drove over the border into Wales. Moel Famau, near Ruthin, was a particular friend. But when I reached Moel Famau the police had closed off the mountain with the same rustling plastic ribbons that they used to mark a crime scene. At home, the public footpaths across the fields, and the woodland tracks, and the hills were all out of bounds. There was nowhere that I could walk, except on asphalt. Six and a half million sheep, cattle and pigs were slaughtered, with over eighty thousand animals being destroyed each week. Smoke drifted from their burning pyres, and the fires lasted for weeks. The foot-and-mouth outbreak would eventually cost the country around eight billion pounds. It cost me my sanity.

The descent began, not with sadness, but with an extraordinary rush of energy. One day I pulled the car into Mum's driveway with over five thousand pounds' worth of goods that I had bought that morning at John Lewis, including a hand-knotted Ziegler carpet, a set of steel pans, and a different-shaped Dyson to the one I already had. I had only gone to buy an iron. Mum came out to the car and asked if I wanted help unloading the goods, but I had simply shaken my head and said: 'It's all got to go back.' I then returned everything to the shop the following day. But quite quickly my high spirits disappeared. After three months I went to see my doctor, convinced that I was suffering from over thirty listed side effects to a topical antibiotic cream and was astonished when he told me I was severely depressed. When I got home, after an indeterminate period of time, for my memory had grown poor, and my ability to concentrate laughable, I looked up the drug the doctor had prescribed for me, and found a set of contraindications not listed by the manufacturer, including suicide and murder. The rock star Michael Hutchence, who a few years earlier had been found dead in his hotel bedroom hanging from a door, was rumoured to have been taking this medication. So had a man in America who murdered his family and then killed himself. I disregarded the obvious fact that both these people were arguably unstable in the first place. But I didn't take the pills. The doctor advised me to cooperate with my treatment before my 'neurotic condition became psychotic'. It was already psychotic. I had seen the devil in the post office and almost caused a car crash in my haste to get away. I noticed that one of my neighbours had the horizontal pupils of a goat. Another lady, I observed, had an extendable neck, her skin like that of a turtle.

I was working on a screenplay at the time, with the Liverpool writer Alan Bleasdale. Because of various hitches the production had slowed down, which was a mercy, so the phone seldom rang. In a moment of lucidity I made a diagram, listing the writer – Alan – the name of the commissioning editor, the broadcaster, the production company, the fact that a director had not yet been appointed, the name of the project and a brief description of the plot, all joined by circles and arrows, so that – if asked – I could sustain a conversation, my forefinger tracing the lines on the paper, which I Sellotaped to my desk.

One morning I found myself staring at the bathroom sink, which was spattered with blood, my hands gripping the sides of the washbasin, a metallic taste in my mouth. Rupert was in the shower, holding his head in both of his hands, weeping. I had no idea what might have occurred, or what I had said, or done. I had deduced that the blood was mine, that it most likely came from a blood vessel in my throat, and that I had therefore, probably, been screaming. I no longer recognised my face in the mirror. In fact, I was terrified of it.

Another day, feeling tired, always so very tired, I decided to make a cup of tea, and then lie down, while Evie had her afternoon nap. I walked over to my bedroom window to close the curtains. In addition to the cup in my hand, there were five other cups, the tea in various stages of cooling, standing in a row on the windowsill. I touched them, the first was tepid, the last only recently made. I watched the sun as it vanished behind our orchard, tangerine and lilac, and I thought it beautiful. The birds had began to chirrup and stir, a last burst of activity before they settled for the night. I listened to the song of a blackbird, the ring-tone of a collared dove. I didn't remember putting the cups of tea on the windowsill. I wondered how long it had taken to make them all. I wondered if it was me that had done it. For the first and only time in my life I understood why suicide might seem reasonable, even sensible, under certain circumstances.

In spite of all this I thought I was doing fine, but could tell from the faces of my friends and family that this probably wasn't so. The fact that I could understand that there was a gap between what I felt and what I saw gave me hope. But I could not trust my senses. Sometimes the walls shifted, or bulged. My greatest fear was that I would go to sleep and wake up mad. Or madder. Evie – the fact that I had to care for her, to feed her, wash her, attend to her every need – was my reason for persevering. She had to be looked after from one moment to the next. She forced me to inhabit the present.

It was a priest who engineered my recovery. I had taken to parking outside the local Catholic church when I went to visit the doctor. The car park was usually empty, except when there was a Mass, and it was easier to negotiate than the crowded surgery car park. One day I knocked on the door of the presbytery, although it had been over twenty years since I had set foot in a church, other than for a wedding or a funeral. The priest invited me inside, and we sat at a table, a glass of water in front of me, while I tried to tell him why I was there.

He looked at me warily, as though at a dog that was known to bite. It was a look to which I had grown accustomed. But the priest was not afraid – of me, or of the condition that I attempted to describe – and this gave me confidence. I found myself telling him how, on the last day of Dad's life, I had watched his spirit leave his body, leave our home. It had begun before dawn. I was sleeping in Mum and Dad's bedroom, a baby monitor at my side, so I could hear Dad breathing in his hospital bed downstairs. Suddenly I was awake, the sound of his voice, the vowel sounds flattened and torn by the monitor. There were no words to speak of. The pain in Dad's bones was almost impossible to relieve. Morphine sedated his mind, but it could not reach into his bones. The day before, I had implored the nurses to leave Dad unwashed, instead of trying to move him, and had smoothed clean linen napkins on either side of his face rather than changing the sweat-soaked pillow. The last word I had heard him utter was *torture*. But now I was too tired to get out of bed. I meant to go to him. I knew Mum was there, resting fitfully in a bed adjacent to his. I could hear her even sleeping breaths crackling through the baby monitor. My sister-in-law, Maria, and I had divided the days and nights into shifts, had taken it in turns looking after Dad, because he didn't want a full-time nurse, none of us wanted a full-time nurse, but I had not slept, other than in brief snatched moments, for five days. I forced myself out of bed and down the stairs, holding onto the wall of the stairwell for support, unable to locate the banister in the darkness. When I got to Dad silence had closed over him, the agony passed for now, his breathing deep and even. I sat next to him and held his hand. Tentatively. Everything hurt. It was the 19th of September

– his father's birthday – and I told him this. I felt that he could hear me. Rupert had shaved Dad's face the previous afternoon, and his skin was smooth and soft. 'No hair on face,' Dad had said. I went to the fridge and opened a bottle of Sancerre. I used cotton wool soaked in cool wine to wash Dad's lips. He could no longer swallow. I cleaned around his teeth and gums with a wine-soaked Q-tip. I poured a glass for myself. It was then that I noticed the light. At first I thought I was mistaken. The light was like the aura around a candle flame, or a street lamp in fine rain. It was orange, and seemed to be emanating from his body. I could only see it from certain angles. As the day uncoiled, the house murmured with people. Dad's breathing remained strong for hours at a time and then, quite suddenly, it would falter, the gaps between each tattered inhalation growing longer. The suspense was extraordinary. Someone brought the Port of Liverpool Tide Table. We consulted the charts, compared the times to the changes in Dad's breathing. 'He'll go out with the tide,' Maria said. At lunchtime we called my brother John, who came from work. But the waters turned again and Dad's strength returned, seamless as the river's bore. So confident were we of his alignment with the water that John went back to work, and returned just before the next high tide, which was due in the early evening. When the tide turned again, Dad's family were gathered about him. Seconds yawned between each breath. The gaps between in-breath and out-breath grew longer. The room had filled with people. At one point there were nineteen of us in the house. The district nurse called by.

'Try to get your mum to leave the room,' she said. 'His love for her binds him to the earth. Even a few moments would do it.' Astonished by the folk wisdom of the nurse, we persuaded Mum to leave Dad's side, on the pretext of having something to eat. John and Rupert took their places on either side of him, and held Dad's two hands. But no sooner had Mum sat down at the table in a room across the hallway, declaring that she had no appetite, than John and Rupert called us back.

As we stood in the doorway a sigh left Dad's body. Mum walked to Dad and took his hand in both of hers. She bent to kiss him, and then sat next to him. There was a terrible sound as my uncle Dennis beat his chest with the backs of his fists, and roared, his head back, mouth open, like a Picasso bull. The room filled with people, they revolved like planets around Dad's awful stillness. Looking down I noticed my own yellow hair, like summer cobwebs, on the floor around the bed. It had been falling out for days. Someone had brought a box of iced buns from the bakery in the village, *for the mourners*. Flipping open the cardboard lid I sat down next to Dad and ate them all. There was a lot of movement in the house, a lot of drinking, tea, whisky, wine. Someone phoned the doctor, the undertaker. Asked if we could keep Dad's body overnight. Yes, we could. I wondered where Evie had got to. Someone had taken her off for the day, but as the hours stretched she had been passed from one friend's house to the next. It was then that I noticed that the orange glow had gone. I wondered if the electric lights rendered it invisible. And then I saw it. No longer emanating from his body, the orange light was now a man-shaped cloud, and it hovered just below the ceiling. I climbed onto the windowsill, and opened the highest window, and then watched as the shape slipped like smoke from a cigarette, into the September sky. That night John slept on the sofa alongside Dad's body. The next day the undertaker came.

The priest looked at me, his fingertips pressed together, making a church of his hands. I wasn't mad, or mentally ill, so far as he could see. He said that if we were Mediterranean it would probably be said that I had *gone mad with grief*. What I had described was not unknown to him. The phenomenon, of a visible aura, wasn't a symptom of psychosis. It had been well documented by the Church over many centuries. The followers of St Francis of Assisi reported just such an orange glow emanating from beneath the door of the saint's cell while he was at prayer. The priest arranged for me to talk to another priest, a Jesuit, and also to a nun, who had trained as both a spiritual director and a counsellor. I don't remember much about this, only that Sister Josephine showed me photographs – of rioting crowds, of deserts, of children, of war, of a river, a fighting bull, and a matador. I began to perceive that there was a world beyond my heartbreak.

I began to cycle, every morning, at dawn, while Rupert looked after Evie. I rode for miles through country lanes. One morning I saw a chubby grey badger slip into a ditch at the sound of my approach. Another day I passed beneath an oak tree heavy with buzzards, and a flock of collared doves, the doves fanned a branch's length from the nine solemn raptors, a temporary truce between them. I saw a family of mute swans at the reed-encircled disc of Hatchmere Lake, the immaculate parents at the side of the road, their muddy-looking cygnets behind them. Often I cycled along the ridged switchback road bisecting the ancient forest of Delamere. I grew back into the world that held me. I learned to reconnect. Gradually I learned to fit.

I stepped back down into the riverbed. It was filled with new grass, brilliant and green, no higher than my foot. I was happy for the companionship of the water. The river was now little wider than a stream, but it was my clue through the labyrinth.

I seemed to have been wandering for hours. I wondered if I had missed the track, which according to the map was about two-thirds of the way along the river's length. Maybe it was a ford, rather than a bridge – and I had passed it, without noticing. The stream was barely more than the span of my arm, and the deer-tracks wandered from one side to the other as the animals sought a straighter path than that of the wriggling stream. I climbed back up onto the heather. A short-eared owl lifted up in front of me with a *he-awe* cry, its black-rimmed eyes as fierce as suns, burning through pale rings, delicate as pansies. The Welsh word for owl means flower-face, after an enchanted woman made from flowers, who was condemned – for her adultery, and for plotting to murder her husband – never to show her face in daylight again. There was no sun now, but neither was it dark, and I tried to dismiss the superstitions linked with the appearance of daytime owls, and to concentrate instead on the fact that short-eared owls are diurnal. After I had passed the spot, the owl returned to its place, and was immediately lost beneath the heather. I walked on. In part I had been unnerved because the owl was sitting on the ground; but there was nowhere else for it – for either of us – to be.

At last I could see the track. It crossed the stream at a bridge made of wooden railway sleepers. There was a square shack with a metal roof and picture windows. As I got closer I saw a kitchen table and some chairs. The stream and the track – two tyre lines across the moor – formed a perfect crossroads. I was still uncomfortable at the thought of being seen. I was too nervous even to put my face to the window of the hut, or to try the door. And yet as soon as I had gone past it, and the stream had curved out of sight of the hut, and out of sight of anyone who might come to it, I felt safe. The transition took moments, not even a minute, because the dwindling stream was now constantly turning, sometimes leaving crescent moons of still water through the gentle cut. There were no more traps. The cleft prints of the deer were for the most part hard and cracked, the black peat baked by the sun. The grass was longer now, and every so often I came across the pressed, indented shapes that marked the place where deer had rested. A golden frog, with a shiny Murano eye, hopped quickly away into the damp grass by the stream.

A hind came down from the moor to drink, her pale face and large ears tuned inquisitively towards me. Uncertain, she changed her mind, and picked her way back onto the peat hag, head pulled back, one eye swivelled in an attempt to keep me in view. And then she turned, and remained there, her ghostly face suspended, waiting for me to pass. She was the first solitary deer that I had come across although I had seen several herds throughout the day.

An eagle. Like the owl, she too must have been resting on the heather, and I heard her before I saw her. When she gained sufficient height to catch the breeze she curled away, black against the still-white sky, which muffled her *pee-oow* call, a white band under her tail attesting to her youth.

It was the time of the evening when the creatures move.

I was relaxed as I walked towards the waterhead, although it seemed extraordinary to me that I still hadn't reached it – the stream was so very narrow. I wondered about settling, soon, for the night, because the boggy water table might not be the most sensible place to sleep. In any case I was hungry. I had apples, chocolate, pumpkin seeds and raisins. And, like *Treasure Island's* Dr Livesey, I carried a block of cheese. I also had the remains of Liz's Rioja in my hip flask. While I was pondering the meal I might make with these things, I heard something.

At first I thought it was an effect of my being alone, a trick my ears were playing caused by the silence of the moor – I wondered if it was tinnitus. But it didn't seem to be coming from inside my head, so I stopped a moment to listen. And as soon as I stopped moving they descended.

Midges!

They filled my eyes, my ears, my nose and mouth with their pointy needle kisses. I breathed them, swallowed them, spat them out, batted at them, and then began to run.

Without ever stopping moving I scanned the ground for somewhere to sleep. A heather-covered ledge had collapsed at the edge of the cut. It was about a yard below the level of the open moor, and yet still a little elevated above the stream. I scrutinised the place as best I could through the stinging cloud. I could see no tracks across it, and found a spot in the middle where I was least likely to be stepped on should a deer descend from the moor in the night. The deer-track along the edge of the stream was around three yards away: I had no desire to find out if *sure-footed as a deer* was a truism.

Having identified my spot, I broke into a furious dance. I pulled off my Wellingtons, pushing them into my bag. I opened out my sleeping bag and wriggled into both it and the bivouac bag before pulling the hoods of both of them over me. I was, mercifully, wearing a muslin T-shirt, and I pulled this over my face like a fencing mask, before killing every one of the horrid little flies that had so comprehensively invaded my bed.

At last it was over. I drank a sip of water from within the safety of the sleeping bag. It was the only one of my supplies that had made it into the sanctuary. I then rearranged the fencing mask. I could feel a space about the size of a fist under my ribs, but hunger was a small price to pay for being safe from the midges. The whole of my body, face and hands stung with their bites. Earlier, as I walked, I had nursed an image of myself sitting by the stream in the long northern night and reading Neil Gunn's book while eating an apple. The electronic-sounding whine was still at full strength, though; I could not even hear the water. And I couldn't see through the muslin fencing mask. In spite of the early hour – it couldn't have been more than nine o'clock – I pushed my body into the heather, which was soft and springy, and didn't even mark the passage into sleep.

A joyful sound awoke me: rain. A light summer rain, but I was warm and dry and the midges were being washed away. When the rain gave way to silence, I peeped out from beneath my mask, then took it off. The darkness was imperfect, and the gentle bubble of the stream replaced the high-pitched hum. A white mist hugged the water, visible as a light area below me. I drifted off.

I felt him before I saw him. It was as though there was a dial in my stomach and an arrow had spun me back to consciousness, accurate and sensitive as a compass. The needle stalled, quivering, in his direction. He coughed and then shifted his footing, and my nose burned with pungent musk. Lying very still, I lifted my face. The stag was standing just behind the crown of my head, his own head held high. His antlers filled the darkness over me; it was like looking at the sky through leaded panes. I could make out the deeper darkness of his body but he was too close, and it was too dark, to see his legs. He seemed unsure about what to do and then, sliding back his head in that tight, reined-in gesture that the hind had exhibited earlier, he delicately stepped down onto the track, and whether he stayed to drink or left immediately I will never know, because sleep once again stopped my senses.

I woke soon after dawn. Thick mist filled the streambed. On either side, in the long grass, cobwebs cast about in all directions, weighted with an early catch of rain. I glanced down at my sleeping bag. I too was covered in a pearly veil. I touched my cheek and my hand came away wet. Even my eyelashes were beaded. I was about to turn over and go back to sleep, wait for the sun to burn it off, when I caught myself. How many times would I ever again wake up alone, at dawn, on a Highland moor? And yet I would sleep the day away!

I took off my clothes and wandered around barefoot, feeling the soft moss and cold peat between my toes. I found a flower which looked like edelweiss, but was really a sprig of sphagnum moss that had dried, rehydrated and then dried again so many times that it had petrified. Stalks of drenched bog-cotton formed an army of white-haired witches, partially transformed into their broomsticks. I got dressed and packed away my bed. I was thrilled to see the place where I had been, the crushed heather dark against the dewy whiteness. I looked up and down the streambed, as though for someone or something with whom to share my excitement at this concrete mark of my existence. But I was alone with the impassive moor. And yet the fact that it was clearly so very much alive reassured me. Made me glad.

I picked up my bag and broke through the cobwebs, feeling certain that the source was close. I smiled at my lack of faith in bringing such a quantity of bottled water to the source of a river.

The stream disappeared into a muddy hole in the ground. Or, rather, it emerged. It hadn't got any narrower. There was no bubbling spring, no crystal well. Just a navel oozing primordial soup: viscous and green. The water seeped, rather than flowed. One half of the damp oval was covered in grass, the height of a finger, preternaturally bright.

There was absolutely nothing there.

I suppose that made sense. That there *was* nothing there. It was the source. Embryonic. The beginning. Although my spirits had sunk when I saw it. I knew that I was fighting to make something out of the discovery, because this was nowhere near the Well at the World's End I'd come to look for. I sat down. I had a flask of hot water, and some sachets of coffee, sugar and milk that I'd taken from the hotel the night before. I made myself a cup and drank it, broke off a piece of chocolate, and all the while gazed at the hole.

The mist blew past in gauzy fragments, sometimes closing, sometimes lifting, and I couldn't really see what lay beyond. I didn't want to move away from the navel. Since reaching the water table the ground had levelled off. I was afraid of getting lost if I left the indentation of the streambed. I was in no hurry to move on.

I took out *Highland River* from my backpack. I still hadn't got beyond the opening chapters. I flicked to the end.

His dismay was vague and ludicrous. From his map-gazing he knew that his river should rise in a loch. He could not have been mistaken . . . And here it was coming out of the earth itself. The realism mocked him.

Vague and ludicrous . . . I took out the map and opened it. I peered at it very closely. There was no loch. I returned to the book.

He went on over the broken ground and came to a round still pool . . . About him the ground was broken and hag-ridden, but he could see he had not yet reached the crest of the watershed. There remained the suggestion of an upward hollow. He came on another small pool like the first. Then another. A primeval no man's land of out-spewings like water-logged shell holes . . . And then all at once before him again was the tiny stream and lifting his eyes he saw the far half of the loch, Loch Braighe na h'Aibhne, the water-head.

I picked up the map again. Stared at it. Yes, the stream *did* disappear, and that could be it re-emerging at the very edge of the page. But there was no loch. I glanced at the back cover of the book as it rested on a peaty knoll. Saw the word *Fiction* in the bottom left-hand corner. Again I scrutinised the map: *Braighe na h'Aibhne* was there, but it described a collection of small pools on the high ground to the south. They looked like a collection of dubh lochs. The book was first published in 1937. Could the loch have disappeared? Was this the result of global warming? Had it sunk into the peat as though through a sponge?

The mountain of Morven that had been hard and bright all afternoon,
its screes and growths now clearly defined, was gathering about it an
imponderable blue.

There was no mountain marked on my map, and no mountain
visible before me. I was puzzled by the discrepancies between the
novel, the Ordnance Survey map, and the place in which I found
myself. The mist continued to blow in ragged wisps and I
contemplated turning back. This hole in the ground was of
limited interest, especially after I had read of a hard bright mountain and a non-existent loch, its shores *of pure ground quartz, paler*
than any woman's face in any old poet's dream. I could try to pick up
the stream again, as did the character in the novel, but I was wary
of setting out over the moor now that a danger more real than
the inconvenience of getting lost in mist had occurred to me.
That is, the possibility of drowning in the bog. And it would
mean walking off the edge of my map. I wanted to cry with
frustration.

But I didn't. It was still early in the morning. I was ravenously
hungry. I made a meal of cheese, apples, raisins and chocolate, and
drank the water that I was happy to have brought with me. I
packed away the book and map and sat down on the peaty knoll.
It was a summer morning in August. I unscrewed the cap of my
hip flask and sipped the chilly, slightly metallic, Rioja.

Half an hour later the sun had chased off the mist. The wide
bowl of the watershed became visible for the first time. It was
filled with heather, and pocked with little pools. The land was still
rising, faintly, and there appeared to be a ridge along one edge of
the bowl. I stepped out of the crease that held the river and headed
for the ridge.

I was anxious as I made my way over the open ground, and kept looking behind me for the dip in the land that marked the head of the strath. Every so often I came across another pool, and circumvented it with anxiety. I couldn't find any deer-tracks and this, too, worried me. And then I stopped, because I could hear a sound I had heard before, a sound like an indrawn breath. Water. A sudden diversity of bright vegetation confirmed the path of the stream. It was flowing just beneath my feet, just beneath the ground, towards the place where I had come from. I followed the sound, bent low so I could hear. Soon I could see it: a trickle barely a hand-span in width. It was leading me towards the ridge. I glanced back to the neck of the valley, anxious lest the mist return. But the visibility held. At the edge of the plateau was a fringe of reeds, and I stepped up onto a bank of peat, before stumbling at the sight before me.

A loch!

The loch. Its surface, soft as pewter, mirrored the clouds. Salt-white boulders lined a powdery shore of crystal sand, unmarked and clean, its whiteness stained to the colour of cork by the peat. Nothing disturbed the water, not a ripple, not a fly. I was choked by its loveliness; my senses flooded. As I watched, the low clouds shifted, lifted, and there, beyond the farthest shore, was the slate-green flank of a mountain. So this was Morven! The sky behind the clouds was as pale as a thrush's egg and the surface of the loch took this new palette for its own. I could see the screes, the grassy slopes, the dark outlines of trees and rocks pencilled in by their elongated shadows. But the vision was momentary and a cloud passed over the mountain, cowling the peak, rearranging the features of the slopes, covering up the sun. My eye returned to the loch. Without the bright reflection I could see to the bottom. The powdered quartz continued beneath the water, a few looping tea-coloured tide-marks as it deepened, the occasional shard of bright white rock. Loch Braighe na h'Aibhne. I sat down on the bank overhanging the shore, my feet dangling above the water, not wanting to spoil its surface.

I don't know how much time passed, but suddenly I felt that I must go. I hadn't swum, or drunk the water, or even walked around the loch. I had presumed, when I first arrived, first knew that it was true, that I would swim to the centre, inhabit the water, make it my own, and yet even as my fingers began to tug at my clothes I knew that it was not going to happen. I straightened my clothing. The strongest sense had settled on me, concrete as the mist that covered the mountain, that, if I once disturbed the surface, or entered the water, I would upset a balance both chemical and physical. I didn't even want to contemplate how long it might take before the stillness of the loch could be recovered.

And yet the rain must do it all the time.

I picked up a handful of the quartz sand and poured it into my pocket, over the silky green hazelnuts that I still had from yesterday. I turned away from the loch and retraced the tiny stream, and this seemed straightforward now, despite its passing underground, and it led me back to the funnel of the valley and the muddy oval where the river re-emerged. It was surprisingly easy walking.

I was following in my footprints, and wondering how long they would remain there, when I was struck by the idea that something was passing, or had ended. I tried to push the feeling away from me, and for the most part I was successful, though I was unable to dismiss it entirely. I again passed the place where I had spent the night, but the dew had vanished and the heather regained its shape. There was nothing to suggest I had ever been there.

I disturbed the eagle, still in her place, and was again unnerved by the owl. The deer came and went as they had throughout my trip. There was no sign of the golden frog. A black seabird rose above me and followed me, crying. I supposed it to be an Arctic skua, we were far enough north, and it remained with me for half an hour, adhering to the path of the stream, and then it circled back across the moor, calling, calling, as though I were a fishing boat and we were at sea, and some good might come from following me. Or perhaps it was curiosity, a desire for companionship, the fascination of living things for one another.

I re-entered the part of the river where the traps were set, and paid careful attention to my footing. But my thoughts ran on independently, looping back now to the loch, and to my decision not to swim. Swimming was one of my passions, one of the ways by which I defined myself. Knew myself. I was also surprised that I had not drunk from it. The idea that had brought me here was the idea that there might just be a well at the end of the world, full of wisdom, and answers, and that I might go and look for it. A lot of the stories associated with the well were about forbidden love. The attempt to explain away, or to cover over, children born of what were often single encounters. Even the miraculous story of the birth of Taliesin – born to an enchantress who had swallowed him whole, while he was a grain of corn, and she was a hen – could be interpreted as a ripping yarn to explain away the need to name a father. Why else would his mother have thrown him into the sea? Then there was the paternity of St Finan Cam of Kinitty, he whose mother successfully maintained that she had been impregnated by a salmon – a big fish tale if ever there was one. St Kentigern's mother claimed her son was miraculously conceived, although his biographer Jocelyn of Furness would have none of it, stating firmly that *that which was born in her womb she received from a human embrace*, although he speculated that she may perhaps have *taken the drink of oblivion*, and therefore been genuinely unable to put together, or to believe, what had happened to her.

Isak Dinesen wrote: 'Love, with very young people, is a heartless business. We drink at that age from thirst, or to get drunk. It is only later in life that we occupy ourselves with the individuality of our wine.' Lovemaking is indeed a heartless business for anyone other than the lovers. It annihilates, blinds, burns, bruises, chokes, consumes, crushes, devours, destroys – and I have only reached D. Cupid pierces our hearts with an arrow, orgasm is a little death. Love is not about personal responsibility, or being considerate of other people's feelings. Love is impulsive, compulsive, addictive. Lovers are selfish, and can be infuriatingly self-righteous, so that more or less anything is felt to be excusable if it is done in the name of love. Consequences have never come into it.

> *A secret well there was* . . . .
> *from which gushed forth every kind of mysterious evil.*
> *There was none that could look to its bottom*
> *But his two bright eyes would burst:*
> *If he should move to left or right,*
> *He would not come from it without blemish.*
> *Therefore none of them dared approach it* . . .

The day unravelled slowly and I followed the thickening ribbon until it again became a brook. I passed the almost ornamental waterfall as it stepped past Poll Roy, and saw it fortified by the tributary at the boundary of the enclosed land, where it once again regained the character of a river. I recovered the Land-Rover track, and the road reasserted itself. I experienced a sense of homecoming as I stepped onto it.

At the farm I came across a rabbit: beheaded and gutted, and left out on the path. I wondered if it was the blind rabbit from yesterday, but could read nothing into the blackening mess, except that a ghillie had been there, and had left the carcass to fatten the hawks against the winter. Soon I was able to make out the cemetery, white as sugar on the green-gold moor. The spidery tombstones again appeared to move.

When I was below the cemetery a glint of light drew my eye. Looking at the place where it had been I caught a second flash, as though someone were signalling across the moors. I listened hard, but could hear nothing above the rustle of the wind, the anxious spill of skylarks. I had regained the place where birds sang. And then a bounced movement: a four-wheel drive was curling up the road; I could hear the constricted voice of an engine in low gear. There were two men inside, one dressed like a country gent, the other in a donkey jacket and woolly hat. They pulled up alongside me.

'Good afternoon!' said the country gent.

'Good afternoon,' I replied.

'Are you walking to Dunbeath?' he asked. When I nodded he told me that they were going to play the pipes for an old friend in the cemetery, and that if I'd like to accompany them they could run me back to the town when they were done.

'Thank you, that's really kind. But I've walked all the way from the sea to the loch. If you don't mind, I'd really like to finish the journey on foot. It's only a few more miles.'

'The loch?'

'Yes. Loch Braighe na h'Aibhne.' I had no idea how to pronounce the Gaelic.

'There's a loch?'

'Yes.' And I pointed to the moor. 'Up there.'

'Well, do you know, I have lived here all my life and I never knew there was a loch!' He turned to the other man, and I missed what he said, but I felt a perfect bubble of delight, because I knew that my journey had been special, and I thanked them again, and bid them goodbye, and continued on my path. When I got to the place where the track bent I glanced back towards the cemetery. I watched the two men search for the key and unlock the iron gate. The man in the donkey jacket raised his pipes; but the wind was against them and all I could hear were the summer bees and the river. In less than an hour I had reached my car, but I continued beyond it, beneath the stone bridge and the boomerang-shaped viaduct, past a dozen or so fishermen's cottages. As I approached the harbour I saw two lovers on a wooden bench, caught in the net of their own arms and legs, their noses almost touching. The tips of their fingers wandered, collecting information, each about the other, as much as their senses could withstand. And then behind them, high above the water, came a flick of silver, a comb of falling droplets, and the arching, turning body of a salmon. It must have entered the river mouth, even as I had reached it. *Did you see?* I wanted to cry to the lovers. *Did you see it?* But of course they didn't, their eyes were closed. But I saw, and my heart filled at this coincidental, timely fish.

It was evening when I got back to the hotel. I had walked thirty miles in the last two days. Then driven two hours back. Although

I had felt almost fluid in Dunbeath, my summer body loose as willow, I ached as I walked from the car park to the lobby, my limbs stiffening in the evening chill. One toe throbbed. I suspected I would lose the nail. The young barman Callum entered the lobby, and without saying a word picked up my holdall and headed up the stairs. At the landing he turned towards the grand rooms at the front of the house and I paused, confused, for I was very much aware of our last interchange. My room had been at the top of the hotel. Realising that I was no longer following him, he also stopped, and turned to me:

'They said you'd gone to follow a river to its source. We said *well, if that's the case, then that lassie's going to be wanting a hot bath . . .'*

I suddenly felt like a warrior queen, from long ago, coming home triumphant from a battle. Callum opened the door to what was probably the best room in the house, and put down my bag; he then nodded towards an open door. There had been no bathroom in the old room, just the communal bath beneath the eaves; but I could already see the lip of a roll-top bath and a pile of fluffy white towels.

'Would you like me to set your table in the bar?'

'Thank you,' I said. 'That would be grand.'

Madryn

wo days later, Evie and I returned to our home on the Llŷn. The Welsh and English schools had, for the most part, begun the autumn term, although there were still a couple of weeks before the Spanish schools went back. We decided to pick up the last part of Afon Geirch, the river that ended at Cable Bay, but which we had failed to follow beyond the golf course at the start of the holiday. We left the cottage on foot, and then set off up a bridle path that spiralled around Garn Fadryn. It took us across the lower reaches of the mountain until we climbed over a stone wall beneath the summit cone. The river, which was now a shallow stream, passed beneath the wall in a specially built granite conduit. A bridge of railway sleepers carried sheep and walkers across the waterway. Watercress and sorrel filled the streambed. Evie called the sleepers Picnic Bridge, and we stopped to eat the eponymous picnic that we had, of course, brought with us. Our legs dangled above the water, which gurgled with a domestic, familiar sound, like bath water passing down a drain.

'Do you know something?' said Evie. 'This is my favourite place in the world.' And we sat there, smiling, eating our sandwiches.

A drone of farm machinery floated up from the plain, then stopped. Beyond the plain was the sea, and it was the same soft blue as the sky, the transition marked by a whitish haze. For a brief moment there was silence, broken only by the occasional *mah* of sheep, until a staccato song of squabbling chaffinches drifted on a sudden breeze: two leaning trees were alive with their chatter, I could just make out their little forms. We put away our picnic and followed the stream up the hill. Evie was adept at picking through thistles and reeds and sphagnum moss, and she soon unearthed the source. Rushes like stiff ribbons festooned the ground, and a bent tree partially obscured the spring. A white boulder marked the place where the water began, two other stones were arranged to either side. It felt unlikely that this rock formation was natural. Evie began to clear the area around the biggest stone, heaping handfuls of moss and leaves, beech nuts and pine needles to one side, until she revealed the well, its water cloudy as she churned the bottom, searching out further debris. She looked up at me while she worked:

'We need to bring gardening things and tidy it up properly,' she said. 'What shall we call it?'

I told her about St Madron's Well in Cornwall. It was a rag well, and people left bits of cloth — often ribbons cut for the purpose, but sometimes the torn hem of a shirt or a hastily removed sock — in the hope that their wishes would be granted, their prayers answered. Our mountain was called Garn Fadryn, known locally as Madryn, after the Welsh mother goddess Modron, and we decided, for the sake of harmony, on St Madryn's Well in English, and Ffynnon Madryn in Welsh. Evie asked me for a piece of paper, and a pen, and I gave her a page of my notebook. She then sat down and wrote for a few moments before spearing the torn-out page onto a branch of the bent tree, as though it were a bill awaiting payment.

I wondered what she had written, and watched for a few moments the square of paper. It shivered like a Buddhist prayer flag at a shrine. She saw me looking, and shot me a glance, and her soft grey eyes conveyed a warning. I stepped back. Evie's business was between her and the well, which was already beginning to clarify.

When we got back to the cottage it was evening. After supper and a bath, Evie went to bed. There was a missed call on my mobile, so I went and sat on the swing in the garden to retrieve the message. It was Rupert. He had heard about a hotel along the Costa Brava, it occupied a curving bay, close by the Catalan/ French border. It had been built to house some archaeologists during the 1930s when they had unearthed a Graeco-Roman city. He thought that if Evie and I were to come back early, and he were to take a few days off work, then perhaps we could go there, the three of us, and spend some time together before school began.

The last time the three of us had been together in a hotel was when we were married, Evie and I unwinding curlers from our hair in the dawn light, her face absolutely serious as she arranged the snowy folds of my dress, and used her licked finger to clean a line of fine dust from the toe of my white cowboy boot. I recalled the furrow of intent between her eyebrows as she wound uneven pearls around my neck and I fastened Navajo silver beads – her gift from Rupert – round hers. Then she ran out in her raw silk skirts and scarlet ballet pumps to Rupert – with our gift to him of an antique turquoise bolo in her hand – calling: *You mustn't look at*

Mummy till we get there. The soles of her feet had been barely insulated against the blistering asphalt footpath. Her excitement at the stretch limousine. Her puzzlement at the empty church. Her delight at our wedding breakfast of sushi. Later, the three of us — lazy as lions — had lain beside the pool, while champagne warmed to the temperature of blood and a golden box of handmade chocolates ran to liquid.

It was the hottest day on record in Las Vegas.

Stars appeared around the summit of Garn Fadryn. A triangle of darkness marked the peak. I dialled the number, waited for the connection, and then listened for the steady pulse of the ring.

PART II

Is it possible to pierce . . . the dark cloud, even for a few moments, and come on the light, the bubbling well at the end of the fairy tale? Do folk still do it, ordinary people?

Neil M. Gunn

All that I have is a river.

Johnny Flynn

Swimming Pool (2)

I was with my friend Eleonora at a café in Barcelona. We were about to collect the children from school.

'There is a big wave coming,' I said, 'and we have to leave before it gets here.'

'A wave? What sort of wave?' she asked.

'A tsunami.'

We collected the children and began our walk to the bus stop. Evie and Matteo, Eleonora's son, climbed onto the fence that surrounded Sofia's garden. Or the garden that had been Sofia's before the summer. Sunlight had split the fence, and I could see through the cracks to the empty pool. The bougainvillea was struggling without water. Dried stalks spilled out of ceramic pots like leftover take-away noodles. The grass was covered in pine cones. Neither of us had heard from Sofia since she'd left Barcelona, though I'd emailed a couple of times.

'It's to do with the banks,' I said, returning to where we'd left off. 'We have to leave while we still can.'

'But you've already left your pretty house!' Her face looked so lovely with her raised eyebrows that I found I was smiling. We had shifted from our eighteenth-century terracotta-roofed house, built around a tiled courtyard, into a tiny flat in a 1970s apartment block, and we lived surrounded by packing boxes.

'It's not enough. I need to go back to London. I need to get a proper job.' A bus came round the corner, and I stuck out my arm, because I couldn't think of anything else to say.

Rupert's livelihood had been shattered by the first hard shock. His American publishers, for the first time in his career, had turned down a book. When the news came we had lain awake all night, holding hands, staring at the ceiling. At about four in the morning Evie appeared in her pyjamas on the terrace that linked our two bedrooms. She tapped on the glass door: 'I can't sleep.' The sky above her head was dense with stars.

Looking overhead he saw that the stars had come out, but why should he seem to see Andromeda, Cepheus, and Cassiopeia? What had become of the constellations of midsummer?

The lines were from a John Cheever story. It was funny what came to mind. I could clearly see Orion's belt. 'Neither can we,' I said, as I opened the glass door for her, and we all three went downstairs and sat around the kitchen table, staring at a pot of tea, and making shrapnel-like toast from the remains of yesterday's baguette.

Rupert had been a writer for almost thirty years. In the UK, the book would win a literary prize. But the prize was a piece of engraved glass. We could no longer afford to pay Evie's school fees, or the mortgage on our home. Every so often I recalled the presentiment I had had as I turned away from the loch at the foot of Morven. The idea that something precious was passing. Had passed. I recalled the headless rabbit on the footpath above Dunbeath. Its rubbery entrails. Presaging what? When Christmas came the three of us went to stay with Mum. Evie and I stayed longer than Rupert who needed to return to his work. In the days following his departure it began to snow. When it was our turn to fly home a taxi took us to the airport in a dawn the colour of unwashed sheets. A man in a luminous yellow jacket waved us away. The airport was closed. The driver turned the slipping car across the hard ridges that marked the edges of other tyre-tracks. I watched his eyes in the rear-view mirror and I felt a fluttering unease.

'I've never driven in anything like this before,' he said, trying to make light of it. He was too young to remember the last serious snowfall.

'Really?' I asked. 'Try not to use the brakes.' His eyes flared in the mirror. Wet flakes clogged up the windshield. He changed down through the gears and we fish-tailed slowly back to Mum's house.

Later that day Evie went sledging with her friend Alice in a sloping field behind their house. I went too, and watched the girls as they shrieked and giggled, bouncing on Alice's scarlet toboggan over snow-filled rabbit holes. Children and grown-ups stood about, laughing, clapping snow from woolly fingers and sharing coffee from a flask. My friend Lucy, who was Alice's mum, offered me a tea tray and I too juddered over the beleaguered rabbit warren and came to rest by a frozen stream at the far edge of the field. But I felt cold, tired and stiff, and I couldn't enter into the spirit of this unexpected extension to our holiday. It wasn't like the surface patina of winter, but an internal ache, that felt colder than the space between the stars. It was as though a plug had been pulled out of my breastbone, just to the right of centre, and my vitality, my life, was passing through it.

In the weeks that followed we began to fold away our Barcelona life. We looked for a new home in London, one we could afford, and a new school, a state school, for Evie. With the help of my brother John, and Evie's godfather Calvin, who paid her school fees, we would be able to stay in Spain until the start of the summer holiday. When the summer term ended we would move to London.

One morning, in late spring, I found myself staring into the bathroom mirror. Despite the sunlight bouncing off the tiles my face looked lined and puffy. A thought presented itself, singular and loud. *You look as though you are dying.* On a Sunday morning at the end of May I noticed a sensation of tightness near my sternum. I massaged the skin. There wasn't anything specific. I worked my fingers into the space between my ribs. There was something, a sort of stiffness, as though chewing gum had been stuck along-side my breastbone. I thought it must be a knot in the muscle. But a week later it still hadn't gone. I made an appointment to see a doctor. She said she thought that it was probably a cyst, but advised me to have a mammogram. She felt fairly certain there was noth-ing urgent. Sometime in the next three months would be fine. I resolved to see a doctor when we arrived in London.

Innominate Stream

School finished. We stayed for the fireworks for the Feast of St John, and then Evie and I flew back to Mum's house, as we had done every summer for the past six years. The three of us meant to spend a week at the cottage, and then I would fly back to help Rupert. Evie would stay with her cousins. The night before we were due to leave for Wales Mum stood outside her house. She was looking at my rental car in the driveway, walking around it, peering through the windows. For some reason she had been adamant that I should hire a car, although God knows I had little enough money, and now, after tapping the roof, she said:

'I think we'll go in my car tomorrow.' I stared at her, unable to fathom her reasoning.

'Well, what do you think we should do with this?' I said.

'We can leave it on the drive until we get back.'

The whole debate about the rental car had seemed bizarre to me, and in order to avoid an argument I went to my room, and started shuffling a deck of cards that Evie had brought with her. Mum was behaving extraordinarily oddly. One card flipped free and slid to the floor. The three of spades. I picked up the card and shuffled again, and then turned over the top card in the pack. The three of spades.

In Tarot, the suit that corresponds to spades is the called the suit of swords. The three shows a scarlet heart with three swords piercing it and rain clouds opening behind it. Black streaks of rain. I shuffled again. The three of spades. I tapped its surface, couldn't resist speculating over its meaning. The first spade, it seemed to me, was the immediate, financial trouble in which we found ourselves. But the second and third pips worried me. I pushed the card back into the centre of the pack, and went to bed, irritated by my superstition.

'Kate? Kate?' It was Mum's voice. I reeled into consciousness, was suddenly wide awake. I listened but could hear nothing more. I disentangled myself from the bed, and ran along the landing to Mum's bedroom, which was empty, the covers thrown back. There was a smell that I could almost touch. Fear.

'Kate?' I looked over the stairwell and there was my little bird, my mother, reaching up the stairs, her eyes spoke where she could not, and I rushed down to her, and helped her to the sofa, her lungs bubbling with liquid. I telephoned 999 and then ran back up the stairs:

'Evie, Grannie is very, very sick and I have called an ambulance, you must get dressed and come down right away.'

Mum waved to us from behind the oxygen mask as she was lifted in a wheelchair into the ambulance. I dropped Evie at my brother's house, and continued to the hospital.

When I got there, Mum was in a bay in Accident and Emergency with two nurses trying to clip heart monitors onto her fingertips. She reached forward, her fingers stretched before her, as though she were trying to find something to hold onto, and pull herself clear of the bed. I touched her hand, but she pushed it away. It was something else that she needed, something more. A doctor appeared at her bedside, and said:

'Prepare for defibrillation.' I was swept aside as a cardiac team gathered around my mother. I saw her fall back on the bed, and her head roll to one side, her hair untidy as a rook's nest. There was a bang, and an electronic whine.

A nurse moved me into a peach-coloured room, with *Bereavement Suite* written on the door.

'It doesn't mean that your mother is dead,' she said, 'but that this is the best place to be while this goes on. There are a lot of people round her.' I heard again the butcher's cleaver bang of the defibrillator behind the door. I telephoned my brother.

When John arrived, trailing Evie and his own family, and we had gathered in the peach-coloured room, the doctor came in to talk to us.

'We have tried to resuscitate your mother three times with the defibrillator, and she has had an adrenalin shot to her heart, but she is unresponsive. Would you like us to continue to try to resuscitate her?' The air in the room seemed to be made of plastic.

'Will she have suffered brain damage?' I asked.

'She has been without oxygen for six minutes, so yes, there will be damage, but what it is I cannot say.'

I looked at John. Mum had never wanted to be revived. She had always been very clear about it. There was a moment where nobody seemed to move, and then one of us must have said something because the door was closing and the doctor had gone. A nurse came in and said that they were preparing Mum's body, taking it to somewhere we could look at it, at her, and would we please wait a few minutes more. I phoned Rupert, and told him that Mum had died. The words sounded very strange to me.

And then the doctor came back. 'This is really very unusual,' he said, his hands raised as though in blessing, 'but your mother's heart has begun to beat of its own accord although she is unable to breathe. We have put her on life support and are moving her to our critical care unit. If there is no improvement in twenty-four hours we will turn off the support. In the meantime we'll try and find out what has caused this.'

Critical care.

I woke in darkness at my brother's house. I was in the spare bed in my nephew Connor's room. He was awake. 'Connor, I'm going to go over to the hospital. Do you want to come?'

'It's OK. I'll stay here and look after Evie. I'll tell the others where you've gone.'

I drove to the hospital and parked Mum's car in the almost empty car park. Trees huffed and nodded. Blue streaks lightened the inky sky. A copy of *Jane Eyre* was tucked beneath my elbow. I made my way through the quiet corridors, their vinyl floors and fluttering fluorescents, and rang the buzzer outside the critical care unit. A nurse admitted me and then rejoined her colleagues sitting peaceably at their station. Mum and two other patients rested, each with their private, internal struggle, each mechanically suspended in a space held open between life and non-life, an opportunity, a place of choosing. Mum was all wired up, with a tube taped to her nose.

There were a lot of pipes. The rhythmic sound of her mechanically controlled breathing was like waves on an artificial beach.

I pulled up a chair and leaned close to Mum's face. Ordinarily she was deaf, and the life support had a range of noises all of its own. I had to lift my voice even to hear myself above it. I read the part where Jane Eyre frightens Mr Rochester's horse and he accuses her of being a fairy. Mum gave no indication of knowing that I was there, but the nurses were very appreciative. After a while, the man in the next bed, who had been in a coma, woke up. There was a choking and whirring as his lungs began to inflate of their own accord, causing a flutter of activity as he fought against the machinery, which suddenly threatened to smother him. Shortly afterwards his wife arrived. He seemed to be trying to say something. His wife translated for him, through his pipes and tubes:

'He wants to know what you were reading,' she said.

'It was *Jane Eyre*.' She looked nonplussed. 'By Charlotte Brontë.'

'He very much enjoyed the story,' she said. Her husband wheezed and rasped. He looked from me to my mum. 'And he wants to know if you're going to come and read again tonight.'

Tonight.

Mum's condition was to be reviewed at four o'clock that afternoon, and if there was no improvement, they would disconnect the breathing apparatus.

'If I'm here, yes, certainly,' I replied.

At some point during the morning Mum's doctor told us that her heartbeat had stabilised, although she was unable to breathe without the machine. He thought she had suffered a thrombosis to her heart, and was almost certain that she would not recover. She had been without oxygen for six minutes before her heart began to beat. It had been damaged by what had happened. He put her chances of recovery at about a million to one. But the medical team agreed that they would postpone turning off the machine until the following afternoon. So Mum was to be given another day. Others came to visit. Evie stayed with the cousins. I went back to Mum's house and collected some personal things. Pyjamas. A photograph of Dad, held in a silver frame. It had been taken on holiday, in France. Feet apart, arms folded. His happy smile as he squinted through bright sunlight at the camera, and at the woman who was taking the picture. He must have been about fifty. I cleaned the glass. It had been Mum's habit to kiss the photograph each night before she went to bed.

When I got back to the hospital and the wide, artificially lit space of the critical care unit, and saw the nurses sitting at their station, it was as though I were looking at it for the first time. I seemed to recognise nothing. Possibly because until this moment I had been focused on Mum, her tiny form, the tubes. Looking at it now, in the middle of the day, it felt more like NASA than a hospital. The intubated patients weren't in space, but they were suspended, several yards apart from one another, each with a bank of equipment and wires maintaining their life on earth. The gasp and bubble of mechanical breath. It took me a while to notice that the man in the next bed, the man who had woken up, and had enjoyed *Jane Eyre*, had gone, and so too had his bed. Only the husk of machinery remained, cracked open like an empty chrysalis. A nurse told me that Mum's condition was stable, but that she was making no effort to breathe.

'She has spent the last nine years waiting to join that man,' I said, and pointed to the photograph of Dad. I had arranged it where Mum would see it if she were to wake. 'You're going to have to try very hard if you want to get her back.' My brother and his wife and I took it in turns sitting with Mum. In the afternoon, the children came too. Evie was fascinated with the tubes. Rupert called from Barcelona. We were already discussing the funeral.

That night, when Evie was in bed, I again returned, alone, to the hospital. I had brought *Jane Eyre* with me, although the empty space where the man had been, and Mum's continued unresponsiveness, made the effort seem pointless. The nurse I had spoken to earlier was sitting in the chair next to the bed. She held Mum's hand.

'Come on, Jean!' she was saying. 'You can do better than that!' When she noticed me standing there we chatted for a moment or two, and the nurse gestured to the photograph of Dad.

'How did they meet?' she asked. I found myself telling her how Mum's best friend had been Dad's sister, and that they had all gone to school together. Dad had decided that he wanted to marry Mum when he saw her playing tennis at the village recreation ground. She must have been about sixteen.

'She was just so *alive!*' he would say.

'What did your dad do?' the nurse asked.

'He was a teacher. At the university. A professor of Mechanical Engineering,' I said.

'You must be very proud of him.'

'Yes,' I said, 'I am.' I had the feeling that the nurse's questions might be in some way therapeutic, though whether intentionally, or accidentally, I couldn't tell. I was very much aware that Mum might hear our voices. So I found myself telling the nurse how when Dad was a boy he had won a scholarship to the local grammar school. I was conscious that I should try to get the story right.

Or more specifically, that the reason I was telling the story at all was in the hope that Mum might recognise it.

Dad had won a scholarship, sponsored by the tannery where his father worked. His grandfather – William – also worked at the tannery. William was a man with forearms like roasted hams, who had been converted to Methodism by John Wesley himself when he crossed the country on horseback.

I looked at the nurse. Then back at Mum. Her face was pale. The breathing apparatus bubbled as her breath condensed in the pipes.

'No, I'm very sorry,' I said. 'That can't possibly be right.' John Wesley died in 1791. Great-Grandfather William must have been born around 1870. I had obviously crossed my wires. I had another go.

From the day of his conversion William Norbury never touched alcohol, and he even turned the other cheek when a fellow-worker struck him. Although, when his assailant hit that cheek also, William had decked him with a single punch to the jaw, saying: 'The Lord said "tha' must turn the other cheek", but he never said owt about what to do if tha's hit on that one.' William had become a lay preacher. He travelled around the county with a suitcase full of sermons, written in a minute, cursive script, and carried by a young man who had incurred some sort of brain damage, but was devoted to William, and would not leave his side. William married and had five children. His first son, Wesley, named after William's hero, had died of meningitis in childhood. The two younger boys had gone into the tannery, where they heaved the stinking hides of cattle into deep salt pits, their sleeves rolled up, rubber boots protecting their legs, their cotton shirts and twill trousers protected by black stuff aprons. This had gone on, day in, day out, until the coming of war in 1914 interrupted a grinding pattern. William remained at the tannery, but my grandfather, Russell, who was the same age as the century, was called up for the fighting. When he came back home again, injured, from France, he was still a teenager. Although his physical injuries healed quite quickly, the war left its mark in other ways. Russell spent four years looking at his face in a mirror, convinced that one side was bigger than the other, and that shrapnel was still embedded in his jaw. Because he was unable to work in the tannery proper, the owner, Mr Posnett, gave Russell a job in the Time Office, where he stamped cards for the workers as they began and ended their shifts. Mr Posnett was often heard to say: 'I saved Russell Norbury's life after the war.' I wasn't sure whether a mind-numbingly dull job in the Time Office constituted saving Granddad's life, or not, but it had certainly provided him with an income. He was plagued by anxiety, although he was always a gentle man, with a fine tenor voice, and was good-humoured about everything except his neuroses.

During the years in which Granddad was unwell, my grand-mother, Doris, worked as a bookie's clerk. She told us of the diminutive jockeys and their bright silks, as the men were weighed in the scales. Throughout the years when Granddad was staring in the mirror, Doris was the only breadwinner.

I stopped again. This, too, seemed far-fetched. What would a Methodist be doing working at a racetrack, and a woman with children at that? And how would she have got there? The nearest racetracks were at Aintree, in Liverpool, and Haydock Park near

Manchester. Without access to transport, they may as well have been on the moon. Maybe Doris had simply worked for a book-keeper, or a local accountant. Perhaps it was I who had made the leap from bookkeeper to bookie, and embellished it with half-remembered scenes from *National Velvet*, in which a young Liz Taylor won the Grand National, or very nearly did, on a farm horse. My time frame for all these events was, in any case, extremely woolly. The fragments of story pulsed and glowed like lumps of molten ore in mud, scattered over an indeterminate period that was punctuated by hardship and war. The stories were familiar to me. But I had never before laid claim to them, or attempted to share them.

Still, somewhere in the hardship years – that came between the war years – Dad won the Highfield Tannery Scholarship. He had gained, briefly, the highest mark in his year at the village school, but a Methodist had never won the School Prize before, and so the examination papers had to be remarked. This meant Dad now had the second highest mark after a girl called Sheila McKnight, who beat him by one per cent. The school wasn't known for its gender equality, but it was clearly better that the prize went to a girl who was an Anglican, than to a boy from Chapel. This, at any rate, was the view expressed by the Methodists and I was aware that it, too, had a ring of legend about it. But Dad quite definitely won the scholarship. Mr Posnett offered, in addition to the bursary, to buy Dad's uniform and books, his protractor and compass, ruler and pens, his Latin grammar, his dictionary. But the tannery work-ers declined the offer and instead they had a whip-round. Fred was one of their own. He had all that he needed for the grammar school. Later he obtained a government bursary to study at the university in Liverpool. The tannery continued to support him.

Mr Posnett made it clear that Dad should ask for whatever he needed. Once again, the villagers made sure he was properly kitted out. There were no summer holidays, on account of the war, and after two years he completed his bachelor's degree in Mechanical Engineering. By the time he had graduated, with first-class honours, peace had broken out, erratic and wild, and Dad was never called upon to fight. When he completed his master's, and Mum was twenty-two, he asked her to marry him at the top of Tryfan, a mountain in Snowdonia. Afterwards they jumped between two monoliths called Adam and Eve, almost ten feet above the ground. This was known as the Tryfan step, and conferred the Freedom of the Mountain on all who successfully completed it.

'My goodness, she must have been fit!' said the nurse. I'd forgotten that she was there.

'She was,' I said. 'She once ran a hundred yards in 11.4 seconds. A research chemist, who had been a Cambridge Blue, saw her race at the ICI recreation ground, and wanted to train her, there'd even been talk of the Olympics. But they weren't able to pursue it, on account of the war.'

Mum didn't stir, and when morning came I took Evie to Liverpool to buy her a dress for the funeral. They would switch off Mum's machine at four o'clock. I could wear the same black Nicole Farhi suit that I'd worn at Dad's funeral. After all, I'd never worn it since. But when we got back to the car there was a message on my phone. Mum had opened her eyes. She looked at her nephew, Peter, who had come to hold her hand. Evie took the bag with her new dress in it and squashed it into the glove compartment. We arrived at the hospital at three o'clock, to find Mum sitting up in bed, a cup of tea in front of her, a slice of buttered toast in her hand.

'I really don't feel very well,' she said.

Mum remained in hospital for weeks. While her astonishing and unlikely recuperation unfolded, I moved between her home, the Welsh cottage, our new home in London, and Barcelona. By the end of the summer we had left Catalunya. Evie began the autumn term at a primary school in Battersea, and I finally took the opportunity to have the mammogram that I had postponed at the start of the summer. I hadn't yet had time to register with a doctor in London, so I went to the same hospital in Chester where Mum was still a patient.

The radiographer said: 'That doesn't look like a cyst.'

It was white, the lump, which meant it was a solid mass, and it had tiny arms that shot out like spider's silks, or pincers. It was uneven, and knobbly. Like a crab.

'Does it look like cancer?' I asked. The radiographer paused.

'Yes.'

'Can you think of anything else, in your experience, that isn't a cyst, and isn't cancer, that this might be?'

This time she didn't hesitate. 'No.'

'I have a ten-year-old daughter,' I said. 'I have to live.' The radiographer took a biopsy. The device sounded like the dead-bolt that vets use to kill a horse. I gasped as it nipped the muscle of my chest wall. The area began to swell. Afterwards I sat and waited with some other ladies, all of us dressed in lilac surgical gowns, outside a nurse's room, our day clothes in plastic crates. I couldn't raise Rupert on the phone. I called my sister-in-law, Maria, who happened to be near by, and she came to sit with me.

'I didn't want to come here.' It was a blonde woman speaking, her roots showing wiry and grey. 'I come here from Caernarfon. They said I should do it on account of my mum. She's died of it.' The rest of us were silent. 'I wouldn't have come if they hadn't told me to. I don't want to be here.' A woman sitting next to me leaned forward. She asked the lady from Caernarfon about her journey, asked if it had been difficult to get to Chester, asked her how long it had taken. A nurse brought me tea in a china cup and saucer, and some custard creams on a doily-covered tray. I noticed that some of the other ladies also had trays. The obvious luxury in an NHS hospital made me feel both special and apprehensive. A nurse told me that the result of the biopsy wouldn't be available until after the weekend, but that eighty per cent of women with breast cancer survived it. Rupert and Evie expected me home in London, but the hospital advised me to wait.

I went back to Mum's empty house, but I was skittish, and couldn't keep still. More than one friend said *I'm sure it will be fine* and this seemed strange to me, because what I'd seen on the ultrasound hadn't looked fine. I recalled the way the radiographer had glanced at the nurse, the way the architecture of the room had appeared to tighten.

I packed an overnight bag and took Mum's car. I drove towards the mountains of Cumbria, two hours north of Chester. When I reached the Lake District I drifted west, towards the Wasdale Valley, and parked the car at the head of the deep lake called Wastwater, beneath the buttressed, stubborn flank of Great Gable and the Scafell Massif. I didn't need a map for this place. I knew it better than anywhere on earth. I had first climbed Scafell with Dad, when I was Evie's age, wearing shorts and thin-soled plimsolls, through which I had felt every stone, Dad's big hand wrapped around my little one.

When Dad had been a doctoral candidate his supervisor, Geoff Calvert, built a cottage in the Lake District out of anything that came to hand. The stones were random rubble. The Crittall windows, which were almost as big as the walls, had been salvaged from a hospital in Liverpool. Geoff told his graduate students that anyone who helped with the construction could have a week's holiday, gratis, for life. And so, every summer, we spent a week at the cottage. There were gas lamps in the early days, run off Calor gas canisters. Later, electricity was provided from a car battery. The water passed through a charcoal filter directly off the mountain behind. And there was a bath beneath the kitchen draining board. We went on expeditions in the day, to the mountains, and the lakes, and laughed and played cards at night.

So I had climbed Scafell, on one of those feted summer days, my hand in Dad's for much of the way, though he had carried me back down on his shoulders, not because I was tired, but because I could feel the stones through my worn-out plimsolls, although my brother had teased me mercilessly for being a baby. Afterwards Mum insisted that we drove to Kendal, so I could have some proper walking shoes. I know that the memory was of Scafell because of a great wall of rock that loomed over us, forbidding as a Cunard liner. The rock-wall led to a passage, and the passage was called Lord's Rake. It rose like a ladder, up and down in a diagonal zigzag, and emerged at the summit of the hill. The combination of the wall, which acted as a landmark, and the narrowness of the passage made Lord's Rake a safe route, even in mist, because you could feel your way, and know exactly where you were, even if you couldn't see. A roughly carved cross at the start of the rake marked the place where, on a warm September afternoon in 1903, four young men, all experienced climbers, 'skilful, careful and modest', had inexplicably fallen to their deaths. But Lord's Rake led beyond the cross, obliquely rising through dips and cols, some as narrow as a horse's saddle, and it carried the traveller across, not over, the buttress.

I had returned to the place many times. When I was twenty-three I ran away from a love affair in New York, and had driven from Heathrow Airport in a rented car wearing a Jean Paul Gaultier suit and ice-pick Jimmy Choo heels. When I arrived at Scafell I rummaged in my travel bag, and then stripped in the National Trust car park, climbing the hill in Converse All Stars, my ex-lover's Levi 501s and a man's black cashmere sweater. I had nestled inside Lord's Rake, and had felt safe, held, the cleft of rock filled with gritty snow, my cheek against the stone, the mist beading in my eyebrows and lashes, and settling in my bleached cropped hair.

This time, as I visited the mountain, I was hopeful, despite what I had seen on the ultrasound. I felt strong, although I also felt sick, and though my thoughts were as skittish as a bird's on a twig peeping down at a lash-tailed cat, my heart sang. Wastwater glowed, a chasm of reflected light. There was a bathtub filled with water for the sheep. The September day was bright although the lower slopes of Scafell were veiled in shadow: the arc of the autumn sun remained low. I followed the footpath over a ridge known as Brown Tongue, walking between two nameless streams, keeping to the bank of the southern one, searching for a place to cross. But the stream was in spate, and at the ford it was not possible. I could see the stepping stones, sunk, conserved, beneath a dark slab of bubbling water. The water looked like glass. I decided to keep to the southern stream, and to follow its northern bank. As I walked higher over the humped side of the mountain I entered the natural amphitheatre that characterised Scafell. I could see Mickledore and Scafell Pike, which is the highest peak in England. Tucked away, to one side, was the summit of Scafell itself. I walked for an hour through bilberry and scattered rocks. In early summer Hollow Stones, for that is what this place is called, is a picture-book tapestry meadow, something from the loom of the Lady of Shalott, where only the unicorns are missing. But today it wore a different coat, the green grass caramelised into brown, a wheezy breath as the wind passed over it, some dried-out blackened seed heads. A dog had slipped its owner's leash and trotted excitedly about, rounding up sheep, its sharp bark and their worried bleats hanging in the air about me, revolving like the shapes on a child's cot mobile. I wondered if the owner was close at hand, or if any of the sheep were pregnant. The farmer might shoot the dog if he saw it. All these 'ifs'. White haze made a ceiling for the sound and my anxiety. And then, quite suddenly, I had reached the spring that was the source of this innominate stream. The water spilled from beneath a rock as big as a car.

The rock is marked on A. Wainwright's iconic guidebook drawing of Scafell, and labelled simply: *Big Boulder*. Beneath it is an 'X' and the word *Spring*. On the other side of the stream, the side of the way-marked footpath, the National Trust were building a staircase of rock in the interest of conserving vegetation and preventing soil erosion. The close proximity of this staircase to the boulder reminded me of the A303, which so narrowly misses the monument at Stonehenge, and where the proximity of heavy traffic to the ancient site mystifies spiritual tourists. The spring was choked with litter. This, too, seemed new. Paper wrappers and plastic crisp packets twirled and snagged in a pool the size of a washing-up bowl. Beyond it was the scree slope that led to the rake, and to the cruise-ship wall of rock.

I searched for a place to drink. There was a channel, litter-free, right underneath the boulder. Reaching in I pulled out handfuls of water, metallic, peaty, cold. I drank because I was thirsty, but also because I wanted something. I wanted the water to wash clean the results that I would receive on Monday. I found two acorns and two hazelnuts in my pocket, souvenirs of other walks, and I dropped them into the water. They were the nearest that I had to pennies. I straightened up, stiffly. An old gentleman with two long sticks appeared. He drew level and then walked past me. He picked his way meticulously and energetically, wiping the sweat from his chin, and pushing his false teeth out when he stopped to catch his breath. After about fifty yards he stared at his map, and then at the wall of rock.

'It's there,' I called. 'Just follow the scree.' He nodded back at me, and after a few more minutes' scrambling, a tall stick in each of his hands, his map on a cord around his neck, he vanished. I followed, then, persevering, until I too had entered the rake. I spread my palms over the cross that was carved in the rock, the memorial to the four dead climbers. The old gentleman had gone. The passage was filled with broken stones. Lemon-coloured saxifrage illuminated the monochromes. Splintered rocks leaned inwards, uncertain as old chimney stacks.

> *Where trouble melts like lemon drops,*
> *High above the chimney tops . . .*

There was a whirring sound: *whop-whop, whop-whop, whop-whop* and a black bird flapped by at nose level. I could see the lie of the feathers on its back. A crow. There was a staggered note to the downbeat, which was bouncing off the ceiling of cloud. The cloud looked close enough to touch. I couldn't go on. I sat down for a moment, and then stood up. I told myself that it was the stress of Mum's illness, and of moving house, and the biopsy that had exhausted me, unwilling to accept the possibility of cancer, or rather, that I might be affected by it in this manner, prevented from completing what I had come to do, and I turned, away from Lord's Rake, away from the summit, and went back down the hill by the same route that I had climbed it.

Thames

had never really got to know the Thames. Even though I had lived in London, on and off, for over twenty years, before moving to Barcelona, I had spent most of that time in Earls Court, and I hardly ever saw the river. But now we lived in Lavender Hill, and I crossed the Thames most days.

We were sitting on the front upstairs seat of a Number 49 bus: Evie, Rupert and I, on our way to an Open Day at one of the secondary schools Evie had chosen. She had only just begun to attend a local primary school, an oasis among the social housing and tangled railway tracks of Battersea. Sacred Heart Primary had chickens in the garden, allotments growing rosemary and chives, chard, sunflowers, sweet peas, sedum and green beans. But she had been there less than a fortnight before we'd had to start thinking about where she might go next. The bus was crossing Battersea Bridge.

'Evie,' I said, 'look at the houseboats!' and I pointed to the pastel-painted boats moored alongside Cheyne Walk. There must have been forty of them, hugging the wall of the Embankment.

Late roses in full bloom nodded around the doorway of the nearest one. The river, at this point, was as wide as a lake.

'Mummy, why do you keep going to visit Grannie, and why is your breast covered in bruises?' I reeled my attention back to Evie. I could feel that Rupert was looking at me, but I didn't meet his gaze. I looked at Evie.

'Because I have breast cancer.'

Her eyes opened wide, her face turned the colour of cream. 'Are you going to die?' she asked.

'Well, yes, eventually, we all are. But I don't know when, and I wouldn't know when if I didn't have cancer. None of us do.' I could see it wasn't the answer she was looking for.

'But are you going to die of this?' Rupert reached for Evie's hand and wrapped it up in his. He looked down at the crown of her hair.

'I don't know, my darling.' The bus had crossed the river and was continuing up Beaufort Street in Chelsea. I glanced back at the coloured houseboats as they slid from view. 'Eighty per cent of women with breast cancer live and I very much hope to be one of them. I've been going to Grannie's because we don't have a doctor in London yet, and I have to have a lot of tests. I'll have to have an operation. It'll be quicker if I have it done in Chester.' Evie seemed satisfied with this, with the idea that something was being done, and turned her attention back to the visit.

The school was like a well-ordered version of St Trinian's. Girls wearing goggles shot home made aeroplanes out of latticed windows above a statue of the Sacred Heart of Jesus. Evie ran about the frescoed cloister, marvelling at the scarlet ceiling with its white-painted wooden beams, like the inside of the divine chest cavity. 'It represents the belly of Jonah's whale!' a rather strict prefect corrected us, and I was happy about this, because the belly of Jonah's whale seemed an excellent place to receive an education.

We all went to stay with Mum for the surgery, although she was barely out of hospital herself. Evie had a week off school. The day of the operation was the Feast Day of St Francis of Assisi, and Evie lent me her gold medallion of the saint, which I am wearing even as I write. I went into what I had thought would be forty minutes of anaesthetic and woke up five hours later. The sun had gone from outside my window, my throat was sore, my neck stiff from being intubated. Nausea rolled around in sticky bales. I had a recollection of a conversation happening around me, but felt sure the cancer had gone. I felt better, so much better, despite the anaesthetic. Evie and Rupert were sitting at my bedside. The next morning the registrar came to visit me. He told me that my surgeon, Claudia, had removed two lymph nodes along with the prickly tumour. She had kept me under anaesthetic while she waited for an initial analysis of the nodes. They had appeared to be disease-free. Had they been otherwise she would have removed all the nodes in my arm. It was this wait that had prolonged the anaesthetic. The survival statistics were woolly for my particular type of cancer, perhaps because so very few people got it. I was aware that the prognosis was 'generally poor'.

'Claudia has done her very best for you,' he said.

'Yes,' I smiled. 'I know she has.'

★

Claudia referred me to the Royal Marsden Hospital in Chelsea, which was exactly two miles from our house. I was excited by this because I believed it to be the best cancer hospital in the country. For a month I kicked my heels and was impatient with my new doctors. I longed to begin chemotherapy. But the pathologists at the Royal Marsden wanted to perform their own examination of the tumour. And there was the idea that I should recover from surgery. There was tension in this waiting. The cares that had resulted in our coming to London in the first place were not about to go away. Obviously, I still wasn't working, and was not in a position to look for work. Rupert's schedule had been completely disrupted. We talked about selling the cottage. Or rather, Rupert did. I couldn't bear to part with it. One night Evie ran to her bedroom, her hands over her ears, as we argued.

Keeping our house warm became a contentious luxury. For the most part the house was cold. We used the heating when Evie got home and if I had visitors, although the moment the door closed behind them I flicked the control to *Off*. Food also required consideration, not helped by my insistence on buying organic produce, and I perfected the art of making a chicken last three days (roast, soup, risotto). Rupert gave up drinking in order to save money, although insisted that I should drink red wine, because it contained something that counteracted cancer. Our lives were pared back, finely honed, absolutely without excess.

What I could do, and did do, every day, was walk. Early one afternoon, towards the end of October, I set off north through Battersea Park until I reached the wide expanse of the river. I left the park at Albert Bridge, and headed west along the Thames Path. A heron flew low over the water. Brake lights winked along the Embankment on the opposite shore. The bronze water appeared to be still. A cormorant splashed clumsily into the middle of the river. One wing was missing a couple of flight feathers, and I thought briefly of the black and white keys on a piano. And then the cormorant remained there, drifting neither east nor west. As I crossed the road at Battersea Bridge a cyclist slammed into me: *What the bloody hell do you think you're doing?* We landed together, on the pavement, and I caught his smell of sweat and 3-IN-ONE OIL, a rich, metallic tang. He got back onto his bike, muttering under his breath, a red light winking on the back of his helmet, and was on his way before I had even got to my feet. I swung my legs out of the road, anxious to avoid the lunchtime traffic. I was winded, and bruised, but inexplicably energised, glad of the contact with another human being, jolted by the impact of the collision.

I rejoined the footpath. Alongside the river wall, in front of St Mary's Church, a line of single shoes hung by their laces. Plane trees, starved of colour, hissed in the breeze. Behind them, the *tick-tick-tick* of a London cab, the yawn and judder of a double-decker bus. A single scarlet leaf, big as a beer mat, blew to my feet and I bent down and picked it up. It was from a Virginia creeper, sometimes called five-finger, although this one only had three. At its base was a lemon-coloured crescent. I pressed the leaf inside the book I was carrying. Other leaves curled like yellow cigarette papers. I picked one up. Rowan. The orange berries hung in clusters over my head. Some late nasturtiums had put out optimistic watery green discs. Pale roses, like balled-up tissues, nodded on browning stems. I listened to the layers of sound, the cars, the clank of a JCB on the northern bank at Chelsea Wharf, the whine of aeroplanes on their way to Heathrow Airport, the whirr of a child's buggy, and the flat rhythmic tread as his mother sped past me, multitasking, running, walking the baby, all the while listening to her iPod on padded headphones. The child's hair floated like the fluffy seeds of willow herb. I worried about his head getting cold. His fingers opened like daisies as they passed.

At Battersea Railway Bridge I stopped. The bridge needed repainting. Undercoat the colour of marigolds showed through a grey, peeling topcoat. Buddleia, fading with the season, waved between metal arches. A weeping willow nodded, its leaves trailing in the water. In the middle of the Thames was a flat tender, containing two men in Day-Glo jackets. The men seemed tiny, and were pointing into a flurry of circling gulls. The whole scene reminded me of a snow-globe paperweight. Suddenly the gulls stopped circling and settled on the water. They began to drift upstream. One of the men threw something, and again the gulls swirled about the boat. And again they settled on the water, and began to drift upstream.

I watched the river settle into this new direction. The sun was shining, the sky pale blue, and the distinctive chalk-milk, clay-grey emulsion was hidden beneath the reflected sky. Etymologists argue that this colour gives the river its name, although they disagree about exactly how. *Thames* derives from the Middle English *Temese*, which in turn grew out of the Celtic name, *Tamesas*, which probably means dark, while a possible Indo-European, but pre-Celtic root implies muddiness, from *tā-*, or *melt*. The water crackled like a stream of newly minted coins. The river had been quite silent, but now a sound appeared, regular as a heartbeat, and every second or two a wave broke along the shore. Common gulls and mallards trimmed the water's edge, each one no more than a yard from the next. The ducks guzzled the soft mud, the emerald and turquoise heads of the drakes giving a beaded, party look, the white gulls soft as sequins. The female mallards were the same colour as the bank, which was spattered in webbed footprints. A great whirring of cormorants landed in the middle of the river, diving below the water, and reappearing back at the surface, each one always in a different place, like the revolving tin birds in a fairground shooting range. By the time I had regained Albert Bridge the river had settled into its new direction, the water coursing inland in sheets, like newspapers slipping off a press. A man and a woman were arguing. The man was holding a map, and then jabbing in the direction of Putney.

'Tower Bridge is that way!' the man insisted. 'Look at the direction of the water.' The man pointed at the river, and then at Battersea Park. 'That is clearly the Royal Hospital in Chelsea.' From where they stood, the iconic Battersea Power Station, which would surely have helped them orientate themselves, was hidden, tucked out of sight. The woman looked uncomfortable, and tugged at her hair. We were far from the Estuary, and yet there was nothing to indicate, as they and I stood and watched the water, that it might ever have behaved in any other way. When they set off in the direction of the Railway Bridge I said:

'Excuse me.' The man looked surprised, and the woman looked relieved. I said: 'The river flows upstream.'

'What?' he said.

'The Thames is tidal. Tower Bridge is behind you. This is the south bank of the river. In about six hours it will flow the other way.' The man looked at me as though I were mad.

I left the couple squabbling about where they thought they were. But I had had the germ of an idea. If this river, the mighty Thames, could flow upstream, could reverse its direction, twice, each day, then surely it was possible that I could survive my cancer.

★

A month later I walked over Albert Bridge. The sugar-pink and lilypad-green and powder-blue suspension bridge was under repair. The road had been taken up to reveal the rotting iron plates below, although there was still a footpath along one side. Men in steel-toed boots and orange jackets and hard plastic hats filtered the pedestrians, and asked cyclists to dismount. Sparks rained down from a welding torch. There was a smell of sea salt and tar. A cormorant skipped and dived through the current, the same colour as the water. When I got to the Royal Marsden I went round to the Fulham Road entrance and marched up the steps to the front door, although the back door had been nearer. I glanced at the coat of arms in passing. The shield was flanked by an owl and a unicorn. Beneath one of the owl's feet there was a crab. I remembered my little diurnal owl on the moors above Dunbeath. But this owl was the owl of Minerva, Athena, daughter of Zeus, who hatched from her father's head fully dressed with her shield, spear and helmet, her free hand flashing lightning bolts. The goddess of wisdom, healing, and war. The one who helped Odysseus come home.

In the clinical day room I began the long wait of blood tests and examinations, weights and measurements, while my customised drugs were mixed and prepared and a canula fixed into my arm. My friend Tessa arrived before the drugs did. Rupert waited at home to look after Evie. Tessa appeared not to notice the women without hair, the women with open sores, the woman whose face had turned metallic green, the woman who would die within the month. She brought me grapes and started eating them, and then laughed and gave them to me. This wasn't a place where we had ever thought to meet. Over the weeks I learned to accept the kindness of our friends. My sister-in-law Jane took me shopping for daffodil and tulip bulbs so that I would have something to look forward to after the winter. My brother and his family took Evie on holiday. Her godfather Calvin flew from New York. He took us to shows in the West End and brought a blue fox-fur hat to keep my bald head warm and a pair of chocolate-coloured UGG boots for Evie. My friend Rob sent the manuscript of his new book and invited me to give him notes. In thanks for these he gave me a map of Buttermere, marked up in his oddly angular hand, blue ink illuminating valleys and rivers, ridges, places to retrieve my strength. My friend Clare spent two weeks in our home so that Rupert could carry on writing. She cooked, shopped, cleaned, organised the Voewood Festival, and ran her literary agency from our living room. Rupert's brother, Robin, planted roses in the front of our house and his agent, Peter, sent us a hamper that lasted for weeks. And Rupert. Rupert folded his life about me. He brought me books and fresh flowers, and hid his fear behind laughter. When I panicked at the thought of dying surrounded by someone else's wallpaper he painted our bedroom a pristine white. He kept Evie close by his side, walked with her to school every morning, and collected her every afternoon. He cared for me, cared for both of us, steadfastly. Since her own illness Mum was, for the most part, unable to remember that I was unwell, and this made me happier than I could say. Although, during one brief moment of clarity, she had looked at me, and said: *You'll be all right. I can feel it in my waters.*

On my first day in hospital I had been asked if there was a history of breast cancer in our family. I explained that I had been adopted, and didn't know. But as the months shunted into one another, and the year turned around, and again became summer, the question of a family medical history appeared again. For the first time it occurred to me that the reason I had never found my birth mother was because she might have died. My friend Caradoc was also an adoptee. He had written a thoughtful memoir about his experience, called *Problem Child*.

'Why don't you talk to Ariel?' he said. He had taken me to lunch at Sheekey's Restaurant, a treat before I left for Wales with Evie. Ariel was the social worker who had helped reunite Caradoc with his own lost family. He rang her on my behalf. The next day, I spoke to Ariel. There were necessary protocols, like proving who I was, and notifying the relevant local authority, but Ariel gave me her assurance that she would rush these through as efficiently as she was able, given the state of my health. I gave her the information that was recorded on my birth certificate, as well as the name of my birth mother's husband, which I knew from their marriage certificate. Shortly afterwards I met with Ariel. I sat on a sofa in her cool white room and glanced at the piece of paper that she had put in front of me. On it was the name, date of birth and address of my birth mother. She had been on the electoral register all along. As were two half-brothers.

I don't know why I hadn't seen her. It seemed ridiculous how easy it had been. When I got back home I replicated the search myself, and found my birth mother in seconds. She lived about a two-hour drive from where I had grown up. I realised, suddenly, obtusely, bizarrely, that I had only ever looked for her under her maiden name. I couldn't believe, hadn't wanted to believe, it had never even occurred to me – that a marriage that took place on the condition that I was given up could succeed.

It had succeeded. Her marriage had lasted forty years but now her husband, the man I believed had turned me out, was dead.

Ariel wrote a letter to her. At the last minute I panicked. I had the strongest feeling that this might be my only chance to communicate with my mother directly. I told Ariel that I wanted to write to her myself. But Ariel reassured me that it was better this way, that the news would come as a shock, and it was kinder to use an intermediary, and I could see this, so I agreed to it. So Ariel wrote to my birth mother to say that she was researching the genealogy of a client, and had reason to believe that we were related. She included the date, and place, of my birth, along with the name on my birth certificate.

Severn

vie and I decided to make a pilgrimage to the source of the River Severn. What had started as a holiday project now lingered as a habit. It was two years ago that I had followed the Dunbeath Water. No longer just a reason for a journey, the rivers had evolved into a metaphor. Each body of water plaited with the next, twisting first into a bubbling thread, and then into a silver rope. When viewed on a map of Britain and Ireland these ropes formed a net, or a ladder. When I was out walking, the waters became my guide, companion and teacher. They marked a border between different states of being: solid, liquid, air. And they kept moving, were — quite literally — defined by their movement. Heraclitus said that 'no man ever steps in the same river twice, because it's not the same river and he's not the same man.' Woman. Wherever I went, I sought them out, and it seemed fitting that the longest river in Britain should rise just a few miles from my birth mother's house.

Evie and I had been staying at the cottage over the summer holiday. Rupert stayed in London to work. Ariel had still not had a reply to the letter she had sent, but I had noticed that our route back to London passed very close to my birth mother's village, which in turn was near the source of the River Severn. We had booked into a pub in the village of Montgomery. We would visit the source of the river the following day. But when we passed the sign for my birth mother's village we giggled, wondered if we should take a look, decided against it, drove twice round a roundabout, and then up and down the same stretch of dual carriageway, before finally pulling into a lay-by and doubling back on ourselves. We decided to make the detour. She lived in an almost inconsequential village that we missed the first time we passed through it. Her house was at the outer edge of the settlement. The door was at the side, which meant we couldn't see it. The curtains were drawn, although it was afternoon. In the garden was an American-style mailbox. A ticking anxiety circled inside me as finely calibrated as a Hornby train set. She was in there, behind the door that we couldn't see. I was sure of it. I felt drunk. A notice in the window said: *Say No to Wind Farms*. The previous summer I had been invited to speak at a public inquiry into a proposed wind farm. A car was parked in the drive, and it was the same make as my own. This woman was familiar to me, even from the scant evidence that was visible of her day-to-day life. She spoke to me in a way that I had never experienced. I could feel a hum of recognition. Three generations of women were within a few yards of one another. But one of them didn't know it. I wondered if she could feel our proximity.

No one went in or out. Evie and I couldn't stop laughing, although I don't know why. Nerves, I suppose. We discussed what we would do if my birth mother appeared, wondered if we should come back with flowers, and chocolates, and pretend to be

Interflora. I was conscious of my boyish hair, only just returning after the months of chemotherapy. I made myself imagine the possibility that, before the end of the week, we might be returning to this very place, and being welcomed into the house as guests.

Alice Oswald had written a poem called 'A Sleepwalk on the Severn'. A part of it was called: 'mother', and two lines kept recurring to me as I looked at the silent house.

> I am waiting for an old frayed queen
> To walk to that window:

So was I. The River Severn (Welsh: *Hafren*, Latin: *Sabrina*) takes its name from the ghost of a little girl, murdered by a bitter queen, who killed her husband and then drowned both his mistress and their love child in the river. The child's name was Hafren. After the drowning, the queen permitted the little girl's name to be given to the river. When the Romans came they Latinised it – Sabrina – and honoured the child as a goddess. I thought the lines of the poem must refer to the queen of the story. But the River Severn was also one of fourteen rivers that came into being when Boand upset the Well of Wisdom, and I wondered if the stories might be connected. They were both about illegitimate children.

No one seemed to be coming into, or going out of, the house. We decided to check into our pub.

The next morning we drove past a dammed-up lake through soft green land, which grew greener, and greyer, as it rose. After a while we came to a wooded area with a circular car park and a Portakabin loo. There were some moss-covered wooden sculptures that looked as though they had been made with a chainsaw. Plastic containers indicated the place where leaflets or maps had been stored. Wooden stairs descended into woodland, and there was a slipway for wheelchair users and pushchair access. A number of wooden posts, with different-coloured collars, indicated the choice of footpath one might take. One of them showed a drawing of a young woman with flowing hair and a medieval gown. Stars encircled her head.

'Look, Evie,' I said, 'that must be Sabrina.'

I had told her the story of the jealous queen, and the drowned child immortalised by the river. How the Romans made little Hafren into a goddess.

'That's like trying to make something good out of something horrible,' Evie said. 'How come she is grown-up in the picture?'

'I don't know,' I said. 'Maybe it's not her.'

The Severn appeared, a flash through the trees, quite wide and flowing fast, amber water over slabs of rock. In a short space of time it became very straight, with coppiced woodland along the opposite bank, and it felt vulnerable, exposed, naked in its canal-like straightness. There was very little sound; low cloud cover muted the river. What birdsong there was seemed to come from far away. A plastic chain-link footpath, brightly coloured, of the sort that are found on golf courses, paved the bank on our side. Every so often there were benches. We caught up with a party of walkers, dressed as though they'd been out for Sunday lunch, incongruous on the woodland trail. We almost stepped on a frog.

The land began to rise, through deeper woodland, quite quickly, and the river narrowed suddenly. It meandered, and so did we.

'It's like bees,' Evie said, 'a tail made out of bees!'

In the past, when we had walked, Evie had been the one to slow down, to reach for my hand to help her. But it was me, now, who followed slowly, me who fought to catch my breath. I had still not recovered my strength from the months of treatment. I had been weakened by chemotherapy, my heart had been affected, and I had had extensive surgery just a few weeks before the summer holidays began, designed to reduce my risk of developing further primary breast cancers. I still had limited use of both my arms, and my stamina returned as slowly as my hair. Every so often I had to stop and rest while Evie ran ahead. She stood on a boulder and waved down at me, threw two sticks into the current, one for each of us, and then raced downriver after them. If they got caught she leaned across the flow, poking until the blockage span free. After a while she found a longer branch, which she stripped of tiny twigs, and this she gave me to use as a walking stick. I took it, happy, grateful for its help. Joint pain was an unexpected side effect of hormone therapy, or perhaps a consequence of a chemically induced meno-pause. Whatever the cause, in medical terms, the practical conse-quence was that my feet, knees, hips and spine protested with every step.

We came to a dirt road. On the other side the river narrowed sharply. The way-marked footpath became a well-trodden track next to the stream. White mist drifted like dragon's breath. Our faces were misted in droplets. They filled our eyelashes and beaded our hair. Evie put her hands to her face: *It's so cold!* I couldn't feel it, because my face was numb, and remains so to this day. Another of the side effects of treatment. But I recognised, from my journey to Dunbeath, the proximity of the waterhead.

As the land rose and the source of the river grew closer the foot-path became boggy and wet. Great stone slabs had been set along the path and for once I didn't complain at the intervention. I wouldn't want to walk out across this moor without very concrete guidance. Suddenly, the stream opened out into a high-sided, bean-shaped black lagoon. A post next to the footpath announced the source of the River Severn. I had that same feeling, of staring into primordial soup, that I had experienced at the hole in the ground at Dunbeath. But this hole was the size of a swimming pool. It was walled around by collapsing peat hags. The river flowed quickly, even from this place. I was amazed that it began with such strong purpose.

Evie looked into the pool, but she too seemed perplexed by it. White mist curtailed the view, although a dim path was visible across the moor. The source of the River Wye was just a few miles away. I wondered if the footpath led to it. But that wasn't what we'd come to do. 'Let's go back,' Evie said. Alice Oswald's poem again returned to me:

> I am waiting for an old frayed queen
> To walk to that window:
> She who shines like the Moon,
> But shits on the walls,
> She whose house has no books in it
> Or bath.
>
> She who stares at her dead child
> And never tidies away
> Its rat-eaten cradle clothes . . .
>
> Waiting for whatever hard worked mother
> Owns those feathery bones.

My fingers caught the stone slab and I hauled myself out of the water. My nose, ears, eyes, lungs were choked with it. Pain seared my chest, from the recent surgery, but I felt that I might drown if I let go of the stone. I could hear Evie shriek behind me. I had stepped off the footpath into a patch of water the size of a puddle. I couldn't help laughing, even as I hauled myself free. Everything that I knew, all I had been told, about the hazards of walking in a bog. The peat around the fixed stone footpath had formed a pocket, and this pocket had worked outwards, but mostly downwards, to form a dubh loch as treacherous as any I might have found in Scotland. Practise what you preach, check the depth of any water with a stick, no matter how small the surface. I laughed even as I tended to the tearing pain across my chest.

Evie hovered, anxious. I was glad that I had done it. I was glad that she had been there, that she had learned, with no harm done, that the moors are not to be fooled with. Once it was clear that I wasn't going to die she became a little sterner.

'You're covered in dirt.'

'It's only water.'

'It's very peaty water. What if we see someone?'

'What if we do?' I said. 'They'll just have to make of it what they will.'

We had planned to drive on to London after our walk. But when we reached the car park Evie telephoned the pub, and asked if we could have our room back. When we arrived we had hot baths, and hot chocolate, and laughed at our adventure. The next day, just as we were leaving, Ariel called to say she had received a letter.

I love you.

There has not been one day when I have not thought of you.

I have been searching for you from the moment we were separated.

The fantasy evaporated, even before Ariel started to read to me. Her tone of voice had given it away. Ariel read words to the effect of:

I have been deeply shocked to receive this correspondence. I do not wish to hear anything else about this matter. Do not pass any information about me to your client. I am sorry she wants to know her family but I grew up without knowing my own father and I am certain your client can survive without knowing her ancestry. This really is the most horrible thing that has ever happened to me and I trust I will hear nothing more on this subject. All I will say is I was in Australia at the time, trying to avoid difficulties of my own.

Yours sincerely

And her name. Let us call her, for the sake of this history, Mrs Thomas. This letter is an approximation because the copyright belongs to Mrs Thomas. The piece of paper on which it was written is the property of Ariel because it was to her that the letter was addressed. The irony of not owning this communication, and of not being able accurately to share the story of my life, in order to protect the privacy of my birth mother, is not lost on me.

Ariel wrote again. She told Mrs Thomas that I already knew what information was publicly available about her, which included where she lived. She said that I had approached her through an intermediary out of consideration for her feelings. I was not searching for her out of idle curiosity but because I had been

248

diagnosed with a rare and aggressive cancer, that I had undergone chemotherapy, bilateral mastectomies, reconstructive surgery and that I had a daughter. In order to make the best possible decision for my daughter's future I would like a full medical history of the family. She also said that I sent Mrs Thomas my very best wishes, and I was irritated by this, because I did no such thing.

The reply came quickly. Mrs Thomas said that she felt terrified, and that there was nowhere where she felt safe. But she would tell us 'what was required'. She then told how she had become engaged to *a wonderful man* just before going to Australia. She had hitch-hiked down the length of the east coast picking up work where she could find it. She said that just before leaving Sydney she had had *a quickie* at a party with someone who belonged to a group of people she hung around with, although she claimed not to know his name. She said she didn't know that she was pregnant until her mother realised her condition after her return to the United Kingdom. A flat was rented for her and she was shut away for the remainder of her pregnancy. She said she had given birth under anaesthetic and never saw the baby *They told me later that it was a girl*. She talked about her husband, the man she said she had betrayed, who had been good enough never to mention *it* in all the long years of their marriage. She did, however, provide a thin medical history and I was happy to find, for Evie's sake, that there had been few deaths through cancer, although several due to acute alcoholism. Mrs Thomas contradicted her first letter, in which she had stated that she did not know her father, by providing details of his and his parents' medical history. Her paternal grandmother, for example, had had the only case of breast cancer in the family, and had survived it. She ended by saying that everyone had rights, even her, and that she wanted to be left alone.

I was struck by her lack of interest, of curiosity. She didn't mention her children. She accepted no social or moral responsibility for her actions. She clearly didn't believe that she had any. I did not believe that she did not know the name of my father. And yet, I felt for her. This woman was, technically, my mother. The tie that had been broken between us is generally regarded as the most powerful bond there is. Certainly, in relation to Evie, that is true. I tried to tell myself that it was not me that Mrs Thomas was rejecting, but a circumstance that had been traumatic for her. I was just an idea to her, and her experience had shaped the rest of her life. One of the two of us had to be the mother, and it clearly wasn't going to be her. I drafted a reply:

Dear Mrs Thomas

My only regret, in approaching you through an intermediary, is that it allowed you to make the first words you said to me a passing reference to 'it'. Had I written to you myself I doubt you would have done this. You say you want to be left alone and, also, that you are terrified. There is nothing here for you to fear. If you truly want to be left alone, then help me, by giving me what I seek.

In your letter you mention rights. I have no right to a relationship with you, or even to meeting you. But I believe I have a moral right to know who I am, and where I come from, and that you have an obligation to tell me what you know. Are we Scottish, English, Welsh or Irish? Norwegian? Sailors or publicans? Gypsies or priests? Are we dark, fair, tall or short? You know the answers to some, if not all, of these things. I invite you to share your story with me, not just the pitiful circumstances of your pregnancy. Let me see something of the fabric of who I am.

Yet this is only half the story. It seems improbable that you neither knew, nor subsequently discovered, the identity of my father. He will

be an old man now – if, indeed, he is still alive – and I would like
to know his name, the colour of his hair, his eyes, what he did for a
living. Was he even Australian? Has it occurred to you that he might
be happy to know he has a child? It need not involve you in any
way.

To go to Australia, alone, in the 1960s, and to travel the length of
the coast, was a brave and wonderful thing to do; you are not so retiring
as you make out.

If you feel unable to help me, then there are other people able to
answer most of my questions. Although it seems unlikely that you have
told your children they have a half-sister.

I wish you well, and send you my best wishes

I wasn't sure if the 'best wishes' were heartfelt or not this time, and I kept the letter, and fiddled with it, for several weeks. Mentioning her children was provocative, but I didn't have much to work with. However you looked at it, I was begging, which was an invidious position to be in. I decided, in the end, not to send it. There didn't seem to be any point. What could possibly be gained from approaching someone who so clearly wanted nothing to do with me? And anyway, I hadn't been honest. What I wanted was to set eyes on a human being who was related to me by blood. Not just Evie. I wanted to meet my birth mother. I was curious about my half-brothers and I wanted to know the identity of my birth father. I wanted to extend the rope back into time and see the genetic tribe from whom I was descended. I wanted to blot out the loneliness. I decided to write to my half-brothers. But there was a problem. There were two boys that I knew of, Ioan and Robert. There were over seventy Robert Thomases in the county where their mother lived and almost as many Ioans. I downloaded the addresses of all of the Roberts from the electoral register. I wrote another letter:

Dear Robert

Forgive me for writing to you out of the blue.

I am researching my family history and have reason to believe that I am closely related to a Robert Thomas, born, I believe, in Caernarfon, and living at some time in Montgomery, Powys. I know the approximate age. I also know the names of other family members, so could easily work out if you are the right one. For my own part I was given up at birth, with the absolute minimum of information regarding my identity. It is my impression that other family members have not been made aware of my existence. I apologise, therefore, for the scattergun and potentially unsettling nature of my enquiry.

If I have got the wrong Robert Thomas (and there are many on the electoral register) then think no more of this, and thank you for your time in reading it. Otherwise, if you think you might be the right one, I would be delighted to hear from you.

With all best wishes

I didn't send that either. If I sent the letter, or rather the seventy-five identical letters, to the seventy-five men in Powys who carried my half-brother's name, and somehow found the right one, then Mrs Thomas would likely become my sworn enemy, whereas now she was simply adamant that she didn't want to know me. Any chance I might have had of finding my natural father would be gone for good. And I felt a growing certainty that any good qualities that I might have inherited had not come from her. Other than a feisty spirit, for it was clear from her two existing letters that she was in possession of that. That, and the ability to string a sentence.

Every so often I took out my birth mother's letters, or rather the photocopies that Ariel had given me, and looked at them. The more familiar they became, the less hurtful they appeared. I was all but incidental to them. But it was becoming less and less clear to me what I might gain from attempting to pursue a relationship with the woman who had written them. The only thing that was apparent was that hearing from me had distressed her.

If she had been prepared to meet me even a small part of the way, this story would have had a different ending. In her second letter she had said something about having made one mistake through ignorance, and not wanting to have to pay for it for the rest of her life. But she hadn't made a mistake when she gave me up for adoption. She had done the best that was possible under the circumstances. Her mistake, it seemed to me, was to refuse the hand of friendship, now.

It was checkmate, or maybe it was check, but the next move wasn't clear to me. I folded away the letters, the photocopies of hers and the drafts of the ones I hadn't sent, and I put them in a file marked: *Mrs Thomas*. I put the file in a box in the attic that contained Rupert's genealogy, researched by his late father, scroll after scroll of family trees, describing a meandering line that wandered back to a sea captain in the 1700s.

And then, just after Christmas, I decided to send the letter that I had drafted to Mrs Thomas. Her reply came quickly. She didn't reveal the identity of my father, or tell me my nationality. Only that she had been 'unimpressed' by the sex, which she described as 'a very brief incident'. She said that her maiden name was different from her father's name, because her mother had remarried. She did not say what my grandfather's name had been. She did say she'd had an illegitimate half-brother who her mother referred to as 'a bastard in both senses of that word'. I wondered why she had chosen to include this, particular, turn of phrase.

I wrote to her again. I told her that I wanted to meet her. No one need know. I gave her my word. I would come to her. If she was unhappy, I would leave at once, and she need never see me again. I hoped with all my heart she could agree to this.

A month later she sent her reply. Certain phrases caught. This was 'the worst kind of emotional bullying'. 'You had parents.' 'You are not mine.'

I knelt down and retrieved the letter from where it had dropped from my open hand, and continued to read.

'My mother said that we could live with her, but I was broke, and had no prospects. You were always going to be adopted.' She didn't mention that she was engaged to be married, and about to embrace the comfortable, middle-class life that her husband made available to her, and which sustains her to this day. I was aware that I had hit her as hard as she hit me. I laughed, dryly, at this family resemblance – not grace, or courage, or wit, or humour – but a sheer bloody-minded determination. Her desire to bury the truth of my existence was exactly mirrored by my own desire, my deepest wish, that she acknowledge it.

> *I never looked at the baby.*
> *They told me later it was a girl.*

> *She who shines like the Moon,*
> *But shits on the walls,*
> *She whose house has no books in it*
> *Or bath.*

A secret well there was
from which gushed forth every kind of mysterious evil.
There was none that would look to its bottom
But his two bright eyes would burst:

Every way the woman went
The cold white water followed
From the Sid to the sea (not weak it was),
So that thence it is called Boand.

That night I tried to laugh it off. Mrs Thomas as the Evil Queen.
Or maybe it was me. I could no longer tell. I wanted my parent to
acknowledge me, my primal scream stuck in my throat. It was
never going to happen. But why should it? She'd given up a baby
that she didn't want on the understanding that she'd never hear of
it again. Why should she cooperate now? Why was what I wanted
more important than what she wanted? She had gone into an
operating theatre pregnant, and had recovered from the anaesthetic no longer so. At some level, her pregnancy had been aborted.
She had never looked at the outcome. The next day I couldn't get
out of bed. Rupert must have got Evie to school, and then gone
to work himself. I drifted in and out of sleep. At lunchtime I awoke
from a dream. In the dream I had been a child again, and I was
standing in front of a door, as though waiting for someone to
come for me. The door was made of red wooden boards and had
been built into the side of a hill. Water seeped constantly from
under it. I watched my dream-self stamp in the mud. Later I
splashed my arms in it and made palm prints on the chipped red
paint, before banging on the door with both my hands. I was
certain that behind the door was *the source*. I could hear it, like a

waterfall, my origin. But the door was locked and had no handle. All I had was the mud on my feet and hands, now drying in pale flakes on the wooden door. I realised, dimly, that the mud was clay, and that something might yet be made of it, although I couldn't see what.

I got out of bed and went to the bathroom. I stood beneath the shower. Some time went by, I don't know how long, and then I reached for a razor, tested the blades. I shaved my legs, my pubis, my armpits and, finally, my head. The lovely new conker-coloured hair that was just beginning to grow clogged up the plughole, choking it. I turned off the shower and walked over to the mirror before starting on my eyebrows. But when I saw my face in the misted glass, the water running off my nose, a wriggle of diluted blood where I had nicked the skin above my ear, I put down the razor, and reached for a towel.

Afon Rhiw

What is existence
but standing patiently for a while
amid flux? Mostly the fish
nibbled out of my reach.
The fly soared, drying its wings
in the March wind before redoubling
its temptations, offering like life itself
a hook hidden among feathers.

R. S. Thomas

Mrs Thomas had addressed the last letter she wrote to me to *Mrs Kate Connelly*. At first I assumed that she had forgotten my name. Later, I began to wonder if this was her father's name. She had told Ariel, when she provided the medical history, that her father was buried in the Beach Head Cemetery at Anzio, in Italy. The Battle of Anzio, in January 1944, was one of the bloodiest battles of the Second World War. Over thirty thousand men lost their lives on the beaches, in the successful attempt to break through the enemy's defences. This awful fact explained the apparent contradiction between Mrs Thomas knowing her father's medical history, yet claiming not to have known the man himself. He had died when she was a baby. I looked up the war records from the Second World War, searched for soldiers called Connelly who'd died at Anzio. I found one. Thomas John Connelly, a member of the Royal Fusiliers. There was a photograph of his white, slightly crooked tombstone. He was buried in the Beach Head Cemetery.

I wrote back to Mrs Thomas, one last note, on a postcard, with a picture of a lion on it. I mentioned the name on her letter to me, *Mrs Kate Connelly*, and I thanked her – if this was my name – for sharing it. I gave her my word that I would never write to her, unsolicited, ever again. I sent her a copy of 'Ash Wednesday' by T.S. Eliot, because she had turned every word that I wrote to her, had prised out a meaning that I had not intended, and I was no longer confident using words of my own. Let her interpret the poet how she will. After posting the letter I lit a candle. I started a novena for the soul of Thomas John Connelly, who died of his wounds at Anzio. Later, Evie and I researched the name. I bought her a Claddagh ring, with a tiny emerald set in the heart, and we laughed that we were descended from the High Kings of Ireland, of whom the Dagda was one.

Three months later Evie and I were in a carwash halfway between Shrewsbury and Newtown.

'Why are we washing the car?' she asked.

'So we don't draw attention to ourselves.' I drove out of the carwash and reversed into a bollard.

'Mum!'

'I'm sorry.'

'Calm down,' Evie said. 'It'll be fine.' When I had been putting the petrol into the car I had noticed that everything added up to eight. Forty-four pounds' worth of fuel. Four and four is eight. The day of the week and the month and the year came to eight; the clock on the dashboard read: *18:08* which, as well as having two eights in it, also added up to eight as did the cost of unleaded petrol at 134.9 pence per litre. I got out of the car to inspect the damage but there was just a faint yellow streak of plastic melded onto the bumper. There was a 1, a 7, and a 4 in our licence plate, which didn't add up to eight but two of the numbers equalled it and another was half of it.

'Mum?'

I got back into the car. We had driven from London to Wales to watch my half-brother, Robert, play rugby.

After giving Mrs Thomas my word that I would not contact her, I had started to think seriously about my half-brothers. Ariel had not seemed keen to trace them, and I had let the correspondence drift. I had promised Mrs Thomas that I wouldn't tell a soul if she would agree to meet me. But she had declined. I had let three months pass by. Three months, in which she might have changed her mind. But there was nothing. So one Friday evening in March, I sat down at our computer, and typed in my half-brothers' names. I added the village where I believed they had grown up, then pressed *Enter*. But there was another word in the search box.

Rupert had been looking up something to do with rugby, and I had failed to delete this one last word. I was about to repeat the search when my eye was caught by the first entry. It was the history of the local rugby club.

'During the '90s brothers Robert and Ioan Thomas went on to play for the league.'

I started looking for a rugby player called Ioan Thomas. I found a reference to one in a club record, but it was years ago and he had retired. I turned my attention to Robert. Instead of looking at clubs I searched through images of rugby players called Robert Thomas. Dozens of faces flashed on the screen, and in the middle of the first page, as the pictures stilled, my eye was caught by a postage-stamp-sized, passport-style image. A kind-looking, good-looking, smiling man, who had my daughter's eyes. Evie came over and stood behind me.

'That's him,' she said.

He was still playing for a Welsh Rugby Union club. I clicked on the image, brought up the website, studied the upcoming fixtures. There was an away match the following evening. Evie and I packed our overnight bags, got into the car, and drove.

We got to the ground early. There was hardly anyone there. A young man came over and tapped on the window of the car. I glanced over at Evie. She was white with apprehension.

'Is it OK to park here?' I asked. 'We've come for the rugby.'

'Over there,' he said, and he pointed. I had driven into the car park of a building supplier next door to the ground, and the man wanted to lock the gate. The floodlights had still not been turned on.

'This is awful!' said Evie. 'I think I'm going to be sick.' I looked at her, chastened. I hadn't stopped to think how she might be feeling. Although I couldn't have imagined it had I tried. There was no emotional signpost by which we might orientate ourselves, although that wasn't an excuse. I had once again walked off the edge of a map, to a place that was completely unknown. I couldn't articulate my feelings. I had little hope of comprehending hers. I parked carefully, close to the exit, with the car facing towards the road.

'We haven't got the right clothes,' Evie said.

'Sorry?'

'Look at us!' Evie was wearing jeans and a brown leather jacket. I was wearing a green plaid duster coat, cut on the bias. It was three months since I had shaved my head. We didn't look as though we were going to a rugby match.

'We look all right. No one is going to be interested in what we are wearing . . . Would you like to go back home?'

'Yes,' she said, and my heart folded like a shot bird. 'No. I want to stay.' I held out my hand, avoiding her gaze.

'Do you want to wait in the car?'

'I'm coming with you,' she said. We squeezed each other's fingers tightly.

We took up a position in the grandstand. There were seventeen people, including us. One young man opened a sports holdall and removed a club flag, and then another, Welsh, flag, and secured them to the back wall of the stand. A young lad with a 1950s cut to his bright red hair ducked in front of us. The man with the flags took out a radio, and began to tune it. A farmer type with flannel trousers tapped a blackthorn walking stick, as though searching for a hidden panel. They all seemed to know one another. I hoped they would assume that we were supporting the visiting team.

There was a training session in progress for the second team. At the edge of the floodlighting, beyond the boundary fence, a horse ran up and down, dipping its head. And then the players came out. I had read the match reports for the previous games and Robert usually wore 6 or 7. I looked for the numbers. Two men, dark-haired, in their twenties.

'He isn't here.'

'That's him!' Evie pointed. 'Number 8.' He was at the other side of the pitch, overexposed in the milky lights, the turf glowing emerald beneath his feet. His hair was longer than in the picture, and he looked stronger than I had imagined; he talked a lot.

'Ah Ref!'

'If I hear one more word from you, Tommo, it's a yellow card!'

'He is *exactly* like you!' Evie said, and giggled. 'Only a boy!'

After that came a tackle which threw him onto his shoulder. He bounced up, tweaked his sleeve, and ran on.

'But, Evie, they're calling him *Tommo*.'

'It's short for Thomas. There's probably another Robert.' I was astonished and delighted by her acumen and detective skills.

Half time came.

We bought milky tea in polystyrene cups. Evie's hands were shaking, though with cold or anticipation she couldn't say. For the first time I began to see how much this secret uncle might mean to her. I had been so caught up in the journey. But Evie had travelled with me. She had lost the hope of having a brother or a sister, at any rate through me. As a result of the treatment I was as barren as the snow. Chemotherapy had damaged my ovaries. Tamoxifen ensured they didn't recover. I had been caught in an early frost. Mum was the only grandparent Evie knew, and she was as frail as apple blossom. Dad had died when she was one. Rupert's parents died long ago. Although there were cousins on both sides of our family, we were not what one might call a dynasty. We moved over to the centre line, and waited for the players to come back. When they filed onto the pitch the man in front of Robert stopped. He chatted for a few moments to the farmer in the flat tweed cap, now leaning on his blackthorn walking stick. The farmer was standing next to us. Robert looked beyond the hold-up, saw there was no virtue in passing, and waited. Then he looked from one to the other of us. He was close enough to touch. I could feel Evie standing next to me. Neither of us seemed able to move. Robert lifted his eyebrows, as though about to speak, and then he grinned at us. It is impossible for me to articulate how I felt.

When the match resumed Robert kept glancing back in our direction. I felt that, if we hadn't gone when he came out of the dressing room, he would come over and speak to us. I watched him shake hands with the referee, the opposing captain, the linesmen and then, as he approached the edge of the pitch, I took Evie by the hand and we flowed down the steps of the stand. Robert glanced briefly in our direction, but he was still talking, and we left the ground.

We checked into a coaching inn in a nearby town. Evie made hot chocolate for both of us – her first time, scrutinising the instructions on the sachet – and poured a generous glass of sherry for me, from a cut-glass decanter on a lace doily. We talked about having hot baths, talked about getting something to eat. Ate the complimentary biscuits instead and curled, a knot of limbs, into the bed.

★

I had seen my half-brother and he had smiled at me. I was indescribably happy. But he had smiled without knowing who I was. This knowledge munched at my equilibrium like a caterpillar inside an apple. In the weeks that followed I veered over what to do. Nothing? Or something? If so, what? Robert was thirty-five years old. It was possible that he might retire. The last match of the season coincided with Evie's half term.

We decided to go back. On the Saturday morning before we left I wrote a letter.

Dear Robert Thomas

I wonder if you remember, at the match against Llangennech, a woman with short hair wearing a long green coat and a young blonde girl with a ponytail. You smiled at us as you walked onto the pitch. We had driven from London to see if the Robert Thomas who played for Llanbeuno might not be the same Robert Thomas we had been seeking. Your smile confirmed it.

I am aware that this letter will come as a surprise to you.

I am a member of your family who was given up at birth. Eighteen months ago I was diagnosed with a rare and aggressive form of cancer. It was for this reason that I wanted to locate my birth family. In part it was because I knew that a family medical history would be invaluable to my daughter. But, in truth, I ached to set eyes on a blood relative. I have approached the older generation of the family and been told, in no uncertain terms, the past is the past. I am sorrier for this than I could ever say, for that past is my 'present continuous'. I do understand that to have had an illegitimate child in the 1960s was considered shameful; though I had hoped that time would soften this.

I have agonised over what to do because no one goes lightly against the wishes of their blood ties, even if it is against the wishes of someone

one has never met. But you are the only blood family I have ever seen,
other than my child, and the questions of what is right and what is
wrong are complex.

I beseech you not to judge those who have known of me and, I
imagine, never spoken of me. It's possible that only one person
now living ever knew of my existence in the first place. I would
ask you to think deeply about whether or not to share this letter
with them.

I have had no way of knowing if you were the 'right' Robert
Thomas. When I saw you across the pitch, though, I knew in an
instant it was you. So did my daughter. She said: That's him!
Number 8. We have come back now to give you this, having no
postal address.

I hope and pray with all my heart that you will view this letter
positively. I pray that we can meet as friends. Whatever happens, your
smile will sustain me for the rest of my life.

With my very best wishes
Kate Norbury
PS. I am staying tonight at the Dragon Inn in Montgomery.

And I added my mobile phone number.

The last match was another away game, in a quiet village, where
the Afon Rhiw, a tributary of the River Severn, was intersected by
an aqueduct. We parked next to the aqueduct, among a strip of
trees between the canal and the river, and made our way to the
ground.

We arrived just a few minutes before full time. When the whistle blew the players walked into the tunnel below the stand. Robert

walked past me, but I was transfixed. Evie said: *Mum!* and I handed the letter to one of the players.

'Could you give this to Robert Thomas, please?'

He looked at the envelope. 'Yeah, all right.'

'Thanks.'

And I walked away from him. Evie caught up with me; I could sense that she wanted to run. We went back to the place where we had left the car, among the trees between the river and the canal, and we climbed the bank onto the aqueduct. Below us, along the lane, people were returning to their cars. Soon there was only a handful of vehicles left. Others walked in the direction of a pub next to a bridge across a bend in the Rhiw.

The riverbed, where it flowed beneath the aqueduct, was paved to protect the supports of the structure from erosion. The river rustled as it slipped across the stones. The trees still seemed bare, but the new leaves were rolled tight, and were bright, making the light beneath the bridge an absinthe green. There was a flick of bronze, a stroke, slight, quick as a meteor. A goldcrest. Above our heads stacked clouds unfurled. Evie said they looked like candlewax.

And then suddenly Robert was there, walking down the lane towards the aqueduct, relaxed, in conversation with another man. He was wearing jeans and a shirt, no sign of a letter, either in his hand or in his pocket. He passed beneath us.

'He hasn't seen it,' I said.

'How do you know?'

'Look at him! That isn't a man who has just been told, after running about for ninety minutes, that he has a long-lost relative.'

'Mum! You must have given it to the wrong man! What if it's in the hands of his enemy!'

'Enemy? Maybe the other guy hasn't come out of the shower yet.'

'What shall we do?' she wailed, her hands on either side of her face.

'Nothing. We'll just hang around here for a bit.'

'How could you go to all that trouble and then give the letter to the wrong man?' she said.

'I don't know! Just be quiet, Evie!'

'You be quiet!'

And then my mobile rang. Unknown caller.

'Hello?'

'Hi Kate, this is Robert. How are you?'

'I'm fine, thank you, Robert. Thank you for ringing me.'

'Where are you?'

'We're in the car park.'

'Well, I'm in the pub, and I would ask you to join me, but there are thirty players in here and you've clearly gone to a great deal of trouble. Do you know where the bridge is?'

It was about five hundred yards away. We'd passed it on the way to the ground.

'Yes,' I said.

'Will you meet me there in five minutes?'

'Yes.'

'Great!'

'Thank you!'

I stared at the phone. Stared at Evie.

'Oh my gosh!' she said.

'Come on.' I reached for her hand. We clambered down the embankment.

As we neared the bridge, Robert was talking on the telephone. When he saw us approaching he finished his call, turned towards us, nodding, smiling, then lifted both arms in greeting. We all shook hands.

'Evie, this is Mr Thomas.'

He laughed, 'It's Robert . . . Please. I am your brother.'

I looked at him. That wasn't what it said in the letter. He raised his hand, stilled the unasked question. 'You don't have to tell me who you are,' he said. 'You are the image of her.'

We stood and chatted for a while on the bridge. 'Obviously this is a surprise,' he said, 'but as far as I'm concerned, it's a good surprise.' Evie went for a walk along the river path. We watched her, looking back at us, and she waved, happy. I may have been the image of Mrs Thomas, but Evie had her uncle's eyes. She held up her iPod and gave a thumbs-up sign. My own eyes kept glancing off the planes of Robert's face, his hands, his body. I was fascinated to meet someone who looked like me, but was a man. He seemed extraordinarily relaxed. Did I mind if he asked me when this happened?

'It was before she married your father,' I said.

'He wasn't your father?'

'I don't know who my father is.'

His eyebrows furrowed. 'Ah! She needs to get this off her chest!'

'I don't think she wants to. She was really very clear.'

He sighed. 'I imagine she was . . . My mother, that is, our mother, is a very hard woman.'

'I think I've worked that out,' I said. A space had opened between us, full of the secret darkness of the years. He saw my fear, and closed the gap.

'Look, we don't have to do all this now,' he said, 'this is just the beginning,' and suddenly he was smiling again. But as I returned the smile his own fell away and he said, 'Look, I'm very sorry for everything that you must have been through. But it's all right now.' The smile had already returned.

We met again a few weeks later, on our way up to the cottage for the summer holiday. Evie and I arrived early in a roadside pub, and were looking around for Robert when a man leaned into Evie, passing her a bundle, soft and fluffy, and smelling of milk and fabric softener.

'Mum!' Evie cried, and I leaned forward, folding her arms about the baby, showing her how to hold her in the crook of her arm. Robert sat next to us. We all peered into the bundle. From beneath a blue hood, covered in roses, two round eyes stared out.

'There you go,' said Robert. 'Here's your cousin, Seren.'

'Oh my goodness!' Evie cried.

'It means star,' he said.

'She's got your nose!' I said. When Evie was born her nose had been a mystery. Now we knew whose side of the family it came from. Seren also had Evie's eyes, and the two girls appraised one another curiously. When Evie looked up her face was glowing. Seren seemed at home and kicked her feet. I waited for it to be my turn for a cuddle.

In the days and weeks that followed, Robert and I pieced together a fragmented history. Robert asked me why I hadn't done this years ago. I told him that I had left messages for our mother. I told him that, when the law changed, and birth parents were free to seek their children, I had put my name on the Adoption Contact Register. I believed that she would come and look for me. In fact, I had expected her to appear on my doorstep the very next day. Naïve, without doubt, but these things are the stuff of fairy tale. It's almost impossible to envisage something sensible, because it falls outside ordinary experience. Still, as the days went by, and slipped into weeks, then months, and finally years, my excitement and resolve had dissipated. After ten years I realised that she wasn't coming, and after that it had seemed hard to know what to do. It took a diagnosis of cancer to bounce me into action.

Robert didn't know who Thomas Connelly was. In fact the name meant nothing to him. He did have a grandfather who was buried in the Beach Head Cemetery at Anzio. Of course, in protecting Robert's identity, I cannot tell you what the name of our grandfather is. But I smiled at the thought of Thomas John Connelly, warmed in his journey through the Underworld, surprised by the gift of an unexpected quiver of arrows in the form of my novena. And I laughed as my Irish heritage evaporated. We discovered that Robert's home was more or less on my way home, if I drove to London from the Llŷn Peninsula. Robert asked me how come I had a cottage there. I said that the purchase had been an impulse. I just felt happy there. Why did he ask? Well, no reason, he said. But his father's relatives all came from the Llŷn, and he still had family on the peninsula.

The next time I was in Cheshire I told my brother John about finding Robert. And then I told Mum. She listened carefully to the story. Although she was often confused now, there was a glint of steel about her, a warning, and I knew I couldn't mention Mrs

Thomas. We had never discussed my birth mother since that one night when I was eleven years old, not even when we had all been to the Convent. But Mum was happy to discuss the idea of Robert. She considered the information for a moment and then said: 'Does that mean there's a brother for Evie?' I thought about Baby Seren, her bright eyes and perky nose.

'More or less,' I said. 'More or less.' I hadn't thought of it that way.

They say you should never play cards with the devil because he always deals you a shitty hand. I had mistaken the hand that Mrs Thomas held. I had no idea what the name *Connelly* signified. It could simply be, as I had first assumed, that Mrs Thomas had forgotten my name. Part of me suspected that Mr Connelly was the man she believed was my natural father, the man she had met in Australia, and that she knew more than she chose to tell. But I had given Mrs Thomas my word that I would never to write to her again – unless she approached me first. Robert and Evie bore an extraordinary likeness to one another. I didn't know how long Mrs Thomas had been in Australia, but it did occur to me, watching Robert and Evie together, that perhaps his father was, after all, my natural father, too, and the whole thing had been a terrible mistake. I wondered if, perhaps, I too had travelled – like the martin, the little blue bird – in a long migratory arc that had brought me to a hillside on the Llŷn Peninsula, to what was, quite literally, the land of my fathers.

But the truth was, I no longer really cared. My father, the only father I could ever need or want, was the man who claimed me when I was a baby, the man to whom I had given my first smile, at the very moment that we met, and who had given me his family's name. Who had laid me down on a rug on the living-room floor and said: 'Now, what are we going to call *you*?' My father was Emeritus Professor John Frederick Norbury, OBE, B.Sc., M.Sc., Ph.D., LLB, Fellow of the Institute of Mechanical Engineers, our Fred, the village boy made good, who had won a Highfield Tannery Scholarship and obtained a first-class honours degree by the time he was nineteen. Who had proposed to Mum on the summit of Tryfan, on one of two rocks called Adam and Eve, and then held her hand as they leapt from one to the other. Who had wrapped his hand around mine and walked with me to the top of Scafell, and then carried me back down on his shoulders. Who had returned our family to the same town in Scotland, so that my brother could defend the trophy he had won playing golf there the year before, when he was only fifteen years old. When I began to read Philosophy as an undergraduate and hated it, I had telephoned home at midnight from a payphone at the end of a rain-filled street to tell Dad how unhappy I was. He had got out of bed, and answered the phone, and said: 'Well done, darling, it's great that you know how you feel about this. Now, don't worry about anything, just go back to bed, and we can make some plans in the morning.' Whenever I had gone to the mountains, because I often walked alone, Dad would telephone the hotel, or pub, where I was staying, every day, to ask how I'd got on. He had welcomed Rupert into our family the first moment they had met, already laughing, his arms held wide, even as Rupert climbed out of his car. His grandchildren he called *my shining diamonds*. When Dad entered a room he had the ability to make everyone in it feel special. You could see it in their faces, and I had been told about it often enough. This lovely, kind, irreplaceable man was, in every way, my father, and if I have a sense of loss, it is because he has died, and there isn't a day when I do not think of him.

The Well at the World's End

R upert and I had gone to a party at the home of the writer, Kirsty Gunn, when *The Well at the World's End* came up in conversation. Kirsty, it turned out, was a distant relative of Neil Gunn. We chatted about the book, and I told her of my journey to Dunbeath, now three summers earlier, and she asked me: 'Did you visit the well?'

'No!' I said, and told her how I had tried to find out where it was but had eventually abandoned the search, and had followed the Dunbeath Water instead.

'My sister lives in Caithness,' she said. 'I'm certain she knows where it is,' and Kirsty promised that she would write to her straight away. She was sure that her sister would be able to draw a map, there was really no mystery about it. But the reply, when it came, was tantalisingly vague and as fruitless as my earlier searches. The sister had forgotten the exact location of the well, and suggested I contact the Heritage Centre in Dunbeath. I had done that three years ago, too. But I did write again, and the same kind lady I had spoken to then now wrote to Neil Gunn's nephew,

Dairmid Gunn. This time Mr Gunn was not away from home, and he wrote to me by return.

Dear Kate (if I may)
I have been asked by Meg Sinclair of the Dunbeath Heritage Centre to
give you directions to reach the well . . .'

It was that easy. Evie and I went together. The road journey, again, took three days to complete. We went first to Dunbeath because I wanted to show her the loch. We stood with our backs to the sea, until a black wave slapped the harbour wall with a crack like a starting pistol. We followed the river until we were high above the town. We passed the cemetery and the waterfall and the abandoned farm and the empty house called Poll Roy. At the farm the wool from a recent shearing clogged the path like sea-foam. We were careful to avoid the rabbit traps. We bent to finger the tangled heads of bog-cotton. Morven, invisible when I had come alone, appeared as a blue wedge on the horizon. The river was the colour of tea. Two pale hinds appeared on the skyline, their leaf-shaped ears revolving like antennae. We slept side by side on the heather. We began walking again just after four the next morning. We saw no birds at all. There were midges. There were *midges*. The only sounds were of the river and our footfalls, the occasional chatter of our voices, and the *swoosh* as we walked through long grass. Mostly, we walked in silence. Once, there was a noise, like a glass of water being knocked over, and a slick black salmon broke the surface of a pool. It made a pattern like a firework before it disappeared beneath the shelter of the bank. Evie stared at the place where the salmon had been. It was the only living thing we had seen all day but for the midges. There was little or no breeze as we followed the river, but above our heads the clouds rolled quickly from the sea, like an autocue of Rorschach inkblots.

We reached the edge of the water table. Clumps of mist in curious shapes appeared like empty dresses. The land was much heavier than when I had come by myself. We had been up to our knees in mud and moss, the peat hags too spongy to be safe, and were now walking barefoot up the streambed. The mist began to press about us, silently stopping up our senses. We perched next to one another on a dryish clump of heather and pondered what to do. The memory of slipping into water that covered my head, on our visit to the source of the Severn, was fresh with me. I couldn't, with good conscience, take Evie across the blasted shell holes between the head of the stream and the unseen loch.

It was as though a blind had been drawn down over our endeavour. It was strange to me how receptive the landscape had felt when I had come here on my own, and how enigmatic, and secretive, it was today. There were no birds, no deer. Only the whine and pin-prick of midges, although the mist – mercifully – had dispersed them for a while. It was like being in an empty theatre between performances. As though the action was happening elsewhere.

'Is this where the well is?' Evie asked.

'No, there's a loch, but we wouldn't see it in this mist. The well is a few miles from Dunbeath. If we turn back now we could find it before nightfall.'

'Let's find the well,' she said.

Later that afternoon Evie reached into the glove compartment of the car and took out Dairmid Gunn's letter and an Ordnance

Survey map. The place Dairmid had described was a few miles south of Golspie. Evie opened the map, and ran her finger down the pink stripe of the A9. We had a grid reference. Evie's finger came to rest on a single letter: W.

Meaning, *Well*.

Evie hated map-reading. We drove up and down the same stretch of road for about half an hour. In Neil Gunn's novel, the well is close to a collection of cottages. The hero has gone to fill his kettle at the well but when he looks at the water it's so clear he can't see it, and so he tells the old woman who lives in the nearby cottage that it's dry. 'That well is never dry,' she replies. We pulled over and I looked at the map. There were two little cubes opposite the 'W' on the map. We'd driven right past them. I turned the car round. The cottages were on a particularly lethal bend in the A9 but they could have been lifted from the book. A band of woodland ran on both sides of the road, and at the northern boundary of the wood, on the opposite side to the cottages, was a lichen-covered wooden gate. We tried to find a place to park. The A9 is the only significant road in that part of the Highlands, and cars fumed like killer bees. I eased the car onto a low grass verge. As I got out I saw a penny. I picked it up and showed it to Evie. She took her bottle of water and emptied what was left of it onto the road.

'For the well water,' she said.

We passed through a wooden gate. A high wicker fence ran alongside a footpath. We could see the woodland between the reeds of the fence, and it seemed to be in a poorly state, black pines leaning against one another. Other trees had been cut down, but not replanted. A chill hung in the air, the only sound came from the creak of the pines, and the occasional buzz from the road. After about fifty yards the path opened out onto a blackened mulchy glade, where a wicker man, wearing a kilt, with a wooden sporran, a tam-o'-shanter and Wellingtons lay alongside an empty stream-bed, pebbled with pine cones and dried leaves. Bronze pine needles covered the earth. The well-keeper scarecrow implied that this was the right place. My heart sank. It seemed as though the well had, after all, dried up. I placed the penny I had found on top of the reclining figure's sporran.

And then I saw it, we both saw it, seemed to notice it together. In a dark bank, a few yards away, surrounded by tendrils of new ferns, was a wooden door. It was made of boards and painted ox-blood red. It wasn't big, more like a cupboard, and on the lintel, in block capitals, had been carved the words:

THE WELL AT THE WORLD'S END

It was similar to the door that I had dreamed about, but unlike that door, which had no handle, there was a ceramic doorknob and a brass bolt. Above the lintel were two chipped enamel cups containing a smattering of pine needles.

We crouched in front of the door.

'You do it,' said Evie. 'Go on.' I slid back the bolt. I was terrified that the well would be empty, filled with broken twigs, like the streambed a few yards to the left of us. I opened the door.

At first I thought that a light had come on. We were looking into a rectangular box, with smooth pale stone sides and a fine whitish sand on the bottom. Looking above it I saw that the roof of the chamber was like a cistern, made of stones the size of apples. A bright fern curled between two of the stones. The water wasn't immediately apparent, but a couple of pine needles that I dislodged on opening the door revealed its surface. The light appeared to be coming from inside the well, and I thought of the words that had inspired our journey: *a well whose water is so clear it is invisible.*

A pulse, like a heartbeat, seemed to move the air in front of us. Without really speaking we fumbled for a cup. Evie passed it to me, and I pressed the cup into the water. A curved meniscus seemed to swell along the rim, to hesitate momentarily before flooding the beaker. I lifted the cup.

'You go first,' she said.

'No, you're my daughter.'

Evie drank off half the water in the cup, and then I finished it. We drank with speed as though we had run a race. It was sweet. Like swallowing light.

A small wind entered the clearing, circling, rising, the trees behind the wicker fence creaking like halyards. We heard the ratchet laughter of crows and then, overhead, a bird with trailing legs flapped slowly above the circle of trees.

'Is that a heron?' Evie asked. The bird flew in an arc.

'No, look at its head. The neck's extended, and it's white. It must be a stork.' The trees were moving around us. The sky had turned porcelain blue. Sunlight streamed to the floor of the glade. The change was so sudden that I found myself laughing, and then a silence fell all about us. A cloud settled over the sun like a dust-sheet. The trees shuffled back into stillness.

'What do you think?' I asked Evie.

'I think the audience is over,' she said.

I closed the door of the well. We hadn't filled our plastic bottle. We walked quickly back the way we had come and as we reached the gate, Evie said: 'Do you feel different?'

I hesitated. 'Yes. Do you?'

'Everything looks clearer,' she said.

We called Rupert to say we were coming home. The journey, as before, took three days. We called to visit Mum. Since her illness her memory had grown extraordinarily patchy and she was surprised to see us, although delighted, and sorry when we had to go. 'Look after yourselves,' she said, 'and ring me when you get home. You children are all I've got!'

'And you're the only mum I've got!' I said.

'And my only granny!' said Evie.

The next night we stayed at the cottage, and then closed it up for the winter. On the third day we headed south through Wales. We drove over mountains and along a tree-lined valley. There was a thunderstorm on the road ahead of us. We passed the signpost to the village where Mrs Thomas lived. I was finding it easier to drive past the turn, knowing that she was there, but suspected that it was never going to be effortless. My phone bleeped and Evie looked at it. It was a message from Robert, he was on his way back from Cardiff. Where were we?

There was a tympanic rumble followed by a bouncing lightning bolt that tore the sky ahead of us into halves. The road was dark, and slick, and shining, although no rain fell. We must have been travelling at the same speed as the storm, because we remained in green light for the whole of our journey, and we counted seven rainbows.

Acknowledgements

would like to thank the following people: At Bloomsbury, my brilliant and unruffleable editor Alexa von Hirschberg, and the lovely Alexandra Pringle for choosing me; Sarah Barlow, Laura Brooke, Michael Fishwick, Helen Flood, David Foy, Greg Heinimann and fierce-eyed Mary Tomlinson, for helping to make this such a pleasing book. Ariel Bruce for her generosity and for finding my birth family; Joanna Comino for her astute notes and her friendship; Clare Conville for being my nurse, and for feeding me; Jane Coward for her constant friendship and excellent company; Mary Doyle and David Austin for looking after our little family when it all looked a bit grim; Tessa Ettedgui for coming to chemotherapy with me; Robin Farquhar Thomson for insisting that I sing; Sr Maria Goretti and Sr Carmel for remembering the story; Dairmid Gunn and the Neil M. Gunn Literary Estate for being consistently supportive of *The Fish Ladder* and for telling me where the well was; Claudia Harding McKean, and her team at the Countess of Chester NHS Trust, for saving my life; Olga Jubany Baucells for reminding me that Minerva is also the goddess of healing; Caradoc King for suggesting I record my wanderings and being my friend, teacher and agent; Robert Macfarlane for mistaking me for a writer, for introducing me to *The Well at the World's End*, and for his encouragement, advice and friendship; Fiona McNeil, her team, and everyone at the Royal Marsden for getting me through the worst of it; Jean McNeil at UEA for her faith in the project; Calvin Mitchell for his overwhelming generosity, tender concern and concrete support; the Norbury family: Jean, John, Maria, Anna, Connor and Lauren, for everything; Oba Nsugbe for his extraordinary care, generosity, wisdom and counsel; Deborah Orr for keeping me company when we had no hair; the dear memory of Dennis Pinnington for a lifetime of love, friendship and encouragement, and for being my second reader, although he died before he got to the end; Polly Samson, for her infectious laughter and for being my first reader; Sue Swift and David Flusfeder for being such welcoming neighbours; my brother 'Robert Thomas,' for being there.

The following people have helped in ways as various as themselves: Louise Allen-Jones; John Bernasconi; Sharon Blackie; Jared Brading and the staff of Sacred Heart Primary School; Harvey Cabaniss; Cynthia and John Carson; Amit Chaudhuri; Simon Chu; Andrew Cowan; Linda Cracknell; Kristin Dean; Amy Elliot; Johnny Flynn; Lucy Geldenhuys; Kirsty Gunn; Judy Herbert; Clare Jolly; Bronwen Jones; Julian Kenyon; Yuko Komiya; Nigel Langford; Michael Lengsfield; Jackie Lomax; Sara Maitland; Bishop Vincent Malone; Chrissie O'Farrell; Mgr Canon Peter O'Neill; Fr Jordi Padro; Jeremy Page; Gwenna Parry Williams; Georgina and William Petty; Noemi Ranz; Jon Riley; Mary Sackville West, Linda Shaughnessy; Meg Sinclair; Peter Straus; Henry Sutton; Gwydion Thomas; Nancy Verrier; Nicola Waddell;

Stuart Webley; Amy Wellesley Wood; Sharon Wilkinson; Peter Womack; Mildred Yuan.

My special thanks go to Evie Thomson, my daughter, for her sparkling companionship and for the brilliant drawings in the book, and to Rupert Thomson – my friend, husband and soul's companion: where can I begin?

Notes

This book is a work of life writing based on the experiences and recollections of Katharine Norbury. In some cases names of people, places, dates, sequences or the detail of events have been changed solely to protect the privacy of others.

NOTES ON SOURCES

Epigraph to Part I

p. 1   'It is no small pity': Teresa of Avila (translated by E. Allison Peers), *The Interior Castle*, Dover Thrift Edition, New York, 2008. Reproduced by kind permission of Dover Publications Inc. on behalf of the E. Allison Peers Literary Estate.

Font del Mont

p. 7   'Places in the heart': Leon Bloy's words, 'Man has places in his heart which do not yet exist, and into them enters suffering, in order that they may have existence', have been made famous as the epigraph to Graham Green's *The End of the Affair*, although no one seems to know when or where Bloy first published them.

Swimming Pool

p. 8   'On a huge hill': John Donne, 'The Third Satire' from *The Complete English Poems*, Penguin Classics, London 1976.

p. 11   'Whose water is so clear': Robert Macfarlane, personal correspondence, 2009. Reproduced by kind permission of Robert Macfarlane.

p. 13, 14   'And what will you do': Neil M. Gunn, *Highland River*, Penguin, London, 1975. Reproduced by kind permission of Dairmid Gunn on behalf of the Neil M. Gunn Literary Estate.

Humber

p. 16   A version of 'Humber' first appeared in *A Wilder Vein*, edited by Linda Cracknell, Two Ravens Press, Port of Ness, 2009.

Mersey

p. 47   'In a dark leathern bag': *The Mabinogion*, translated by Lady Charlotte E. Guest, Dover Thrift Editions, New York, 2000.

Afon Geirch

p. 56   'Matthew, Mark, Luke and John': This is a version of the English language prayer and nursery rhyme also known as the 'Black Paternoster', traditionally said by children as they go to bed. It has a Roud Folk Song Index number of 1704. It may have origins in ancient Babylonian prayers and was being used in a Christian version in late Medieval Germany. The earliest extant version in English can be traced to the mid-sixteenth century.

p. 61   There are many variants of this story: Jan Morris recounts one in her book *Wales*, in which all the revellers but one drown as the waters rise around a castle, but it also shares a family likeness with the story of Odysseus's revenge on Persephone's suitors, when the hero enters his besieged home disguised as a beggar, then kills the suitors with the help of his son and a trusty swineherd.

p. 63   'Time held me green and dying': Dylan Thomas, 'Fern Hill' from *The Collected Poems of Dylan Thomas: The Original Edition*, New Directions, 2010. Copyright 1945 by The Trustees for the Copyrights of Dylan Thomas. Reproduced by kind permission of David Higham Associates and New Directions Publishing Corp.

Ffynnon Fawr

p. 72   'They did not divine it': R.S. Thomas, 'Ffynnon Fair' from *Collected Poems 1949–1990*, Phoenix, 2000. Reproduced by kind permission of Gwydion Thomas on behalf of the R. S. Thomas Literary Estate.

p. 73   'St. Mary's cave': Ieuan Lleyn (1769–1832), also known as Evan Pritchard, was a renowned bard, poet and writer of hymns. This extract is from a letter to his friend Dafydd Ddu Eryri, 1799. Translation reproduced by kind permission of Gwenllian Jones on behalf of Rhiw.com.

Caherdaniel

p. 99   'But Hermes did not find': *The Odyssey of Homer*, translated and with an introduction by Richmond Lattimore, Harper Perennial, New York, 1999. Copyright 1965, 1967 by Richmond Lattimore; Renewed 1995 by Alice B. Lattimore. Reproduced by kind permission of HarperCollins Publishers.

p. 101   'That unnameable something': C.S. Lewis, Foreword to *The Pilgrim's Regress*, Fount, London, 1998. Copyright C.S. Lewis Pte Ltd 1933. Reproduced by kind permission of The C.S. Lewis Company Ltd.

Skell

p. 106, 107   'Hither came on a day': 'Every way the woman went': *Irish Metrical Dindshenchas*, translated by Edward John Gwynn, CELT, University College, Cork, 2004

p. 110   'That state of highly respectful sulkiness': Wilkie Collins, *The Woman in White*, Penguin Classics, London, 2007.

p. 120   'Should th' ungenerous world': Georgiana, Duchess of Devonshire, letter to Eliza Gray, from *Verses copied by Lady Charlotte Cholmondeley in her common place book*, c. 1816.

Tummell

p. 133   'A very fundamental human attribute': Sara Maitland, *Gossip from the Forest*, Granta, London, 2013. Reproduced by kind permission of Sara Maitland.

p. 135   'Over the Rainbow': Words and Music by Harold Arlen and EY Harburg © 1938. Reproduced by permission of EMI Feist Catalog, London, W1F 9LD.

Spey

p. 141   A version of 'Spey' first appeared in the *UEA Creative Writing Anthology*, foreword by Andrew Motion, Eggbox Publishing, Norwich, 2012.

p. 150   'We fulfil the demands of nature': Cassius Dio, *Roman History*, published in Vol. IX of the Loeb Classical Library edition, Harvard, 1927.

p. 153   'A curious mood of fatalism': Neil M. Gunn, *Highland River*, Penguin, London, 1975. Reproduced by kind permission of Dairmid Gunn on behalf of the Neil M. Gunn Literary Estate.

Dunbeath

p. 162, 163, 164, 195   'Who turned her eyes onto', 'restraining her feet', 'Truly we think the matter', 'That which was born in her womb': *Jocelyn, A monk of Furness: The Life of Kentigern* (Mungo), translated by Cynthia Whiddon Green, as part of an MA Thesis, University of Houston, 1998, from the Internet Mediaeval Sourcebook, a collection of public domain and copy-permitted historical texts edited by Paul Halsall.

p. 190   'His dismay was vague': Neil M. Gunn, *Highland River*, Penguin, London, 1975. Reproduced by kind permission of Dairmid Gunn on behalf of the Neil Gunn Literary Estate.

p. 195   'Love, with very young people': Isak Dinesen, 'The Old Chevalier' from *Seven Gothic Tales*, Penguin, 2002.

p. 195   'A secret well there was': *Irish Metrical Dindshenchas*, translated by Edward John Gwynn, CELT, University College, Cork, 2004.

Epigraphs to Part II

p. 205   'Is it possible to pierce': Neil M. Gunn from a letter to Geoffrey Faber, 1950. Reproduced by kind permission of Dairmid Gunn on behalf of the Neil Gunn Literary Estate.

p. 205   'The Water' by John Patrick Vivian Flynn © Transgressive Publishing Ltd (PRS) (NS). All rights administered by Warner/Chappell Music Publishing Ltd. All rights reserved.

Swimming Pool (2)

p. 208   'Looking overhead he saw': John Cheever, 'The Swimmer' from *Collected Stories*, Vintage Classics, 1990. Reproduced by kind permission of Penguin Random House UK on behalf of the John Cheever Literary Estate.

Innominate Stream

p. 225   'Skilful, careful and modest': from *The Scawfell Accident*, Climbers' Club Journal No 21, 1903.

Severn

p. 243, 246, 254   'I am waiting for an old frayed queen', 'She who shines': Alice Oswald, *A Sleepwalk on the Severn*, Faber and Faber, London, 2009. Reproduced by kind permission of United Agents LLP (www.unitedagents.co.uk) and Faber and Faber Ltd on behalf of Alice Oswald.

p. 250   'The connection between biological mother and child is primal, mystical, mysterious, and everlasting. Far more than merely biological and historical, this primal connection is also cellular, psychological, emotional, and spiritual. So deep runs the connection between a child and its mother that the severing of that bond results in a profound wound for both, a wound from which neither fully recovers. In the case of adoption, the wound cannot be avoided, but it can and must be acknowledged and understood'. Nancy Verrier, 'Position Statement', www.nancyverrier.com/position-statement. Reproduced by kind permission of Nancy Verrier.

p. 255   'A secret well there was', 'Every way the woman went': *Irish Metrical Dindshenchas*, translated by Edward John Gwynn, CELT, University College, Cork, 2004.

Afon Rhiw

p. 258   'What is existence': R. S. Thomas, 'Mass for Hard Times' from *Selected Poems*, Penguin Modern Classics, London, 2003. Reproduced by kind permission of Gwydion Thomas on behalf of the R.S. Thomas Literary Estate.

p. 279   'That well is never dry': Neil M. Gunn, *The Well at the World's End*, Faber and Faber, London, 1951. Reproduced by kind permission of Dairmid Gunn on behalf of the Neil M. Gunn Literary Estate.

A Note on the Author

Katharine Norbury trained as a film editor with the BBC and has worked extensively in film and television drama. She is a graduate of the Creative Writing MA programme at UEA and a doctoral candidate at Goldsmiths. She lives in London with her family. *The Fish Ladder* is her first book.

@kjnorbury

A Note on the Type

The text of this book is set in Bembo. This type was first used in 1495 by the Venetian printer Aldus Manutius for Cardinal Bembo's *De Aetna*, and was cut for Manutius by Francesco Griffo. It was one of the types used by Claude Garamond (1480–1561) as a model for his Romain de L'Université, and so it was the forerunner of what became standard European type for the following two centuries. Its modern form follows the original types and was designed for Monotype in 1929.